Irene C. Haley

THE AMENITIES OF BOOK-COLLECTING
AND
KINDRED AFFECTIONS

CARICATURE OF TWO GREAT VICTORIANS
W. M. THACKERAY AND CHARLES DICKENS

THE AMENITIES
OF BOOK-COLLECTING

AND

KINDRED AFFECTIONS

BY
A. EDWARD NEWTON

WITH ILLUSTRATIONS

BOSTON
LITTLE, BROWN, AND COMPANY
1929

First Impression, August, 1918
Second Impression, March, 1919
Third Impression, August, 1920
Fourth Impression, May, 1922
Fifth Impression, March, 1924
Sixth Impression, May, 1929

THE ATLANTIC MONTHLY PRESS PUBLICATIONS
ARE PUBLISHED BY
LITTLE, BROWN, AND COMPANY
IN ASSOCIATION WITH
THE ATLANTIC MONTHLY COMPANY

PRINTED IN THE UNITED STATES OF AMERICA

DEDICATION

*If, as Eugene Field suggests, womenfolk
are few in that part of paradise especially
reserved for book-lovers I do not care. One
woman will be there, for I shall insist that
eight and twenty years probation entitles
her to share my biblio-bliss above as she
has shared it here below. That woman is
my wife.*   A. EDWARD NEWTON

OCTOBER, 1918

A FIFTH EDITION

THE *fourth edition was not born to a long life. **Mr**. Newton, now abroad, cannot be reached for consultation about the fifth. If he could, we should hardly want to ask him to repeat himself. What he said less than two years ago about his "blunders" is still valid. We can guarantee that no more have crept into his pages since then.*

THE PUBLISHERS.

JANUARY 1924

INTRODUCING A FOURTH EDITION

WHEN, *owing to the continued demand for "The Amenities of Book-Collecting," we decided to print a fourth edition, we wrote Mr. Newton and asked him if he desired any corrections or changes made in the new edition. His reply was characteristic: "Certainly not. Evidently people buy my book on account of the blunders in it, and I would n't have 'em disappointed for worlds."*

THE PUBLISHERS.

MAY 1922

PREFACE TO THIRD EDITION.

"BEWILDERING!" I exclaimed to myself as I laid down the letter. It was from my publisher, telling me that a third edition of six thousand copies of the "Amenities" would go to press shortly (making fifteen thousand in all), and saying that, if there were "no objections or corrections, it would stand approved as read." I looked about my little office in which so many (to me) important matters had been decided, and said, as I have so often said, "It is so ordered. Is it moved we adjourn? All in favor —"; and as the meeting broke up, I reached for my hat and coat and took the next train for New York, there to join my wife in celebrating, as merrily as we could on White Rock, our thirtieth wedding anniversary.

Going over on the train, I wondered whether I was not running away from duty unperformed, having in mind several little blunders that remained uncorrected. I decided that I was, and that added zest to the journey. But if blunders have been permitted to remain, a crime shall be pointed out; it was committed in ignorance. "But ignorance is no excuse," I hear a fledgling lawyer say. It is, however, the only excuse I have.

One day there came a letter from a schoolteacher, who began by praising my book; then quietly and by degrees its defects were noted, until finally I was accused of a crime. "On page 99, second line from the bottom," my correspondent said, "You have left what we grammarians call a participle dangling. Infinitives may be split occasionally and an author retain his self-respect, but participles must not be allowed to dangle."

I read no further; seizing the book, I turned to the offending sentence; there seemed to be something queer about it, but I could not say just what it was, but I determined to go to the rescue of that dangling participle as I would go to a damsel in distress. But first I must know what was the matter with it. Grasping the telephone I got "long distance," and finally my friend Osgood, the head of the English Department at Princeton. "Charlie," I said, "I have been detected in a crime."

"I'm not surprised, Ned," he answered; "I've been expecting it for years. What have you been doing?"

"Hanging a participle," I replied.

"Hanging a what?" he cried.

"A participle," I screamed. "I have left a participle dangling in my book. You remember my 'Amenities of Book-Collecting'?"

"Of course," he said.

"Well," said I, "on page 99, second line from the bottom, there is a sentence which reads, 'Turning to a book-seller's catalogue, published a year or two ago, there is a copy in original calf binding, and the price is twenty-five hundred dollars.' What's the matter with that sentence?"

"Why, don't you see," said Charlie, "the sentence turns automatically, as it were. You don't say who does the turning. It's the second line from the bottom of the page you say, well then," (with a chuckle) "it don't dangle very far. It would be more noticeable if it dangled from the second line from the top. I would not suppress the book on that account. Who made the discovery?"

"A teacher at the H—— School," I replied.

"Think of it!" said Charlie, "I wonder where he got the money to buy the book."

"He gave the book to his wife instead of a new frock, I suppose," I said; "that's the way I get most of my books." Then there was something about a Blake item I had just bought, and I hung up the telephone.

I am relieved to have this matter off my mind.

The "Amenities" has been received so well, in spite of its faults,— perhaps I should say by reason of them,— that it is inevitable that its readers should be rewarded or punished by another volume in a similar vein. It now only remains for me to write the papers, select the title, and attend to some, at present, very troublesome and expensive mechanical details, and the book will be ready for publication. Until then, I trust that the discriminating reader will remain satisfied with the third edition of this one.

A. EDWARD NEWTON

July 12, 1920.

ESSAY INTRODUCTORY

A MAN (or a woman) is the most interesting thing in the world; and next is a book, which enables one to get at the heart of the mystery; and although not many men can say why they are or what they are, any man who publishes a book can, if he is on good terms with his publisher, secure the use of a little space to tell how the book came to be what it is.

Some years ago a very learned friend of mine published a book, and in the introduction warned the "gentle reader" to skip the first chapter, and, as I have always maintained, by inference suggested that the rest was easy reading, which was not the case. In point of fact, the book was not intended for the "gentle reader" at all: it was a book written by a scholar for the scholar.

Now, I have worked on a different plan. My book is written for the "tired business man" (there are a goodly number of us), who flatters himself that he is fond of reading; and as it is my first book, I may be permitted to tell how it came to be published.

One day in the autumn of 1913, a friend, my partner, with whom it has been my privilege to be associated for so many years, remarked that it was time for me to take a holiday, and handed me a copy of the " Geographical Magazine." The number was devoted to Egypt; and, seduced by the charm of the illustrations, on the spur of the moment I decided on a trip up the Nile.

Things moved rapidly. In a few weeks my wife and I were in the Mediterranean, on a steamer headed for Alexandria. We had touched at Genoa and were soon to reach Naples, when I discovered a feeling of homesickness stealing over me. I have spent my happiest holidays in London. Already I had tired of Egypt. The Nile has been flowing for centuries and would continue to flow. There were books to be had in London, books which would not wait. Somewhat shamefacedly I put the matter up to my wife; and when I discovered that she had no insuperable objection to a change of plan, we left the steamer at Naples, and after a few weeks with friends in Rome, started *en grande vitesse* toward London.

By this time it will have been discovered that I am not much of a traveler; but I have always loved London — London with its wealth of literary and historic association, with its countless miles of streets lined with inessential shops overflowing with things that I don't want, and its grimy old book-shops overflowing with things that I do.

One gloomy day I picked up in the Charing Cross Road, for a shilling, a delightful book by Richard Le Gallienne, "Travels in England." Like myself, Le Gallienne seems not to have been a great traveler — he seldom reached the place he started for; and losing his way or changing his mind, may be said to have arrived at his destination when he has reached a comfortable inn, where, after a simple meal, he lights his pipe and proceeds to read a book.

Exactly my idea of travel! The last time I read "Pickwick" was while making a tour in Northern Italy. It is wonderful how conducive to reading I found the stuffy smoking-rooms of the little steamers that dart like water-spiders from one landing to another on the Italian Lakes.

It was while I was poking about among the old book-shops that it occurred to me to write a little story about my books — when and where I had bought them, the prices I had paid, and the men I had bought them from, many of whom I knew well; and so, when my holiday was done, I lived over again its pleasant associations in writing a paper that I called "Book-Collecting Abroad." Subsequently I wrote another, — "Book-Collecting at Home," — it being my purpose to print these papers in a little volume to be called "The Amenities of Book-Collecting." I intended this for distribution among my friends, who are very patient with me; and I sent my manuscript to a printer in the closing days of July, 1914. A few days later something happened in Europe, the end of which is not yet, and we all became panic-stricken. For a moment it seemed unlikely that one would care ever to open a book again. Acting upon impulse, I withdrew the order from my printer, put my manuscript aside, and devoted myself to my usual task — that of making a living.

Byron says, "The end of all scribblement is to amuse." For some years I have been possessed of an itch for "scribblement"; gradually this feeling reasserted itself, and I came to see that we must become accustomed to working in a world at war, and to realizing that life must be permitted to resume, at least to some extent, its regular course; and the idea of my little book recurred to me.

It had frequently been suggested by friends that my papers be published in the "Atlantic." What grudge they bore this excellent magazine I do not know, but they always said the "Atlantic"; and so, when one day I came across my manuscript, it occurred to me that it would cost only a few cents to lay it before the editor. At that time I did not know the editor of the "Atlantic" even by name. My pleasure then can be imagined when, a week or so later, I received the following letter: —

Oct. 30, 1914.

DEAR MR. NEWTON: —
The enthusiasm of your pleasant paper is contagious, and I find myself in odd moments looking at the gaps in my own library with a feeling of dismay. I believe that very many readers of the "Atlantic" will feel as I do, and it gives me great pleasure to accept your paper.

Yours sincerely,
ELLERY SEDGWICK.

Shortly afterward, a check for a substantial sum fluttered down upon my desk, and it was impossible that I should not remember how much Milton had received for his "Paradise Lost," — the receipt for which is in the British Museum, — and draw conclusions therefrom entirely satisfactory to my self-esteem. My paper was published, and the magazine, having a hardy constitution, survived; I even received some praise. There was nothing important enough to justify criticism, and as a result of this chance publication I made a number of delightful acquaintances among readers and collectors, many of whom I might almost call friends although we have never met.

Not wishing to strain the rather precarious friendship with Mr. Sedgwick which was the outcome of my first venture, it was several years before I ventured to try him with another paper. This I called "A Ridiculous Philosopher." I enjoyed writing this paper immensely, and although it was the reverse of timely, I felt that it might pass editorial scrutiny. Again I received a letter from Mr. Sedgwick, in which he said: —

Two days ago I took your paper home with me and spent a delightful half-hour with it. Now, as any editor would tell you, there is no valid reason for a paper on Godwin at this time, but your essay is so capitally seasoned that I cannot find it in my heart to part with it. Indeed I have been gradually making the editorial discovery that, if a paper is sufficiently readable, it has some claim upon the public, regardless of what the plans of the editor are. And so the upshot of my deliberation is that we shall accept your paper with great pleasure and publish it when the opportunity occurs.

The paper appeared in due course, and several more followed. The favor with which these papers were received led the "Atlantic" editors to the consideration of their reprint in permanent form, together with several which now appear for the first time. All the illustrations have been made from items in my own collection. I am thus tying a string, as it were, around a parcel which contains the result of thirty-six years of collecting. It may not be much, but, as the Irishman said of his dog, "It's mine own." My volume might, with propriety, be called "Newton's Complete Recreations."

I have referred to my enjoyment in writing my "Ridiculous Philosopher." I might say the same of all my papers. I am aware that my friend, Dr. Johnson, once remarked that no man but a blockhead writes a book except for money. At some risk, then, I admit that I have done so. I have written for fun, and my papers should be read, if read at all, for the same purpose, not that the reader will or is expected to laugh loud. The loud laugh, in Goldsmith's phrase, it may be remembered, bespeaks the vacant mind. But I venture to hope that the judicious will pass a not unpleasant hour in turning my pages.

One final word: I buy, I collect "Presentation Books"; and I trust my friends will not think me churlish when I say that it is not my intention to turn a single copy of this, my book, into a presentation volume. Whatever circulation it may have must be upon its own merits. Any one who sees this book in the hands of a reader, on the library table, or on the shelves of the collector, may be sure that some one, either wise or foolish as the event may prove, has paid a substantial sum for it, either in the current coin of the realm, or perchance in thrift stamps. It may, indeed, be that it has been secured from a lending library, in which case I would suggest that the book be returned instantly. "Go ye rather to them that sell and buy for yourselves." And having separated yourself from your money, in the event that you should feel vexed with your bargain, you are at liberty to communicate your grievance to the publisher, securing from him what redress you may; and in the event of failure there yet remains your inalienable right, which should afford some satisfaction, that of damning

THE AUTHOR.

"OAK KNOLL,"
DAYLESFORD, PENNSYLVANIA,
April 7, 1918.

TABLE OF CONTENTS

LIST OF ILLUSTRATIONS

LIST OF ILLUSTRATIONS

THE AMENITIES OF BOOK–COLLECTING

AND

KINDRED AFFECTIONS

I

BOOK-COLLECTING ABROAD

IF my early training has been correct, which I am much inclined to doubt, we were not designed to be happy in this world. We were simply placed here to be tried, and doubtless we are — it is a trying place. It is, however, the only world we are sure of; so, in spite of our training, we endeavor to make the best of it, and have invented a lot of little tricks with which to beguile the time.

The approved time-killer is work, and we do a lot of it. When it is quite unnecessary, we say it is in the interest of civilization; and occasionally work is done on so high a plane that it becomes sport, and we call these sportsmen, "Captains of Industry." One of them once told me that making money was the finest sport in the world. This was before the rules of the game were changed.

But for the relaxation of those whose life is spent in a persistent effort to make ends meet, games of skill, games of chance, and kissing games have been invented, and indoor and outdoor sports. These are all very well for those who can play them; but I am like the little boy who declined to play Old Maid because he was always "it." Having early discovered that I was always "it" in every game, I decided to take my recreation in another way. I read occasionally and have always been a collector.

Many years ago, in an effort to make conversation on a train, — a foolish thing to do, — I asked a man what he did with his leisure, and his reply was, "I play cards. I used to read a good deal but I wanted something to occupy my mind, so I took to cards." It was a disconcerting answer.

It may be admitted that not all of us can read all the time. For those who cannot and for those to whom sport in any form is a burden not to be endured, there is one remaining form of exercise, the riding of a hobby — collecting, it is called; and the world is so full of such wonderful things that we collectors should be as happy as kings. Horace Greeley once said, "Young man, go West." I give advice as valuable and more easily followed: I say, Young man, get a hobby; preferably get two, one for indoors and one for out; get a pair of hobby-horses that can safely be ridden in opposite directions.

We collectors strive to make converts; we want others to enjoy what we enjoy; and I may as well confess that the envy shown by our fellow collectors when we display our treasures is not annoying to us. But, speaking generally, we are a bearable lot, our hobbies are usually harmless, and if we loathe the subject of automobiles, and especially discussion relative to parts thereof, we try to show an intelligent interest in another's hobby, even if it happen to be a collection of postage-stamps. Our own hobby may be, probably is, ridiculous to some one else, but in all the wide range of human interest, from postage-stamps to paintings, — the sport of the millionaire, — there is nothing that begins so easily and takes us so far as the collecting of books.

And hear me. If you would know the delight of book-collecting, begin with something else, I care not what. Book-collecting has all the advantages of other hobbies without their drawbacks. The pleasure of acquisition is common to all — that's where the sport lies; but the strain of the possession of books is almost nothing; a tight, dry closet will serve to house them, if need be.

It is not so with flowers. They are a constant care. Some one once wrote a poem about "old books and fresh flowers." It lilted along very nicely; but I remark that books stay old, indeed get older, and flowers do not stay fresh: a little too much rain, a little too much sun, and it is all over.

Pets die too, in spite of constant care — perhaps by reason of it. To quiet a teething dog I once took him, her, it, to my room for the night and slept soundly. Next morning I found that the dog had committed suicide by jumping out of the window.

The joys of rugs are a delusion and a snare. They cannot be picked up here and there, tucked in a traveling-bag, and smuggled into the house; they are hard to transport, there are no auction records against them, and the rug market knows no bottom. I never yet heard a man admit paying a fair price for a rug, much less a high one. "Look at this Scherazak," a friend remarks; "I paid only nine dollars for it and it's worth five hundred if it's worth a penny." When he is compelled to sell his collection, owing to an unlucky turn in the market, it brings seventeen-fifty. And rugs are ever a loafing place for moths — But that's a chapter by itself.

Worst of all, there is no literature about them. I know very well that there are books about rugs; I own some. But as all books are not literature, so all literature is not in books. Can a rug-collector enjoy a catalogue? I sometimes think that for the overworked business man a book-catalogue is the best reading there is. Did you ever see a rug-collector, pencil in hand, poring over a rug-catalogue?

Print-catalogues there are; and now I warm a little. They give descriptions that mean something; a scene may have a reminiscent value, a portrait suggests a study in biography. Then there are dimensions for those who are fond of figures and states and margins, and the most ignorant banker will tell you that a wide margin is always better than a narrow one. Prices, too, can be looked up and compared, and results, satisfactory or otherwise, recorded. Prints, too, can be snugly housed in portfolios. But for a lasting hobby give me books.

Book-collectors are constantly being ridiculed by scholars for the pains they take and the money they spend on first editions of their favorite authors; and it must be that they smart under the criticism, for they are always explaining, and attempting rather foolishly to justify their position. Would it not be better to say, as Leslie Stephen did of Dr. Johnson's rough sayings, that "it is quite useless to defend them to any one who cannot enjoy them without defense"?

I am not partial to the "books which no gentleman's library should be without," fashionable a generation or two ago. The works of Thomas Frognall Dibdin do not greatly interest me, and where will one find room to-day for Audubon's "Birds" or Roberts's "Holy Land" except on a billiard-table or under a bed?

The very great books of the past have become so rare, so high-priced, that it is almost useless for the ordinary collector to hope ever to own them, and fashion changes in book-collecting as in everything else. Aldines and Elzevirs are no longer sought. Our interest in the Classics being somewhat abated, we pass them over in favor of books which, we tell ourselves, we expect some day to read, the books written by men of whose lives we know something. I would rather have a "Paradise Lost" with the first title-page,[1] in

[1] The facsimile (page 6) is from the first edition, with the first title-page. From the Hagen collection. Mr. Hagen has written on the fly-leaf, "Rebound from original calf binding which was too far gone to repair." In the process of binding it was seen that the title-page was part of a signature and not a separate leaf as in the case of the issue with the "Second" title, 1667, which would seem to settle the priority of these two titles.

Paradiſe loſt.

A
POEM
Written in
TEN BOOKS

By *JOHN MILTON.*

Licenſed and Entred according
to Order.

LONDON
Printed, and are to be ſold by *Peter Parker*
under *Creed* Church neer *Aldgate*; And by
Robert Boulter at the *Turks Head* in *Biſhopſgate-ſtreet*;
And *Matthias Walker*, under St. *Dunſtons* Church
in *Fleet-ſtreet*, 1667.

contemporary binding, or an "Angler," than all the Aldines and Elzevirs ever printed.

That this feeling is general, accounts, I take it, for the excessively high prices now being paid for first editions of modern authors like Shelley, Keats, Lamb, and, to come right down to our own day, Stevenson. Would not these authors be amazed could they know in what esteem they are held, and what fabulous prices are paid for volumes which, when they were published, fell almost stillborn from the press? We all know the story of Fitzgerald's "Rubaiyat": how a "remainder" was sold by Quaritch at a penny the copy. It is now worth its weight in gold, and Keats's "Endymion," once a "remainder" bought by a London bookseller at fourpence, now commands several hundred dollars. I paid three hundred and sixty dollars for mine — but it was once Wordsworth's and has his name on the title-page.

But it is well in book-collecting, while not omitting the present, never to neglect the past. "Old books are best," says Beverly Chew, beloved of all collectors; and I recall Lowell's remark: "There is a sense of security in an old book which time has criticized for us." It was a recollection of these sayings that prompted me, if prompting was necessary, to pay a fabulous price the other day for a copy of "Hesperides, or the Works both Humane and Divine of Robert Herrick, Esq.," a beautiful copy of the first edition in the original sheep.

We collectors know the saying of Bacon: "Some

books are to be tasted, others to be swallowed and some few to be chewed and digested"; but the revised version is, Some books are to be read, others are to be collected. Mere reading books, the five-foot shelf, or the hundred best, every one knows at least by name. But at the moment I am concerned with collectors' books and the amenities of book-collecting; for, frankly, —

> I am one of those who seek
> What Bibliomaniacs love.

Some subjects are not for me. Sydney Smith's question, "Who reads an American book?" has, I am sure, been answered; and I am equally sure that I do not know what the answer is. "Americana" — which was not what Sydney Smith meant — have never caught me, nor has "black letter." It is not necessary for me to study how to tell a Caxton. Caxtons do not fall in my way, except single leaves now and then, and these I take as Goldsmith took his religion, on faith.

Nor am I the rival of the man who buys all his books from Quaritch. Buying from Quaritch is rather too much like the German idea of hunting: namely, sitting in an easy chair near a breach in the wall through which game, big or little, is shooed within easy reach of your gun. No, my idea of collecting is "watchful waiting," in season and out, in places likely and unlikely, most of all in London. But one need not begin in London: one can begin wherever one has pitched one's tent.

I have long wanted Franklin's "Cato Major." A copy was found not long ago in a farmhouse garret in my own county; but, unluckily, I did not hear of it until its price, through successive hands, had reached three hundred dollars.

But if one does not begin in London, one ends there. It is the great market of the world for collectors' books — the best market, not necessarily the cheapest.

My first purchase was a Bohn edition of Pope's Homer, the Iliad and the Odyssey in two volumes — not a bad start for a boy; and under my youthful signature, with a fine flourish, is the date, 1882.

I read them with delight, and was sorry

M. T. CICERO's

CATO MAJOR,

OR HIS

DISCOURSE

O F

OLD-AGE:

With Explanatory NOTES.

PHILADELPHIA:

Printed and Sold by B. FRANKLIN,
MDCCXLIV.

when I learned that Pope is by no means Homer. I have been a little chary about reading ever since. We collectors might just as well wait until scholars settle these questions.

I have always liked Pope. In reading him one has the sense of progress from idea to idea, not a mere floundering about in Arcady amid star-stuff. When

Dr. Johnson was asked what poetry is, he replied, "It is much easier to say what it is not." He was sparring for time and finally remarked, "If Pope is not poetry it is useless to look for it."

Years later, when I learned from Oscar Wilde that there are two ways of disliking poetry, — one is to dislike it, and the other, to like Pope, — I found that I was not entirely prepared to change my mind about Pope.

In 1884 I went to London for the first time, and there I fell under the lure of Dr. Johnson and Charles Lamb. After that, the deluge!

The London of 1884 was the London of Dickens. There have been greater changes since I first wandered in the purlieus of the Strand and Holborn than there were in the hundred years before. Dickens's London has vanished almost as completely as the London of Johnson. One landmark after another disappeared, until finally the County Council made one grand sweep with Aldwych and Kingsway. But never to be forgotten are the rambles I enjoyed with my first bookseller, Fred Hutt of Clement's Inn Passage, subsequently of Red Lion Passage, now no more. Poor fellow! when, early in 1914, I went to look him up, I found that he had passed away, and his shop was being dismantled. He was the last of three brothers, all booksellers.

From Hutt I received my first lesson in bibliography; from him I bought my first "Christmas Carol," with "Stave 1," not "Stave One," and with the green end-papers. I winced at the price: it was thirty shillings. I saw one marked twenty guineas not long ago. From Hutt, too, I got a copy of Swinburne's "Poems and Ballads," 1866, with the Moxon imprint, and had pointed out to me the curious eccentricity of type on page 222. I did not then take his advice and pay something over two pounds for a copy of "Desperate Remedies." It seemed wiser to wait until the price reached forty pounds, which I subsequently paid for it. But I did buy from him for five shillings an autograph letter of Thomas Hardy to his first publisher, "old Tinsley." As the details throw some light on the subject of Hardy's first book, I reproduce the letter, from which it will be seen that Hardy financed the publication himself.

When, thirty years ago, I picked up my Hardy letter for a few shillings, I never supposed that the time would come when I would own the complete manuscript of one of his most famous novels. Yet so it is. Not long since, quite unexpectedly, the original draft of "Far from the Madding Crowd" turned up in London. Its author, when informed of its discovery, wrote saying that he had "supposed the manuscript had been pulped ages ago." One page only was missing; Mr. Hardy supplied it. Then arose the question of ownership, which was gracefully settled by sending it to the auction-room, the proceeds of the sale to go to the British Red Cross. I cannot say that the bookseller who bought it gave it to me exactly, but we both agree that it is an item

Bockhampton
Dorchester
Dec 20: 1870

Sir,

I believe I am right in under=
standing your terms thus — that if the gross
receipts reach the costs of publishing I shall
receive the £75 back again, & if they are
more than the costs I shall have £75,
added to half the receipts beyond the costs
(i.e. assuming the expenditure to be £100
& the receipts £200 I should have returned
to me £75 + 50 = 125.) Will you be
good enough to say too if the sum includes
advertising to the customary extent, &
about how long after my paying the money
the book would appear?

Yours faithfully
Thomas Hardy.

LETTER OF THOMAS HARDY TO HIS FIRST PUBLISHER, "OLD TINSLEY"

I paid five shillings for this letter many years ago, in London. Maggs, in his last
catalogue, prices at fifteen guineas a much less interesting letter from Hardy to
Arthur Symons, dated December 4, 1915, on the same subject.

which does honor to any collection. Although it is the original draft, there are very few corrections or interlineations, the page reproduced (see next page) being fairly representative.

Only those who are trying to complete their sets of Hardy know how difficult it is to find "Desperate Remedies" and "Under the Greenwood Tree" "in cloth as issued."

My love for book-collecting and my love for London have gone hand in hand. From the first, London with its wealth of literary and historic interest has held me; there has never been a time, not even on that gloomy December day twenty years ago, when, with injuries subsequently diagnosed as a "compound comminuted tibia and fibula," I was picked out of an overturned cab and taken to St. Bartholomew's Hospital for repairs, that I could not say with Boswell, "There is a city called London for which I have as violent an affection as the most romantic lover ever had for his mistress."

The book-shops of London have been the subject of many a song in prose and verse. Every taste and pocket can be satisfied. I have ransacked the wretched little shops to be found in the by-streets of Holborn one day, and the next have browsed in the artificially stimulated pastures of Grafton Street and Bond Street, and with as much delight in one as in the other.

I cannot say that "I was 'broke' in London in the fall of '89," for the simple reason that I was not in

may be called a small silver clock: in other words it
was a watch as to shape & intention, & a small clock as to
size. This instrument, being several years older than Oak's
grandfather, had the peculiarity of going either too fast or not
at all. The smaller of its hands, too, occasionally slipped round
on the pivot, & thus, though the minutes were told with the greatest
precision, nobody could be quite certain of the hour they belonged
to. The stopping peculiarity of this watch Oak remedied by
thumps & shakes, when it always went on again immediately,
& he escaped any evil consequences from the other two defects
by constant comparisons with & observations of the sun & stars,
& by pressing his face close to the glass of his neighbour's windows
when passing by their houses, till he could discern the hour
marked by the green-faced timekeepers within.. It may be
mentioned that Oak's fob, being painfully difficult of access
by reason of its somewhat high situation in the waistband of
his trousers (which also lay at a remote height under his
waistcoat) the watch was as a necessity pulled out by
throwing the body extremely to one side, compressing the
mouth & face to a mere mass of wrinkles on account of the exertion required, & drawing
up the watch by its chain, like a bucket from a well.

But some thoughtful persons, who had seen him walking
across one of his fields on a certain December morning—
sunny, & exceptionally mild — might have regarded
                           Gabriel Oak

FACSIMILE OF A PAGE OF HARDY'S "FAR FROM THE MADDING CROWD," MUCH REDUCED IN SIZE

BERNARD QUARITCH

"The extensive literature of catalogues is probably little known to most readers. I do not pretend to claim a thorough acquaintance with it but I know the luxury of reading good catalogues and such are those of Bernard Quaritch." — OLIVER WENDELL HOLMES.

London that year; but I am never long in London without finding myself as light in heart and pocket as Eugene Field — the result of yielding to the same temptations.

I knew the elder Quaritch well, and over a cup of tea one winter afternoon years ago, in a cold, dingy little room filled with priceless volumes in the old shop in Piccadilly, he confided to me his fears for his son Alfred. This remarkable old man, who has well been called the Napoleon of booksellers, was certain that Alfred would never be able to carry on the business when he was gone. "He has no interest in books, he is not willing to work hard as he will have to, to maintain the standing I have secured as the greatest bookseller in the world." Quaritch was very proud, and justly, of his eminence.

How little the old man knew that this son, when the time came, would step into his father's shoes and stretch them. Alfred, when he inherited the business, assumed his father's first name and showed all his father's enthusiasm and shrewdness. He probably surprised himself, as he surprised the world, by adding lustre to the name of Bernard Quaritch, so that, when he died, the newspapers of the English-speaking world gave the details of his life and death as matters of general interest.

The book-lovers' happy hunting-ground is the Charing Cross Road. It is a dirty and sordid street, too new to be picturesque; but almost every other shop on both sides of the street is a bookshop, and the patient man is frequently rewarded by a find of peculiar interest.

One day, a few years ago, I picked up two square folio volumes of manuscript bound in old, soft morocco, grown shabby from knocking about. The title was "Lyford Redivivus, or A Grandame's Garrulity."

Lyford Redivivus

or

A Grandame's Garrulity.

By   An Old Woman

Examination showed me that it was a sort of dictionary of proper names. In one volume there were countless changes and erasures; the other was evidently a fair copy. Although there was no name in either volume to suggest the author, it needed no second glance to see that both were written in the clear, bold hand of Mrs. Piozzi. The price was but trifling, and I promptly paid it and carried the volumes home. Some months later, I was reading a little volume, "Piozziana," by Edward Mangin, — the first book about Mrs. Thrale-Piozzi, — when, to my surprise, my eye met the following: —

BERNARD ALFRED QUARITCH

"He probably surprised himself as he surprised the world by adding lustre to the name of Bernard Quaritch."

Early in the year 1815, I called on her [Mrs. Piozzi] then resident in Bath, to examine a manuscript which she informed me she was preparing for the press. After a short conversation, we sat down to a table on which lay two manuscript volumes, one of them, the fair copy of her work, in her own incomparably fine hand-writing. The title was "Lyford Redivivus"; the idea being taken from a diminutive old volume, printed in 1657, and professing to be an alphabetical account of the names of men and women, and their derivations. Her work was somewhat on this plan: the Christian or first name given, Charity, for instance, followed by its etymology; anecdotes of the eminent or obscure, who have borne the appellation; applicable epigrams, biographical sketches, short poetical illustrations, &c.

I read over twelve or fourteen articles and found them exceedingly interesting; abounding in spirit, and novelty; and all supported by quotations in Hebrew, Greek, Latin, Italian, French, Celtic, and Saxon. There was a learned air over all, and in every page, much information, ably compressed, and forming what I should have supposed, an excellent popular volume. She was now seventy-five; and I naturally complimented her, not only on the work in question, but on the amazing beauty and variety of her hand-writing. She seemed gratified and desired me to mention the MS. to some London publisher. This I afterwards did, and sent the work to one alike distinguished for discernment and liberality, but with whom we could not come to an agreement. I have heard no more of "Lyford Redivivus" since, and know not in whose hands the MS. may now be.

A moment later it was in mine, and I was examining it with renewed interest.

My secret is out. I collect, as I can, human-interest books — books with a *provenance*, as they are called;

but as I object to foreign words, I once asked a Bryn Mawr professor, Dr. Holbrook, to give me an English equivalent. "I should have to make one," he said. "You know the word *whereabouts*, I suppose." I admitted that I did. "How would *whenceabouts* do?" I thought it good.

In recent years, presentation, or association, books have become the rage, and the reason is plain. Every one is unique, though some are uniquer than others. My advice to any one who may be tempted by some volume with an inscription of the author on its flyleaf or title-page is, "Yield with coy submission" — and at once. While such books make frightful inroads on one's bank account, I have regretted only my economies, never my extravagances.

I was glancing the other day over Arnold's "Record of Books and Letters." He paid in 1895 seventy-one dollars for a presentation Keats's "Poems," 1817, and sold it at auction in 1901 for five hundred.[1] A few years later I was offered a presentation copy of the work, with an inscription to Keats's intimate friends, Charles and Mary Cowden Clarke, for a thousand dollars, and while I was doing some preliminary financing the book disappeared, and forever; and I have never ceased regretting that the dedication copy of Boswell's "Life of Johnson," to Sir Joshua Reynolds, passed into the collection of my lamented

[1] See *infra*, chapter III, p. 104, where the further adventures of this book are related, and where its price at the Hagen sale, May 14, 1918, becomes $1950, with A. E. N. as the bidder-up.

friend, Harry Widener, rather than into my own. "I shall not pass this way again" seems written in these volumes.

But my record is not all of defeats. The "whenceabouts" of my presentation "Vanity Fair" is not without interest — its story is told in Wilson's "Thackeray in the United States."

The great man took particular delight in schoolboys. When, during his lecturing tour, he visited Philadelphia, he presented one of these boys with a five-dollar goldpiece. The boy's mother objected to his pocketing the coin, and Thackeray vainly endeavored to convince her that this species of beneficence was a thing of course in England. After a discussion the coin was returned, but three months later the lad was made happy by the receipt of a copy of "Vanity Fair," across the title-page of which he saw written, in a curiously small and delicate hand, his name, Henry Reed, with W. M. Thackeray's kind regards, April, 1856.

One day, some years ago, while strolling through Piccadilly, my attention was attracted by a newspaper clipping posted on the window of a bookshop, which called attention to a holograph volume of Johnson-Dodd letters on exhibition within. I spent several hours in careful examination of it, and, although the price asked was not inconsiderable, it was not high in view of the unusual interest of the volume. I felt that I must own it.

When I am going to be extravagant I always like the encouragement of my wife, and I usually get it. I determined to talk over with her my proposed pur-

chase. Her prophetic instinct in this instance was
against it. She reminded me that the business out-
look was not good when we left home, and that the
reports received since were anything but encouraging.
"That amount of money," she said, "may be very
useful when you get home." The advice was good;
indeed, her arguments were so unanswerable that I
determined not to discuss it further, but to buy it
anyhow and say nothing. Early the next morning I
went back, and to my great disappointment found
that some one more forehanded than I had secured
the treasure. My regrets for a time were keen, but
on my return to this country I found myself in the
height of the 1907 panic. Securities seemed almost
worthless and actual money unobtainable; then I congratulated my wife on her wisdom, and pointed out
what a fine fellow I had been to follow her advice.

Six months later, to my great surprise, the collection was again offered me by a bookseller in New
York at a price just fifty per cent in advance of the
price I had been asked for it in London. The man who
showed it to me was amazed when I told him just
when he had bought it and where, and the price he
had paid for it. I made a guess that it was ten per
cent below the figure at which it had been offered to
me. "I am prepared," I said, "to pay you the same
price I was originally asked for it in London. You
have doubtless shown it to many of your customers
and have not found them as foolish in their enthusiasm over Johnson as I am. You have had your

PORTRAIT OF DR. JOHNSON BY SIR JOSHUA REYNOLDS. PAINTED ABOUT 1770
FOR JOHNSON'S STEPDAUGHTER, LUCY PORTER

Engraved by Watson

chance to make a big profit; why not accept a small
one?" There was some discussion; but as I saw my
man weakening, my firmness increased, and it finally
ended by my handing him a check and carrying off the
treasure.

The collection consists of original manuscripts relating to the forgery of Dodd, twelve pieces being
in Dr. Johnson's handwriting. In 1778 Dr. William
Dodd, the "unfortunate" clergyman, as he came to
be called, was condemned to death for forging the
name of his pupil, Lord Chesterfield, to a bond for
forty-two hundred pounds. Through their common
friend Edmund Allen, Johnson worked hard to secure
Dodd's pardon, writing letters, petitions, and addresses, to be presented by Dodd, in his own or his
wife's name, to the King, the Queen, and other important persons, Johnson taking every care to conceal his own part in the matter. In all there are
thirty-two manuscripts relating to the affair. They
were evidently used by Sir John Hawkins in his "Life
of Johnson," but it is doubtful whether Boswell, although he quotes them in part, ever saw the collection.[1]

Pearson, from his shop in Pall Mall Place, issues
catalogues which for size, style, and beauty are unexcelled — they remind one more of publications *de
luxe* than of a bookseller's catalogue. It is almost
vain to look for any item under a hundred pounds,
and not infrequently they run to several thousand.

[1] See *infra*, chapter xi, pp. 307*ff*.

A catalogue now on my writing table tells me of a Caxton: "Tully, His Treatises of Old Age and Friendship," one of four known copies, at twenty-five hundred pounds; and I'd gladly pay it did my means allow.

From Pearson I secured my holograph prayer of Dr. Johnson, of which Birkbeck Hill says: "Having passed into the cabinet of a collector it remains as yet unpublished." It is dated Ashbourne, September 5, 1784 (Johnson died on December 13 of that year), and reads: —

Almighty Lord and Merciful Father, to Thee be thanks, and praise for all thy mercies, for the awakening of my mind, the continuance of my life, the amendment of my health, and the opportunity now granted of commemorating the death of thy Son Jesus Christ, our Mediator and Redeemer. Enable me O Lord to repent truly of my sins — enable me by thy Holy Spirit to lead hereafter a better life. Strengthen my mind against useless perplexities, teach me to form good resolutions and assist me that I may bring them to effect, and when Thou shalt finally call me to another state, receive me to everlasting happiness, for the sake of our Lord Jesus Christ, Amen.

Prayers in Dr. Johnson's hand are excessively rare. He wrote a large number, modeled evidently upon the beautiful Collects — prose sonnets — of the Church of England Prayer Book; but after publication by their first editor, Dr. George Strahan, in 1785, most of the originals were deposited in the Library of Pembroke College, Oxford; hence their scarcity.

From Pearson, too, came my beautiful uncut copy

Ashbourn Sept. 7. 1784

Almighty Lord and merciful Father, to Thee be thanks and praise for all thy mercies, for the awakening of my mind, the continuance of my life, the amendment of my health, and the opportunity now granted of commemorating the death of thy Son Jesus Christ, our Mediator and Redeemer. Enable me O Lord to repent truly of my sins ✝ Enable me by thy Holy Spirit to lead hereafter a better life. Strengthen my mind against useless perplexities, teach me to form good

of "A Journey to the Western Islands of Scotland,"
with a receipt for one hundred pounds in Johnson's
handwriting on account of the copyright of the
book, and, more interesting still, a brief note to
Mrs. Horneck (the mother of Goldsmith's "Jessamy
Bride"), reading: "Mr. Johnson sends Mrs. Horneck
and the young ladies his best wishes for their health
and pleasure in their journey, and hopes his Wife
[Johnson's pet name for the young lady] will keep
him in her mind. Wednesday, June 13." The date
completes the story. Forster states that Goldsmith, in
company with the Hornecks, started for Paris in the
middle of July, 1770. This was the dear old Doctor's
good-bye as the party was setting out.

To spend a morning with Mr. Sabin, the elder, in
his shop in Bond Street is a delight never to be forgotten. The richest and rarest volumes are spread
out before you as unaffectedly as if they were the last
best-sellers. You are never importuned to buy; on
the contrary, even when his treasures are within
your reach, it is difficult to get him to part with them.
One item which you particularly want is a part of a
set held at a king's ransom; some one has the refusal
of another. It is possible to do business, but not
easy.

His son, Frank, occasionally takes advantage of
his father's absence to part with a volume or two.
He admits the necessity of selling a book sometimes
in order that he may buy another. This, I take it,
accounts for the fact that he consented to part with a

THE
WORKS

Of that

Famous English

P O E T,

Mr. Edmond Spenſer.

Viz.
- The FAERY QUEEN,
- The SHEPHERDS CALENDAR,
- The HISTORY of IRELAND, &c.

Whereunto is added,

An ACCOUNT of his LIFE;

With other new ADDITIONS
Never before in PRINT.

Licenſed, *October* 24th 1678. *Roger L'Eſtrange.*

L O N D O N:
Printed by *Henry Hills* for *Jonathan Edwin*, at the
Three Roſes in *Ludgate-ſtreet.* 1679.

JOHN KEATS'S COPY OF SPENSER'S WORKS

copy of "The Works of that Famous English Poet, Mr. Edmond Spenser" — the fine old folio of 1679, with the beautiful title-page. A "name on title" ordinarily does not add to a book's value; but when that name is "John Keats" in the poet's hand, and in addition, "Severn's gift, 1818," one is justified in feeling elated.

John Keats! who in the realm of poetry stands next to the great Elizabethans. It was Spenser's "Fairy Queen" which first fired his ambition to write poetry, and his lines in imitation of Spenser are among the first he wrote. At the time of the presentation of this volume, Severn had recently made his acquaintance, and Keats and his friends were steeped in Elizabethan literature. The finest edition of the works of Spenser procurable was no doubt selected by Severn as a gift more likely than any other to be appreciated by the poet.

Remember that books from Keats's library, which was comparatively a small one, are at the present time practically non-existent; that among them there could hardly have been one with a more interesting association than this volume of Spenser. Remember too that Keats's poem, —

> Sweet are the pleasures that to verse belong,
> And doubly sweet a brotherhood in song, —

was addressed to my great-great-uncle, George Felton Mathew; and let me refer to the fact that on my first visit to England I had spent several days with his sister, who as a young girl had known Keats well, and it will be realized that the possession of this treasure made my heart thump.

Stimulated and encouraged by this purchase, I successfully angled for one of the rarest items of the recent Browning sale, the portrait of Tennyson reading "Maud," a drawing in pen and ink by Rossetti, with a signed inscription on the drawing in the artist's handwriting: —

> I hate the dreadful hollow behind the little wood.

Browning's inscription is as follows: —

Tennyson read his poem of Maud to E.B.B., R.B., Arabel and Rossetti, on the evening of Thursday, Septr. 27, 1855, at 13 Dorset St., Manchester Square. Rossetti made this sketch of Tennyson as he sat reading to E.B.B., who occupied the other end of the sofa.

R.B. March 6, '74.

19 Warwick Crescent.

W. M. Rossetti and Miss Browning were also present on this famous evening, which is vivaciously described by Mrs. Browning in an autograph letter to Mrs. Martin inserted in the album.

One of the pleasantest things which has happened to us here is the coming down on us of the Laureate, who, being in London for three or four days from the Isle of Wight, spent two of them with us, dined with us, smoked with us, opened his heart to us (and the second bottle of port), and ended by reading "Maud" through from end to end, and going away at half-past two in the morning. If I had had a heart to spare, certainly he would have won mine. He is captivating with his frankness, confidingness, and unexampled naïveté! Think of his stopping in "Maud" every

I hate the dreadful hollow behind the little wood

PORTRAIT OF TENNYSON, READING "MAUD" TO ROBERT
AND MRS. BROWNING, BY ROSSETTI

now and then — "There's a wonderful touch! That's very tender. How beautiful that is!" Yes, and it was wonderful, tender, beautiful, and he read exquisitely in a voice like an organ, rather music than speech.

Thus are linked indissolubly together the great Victorians: Browning, Tennyson, Rossetti, and Mrs. Browning. It would be difficult to procure a more interesting memento.

At 27 New Oxford Street, West, is a narrow, dingy little shop, which you would never take to be one of the most celebrated bookshops in London — Spencer's. How he does it, where he gets them, is his business, and an inquiry he answers only with a smile; but the fact is, there they are — just the books you have been looking for, presentation copies and others, in cloth and bound. Spencer owes it to book-collectors to issue catalogues. They would make delightful reading. He has always promised to do it, but he, as well as we, knows that he never will.

But he is kind in another way, if kindness it is: he leaves you alone for hours in that wonderful second-story room, subjected to temptation almost too great to be resisted. Autograph letters, first drafts of well-known poems, rare volumes filled with corrections and notes in the hand of the author, are scattered about; occasionally, such an invaluable item as the complete manuscript of "The Cricket on the Hearth."

It was from the table in this room that I picked up one day a rough folder of cardboard tied with red tape and labeled "Lamb." Opening it, I found a letter from Lamb to Taylor & Hessey, "acknowledging with thanks receit of thirty-two pounds" for the copyright of "Elias (Alas) of last year," signed and dated, June 9, 1824. I felt that it would look well in my presentation "Elia," in boards, uncut, and was not mistaken.

My acquaintance with Mr. Dobell I owe to a paragraph that I read many years ago in Labouchere's "Truth." One day this caught my eye: —

From the catalogue of a West End Bookseller I note this: "Garrick, David. 'Love in the Suds. A Town Eclogue,' first edition. 1772. Very rare. 5 guineas." The next post brought me a catalogue from Bertram Dobell, the well-known bookseller in the Charing Cross Road. There I read, "Garrick, David. 'Love in the Suds. A Town Eclogue,' first edition, 1772, boards, 18 pence." The purchaser of the former might do well to average by acquiring Mr. Dobell's copy.

Old Dobell is in a class by himself — scholar, antiquarian, poet, and bookseller.[1] He is just the type one would expect to find in a shop on the floor of which books are stacked in piles four or five feet high, leaving narrow tortuous paths through which one treads one's way with great drifts of books on either side. To reach the shelves is practically impossible, yet out of this confusion I have picked many a rare item.

[1] I had a letter from Mr. Dobell early in the war, telling me that business was very bad in his line, and that he had taken to writing bad war-poems, which, he said, was a harmless pastime for a man too old to fight. I am not sure that the writing of bad poetry is a harmless pastime, and I was just about to write and tell him so, when I read in the *Athenæum* that he had passed away quite suddenly.

Don't be discouraged if, on your asking for a certain volume, Mr. Dobell gently replies, "No, sorry." That means simply that he cannot put his mental eye on it at the moment. It, or something as interesting, will come along. Don't hurry; and let me observe that the prices of this eighteenth-century bookshop are of the period.

I once sought, for years, a little book of no particular value; but I wanted it to complete a set. I had about given up all hope of securing a copy when I finally found it in a fashionable shop on Piccadilly. It was marked five guineas, an awful price; but I paid it and put the volume in my pocket. That very day I stumbled across a copy in a better condition at Dobell's, marked two and six. I bethought me of Labby's advice and "averaged."

From Dobell came Wordsworth's copy of "Endymion"; likewise a first edition of the old-fashioned love-story, "Henrietta Temple," by Disraeli, inscribed, "To William Beckford with the author's compliments," with many pages of useless notes in Beckford's hand; he seems to have read the volumes with unnecessary care. Nor should I forget a beautiful copy of Thomson's "Seasons," presented by Byron "To the Hon'ble Frances Wedderburne Webster," with this signed impromptu: —

> Go! — volume of the Wintry Blast,
> The yellow Autumn and the virgin Spring.
> Go! — ere the Summer's zephyr 's past
> And lend to loveliness thy lovely Wing.

The morning's mail of a busy man, marked "personal," takes a wide scope, ranging all the way from polite requests for a loan to brief statements that "a prompt remittance will oblige"; but at the bottom of the pile are the welcome catalogues of the second-hand booksellers — for books, to be interesting, must at least be second-hand. Indeed, as with notes offered for discount, the greater the number of good indorsers the better. In books, indorsements frequently take the form of bookplates. I am always interested in such a note as this: "From the library of Charles B. Foote, with his bookplate."

Auction catalogues come, too. These also must be scanned, but they lack the element which makes the dealers' catalogues so interesting — the prices. With prices omitted, book-auction catalogues are too stimulating. The mind at once begins to range. Doubt takes the place of certainty.

The arrival of a catalogue from the Sign of the Caxton Head, Mr. James Tregaskis's shop in High Holborn, in the parish of St.-Giles's-in-the-Fields, always suspends business in my office for half an hour; and while I glance rapidly through its pages in search of nuggets, I paraphrase a line out of Boswell, that "Jimmie hath a very pretty wife." Why should n't a book merchant have a pretty wife? The answer is simple: he has, nor are good-looking wives peculiar to this generation of booksellers.

Tom Davies, it will be remembered, who, in the back parlor of his little bookshop in Russell Street,

Covent Garden, first introduced Boswell to Johnson, had a wife who, we are told, caused the great Doctor to interrupt himself in the Lord's Prayer at the point, "Lead us not into temptation," and whisper to her, with waggish and gallant good humor, "You, my dear, are the cause of this." Like causes still produce like effects.

From Tregaskis I secured my "Memoirs of George Psalmanazar," 1764, an interesting book in itself; but its chief value is the signature and note, "Given to H. L. Thrale by Dr. Sam Johnson," I suppose about 1770. Following Mrs. Thrale's usual practice, there are scattered through the volume a number of notes and criticisms in her handwriting. It

DR. JOHNSON'S CHURCH, ST. CLEMENT
DANES

*From a pen-and-ink sketch by
Charles G. Osgood*

was Psalmanazar, afterwards discovered to be a notorious old scamp, whose apparent piety so impressed Dr. Johnson that he "sought" his company;

and of whom he said, "Sir, contradict Psalmanazar! I should as soon think of contradicting a Bishop."

Given to H: L: Thrale by Dr Sam: Johnson

Side by side with this volume on my shelves stands the "Historical and Geographical Description of Formosa," a work of sheer imagination if ever there was one.

My "Haunch of Venison," 1776, in wrappers, uncut, with the rare portrait of Goldsmith drawn by Bunbury (he married Goldsmith's Little Comedy, it will be remembered), also came from him, as did my "London, A poem in imitation of the third Satire of Juvenal," and the first edition of the first book on London, Stow's "Survay," 1598.

From another source came one of the last books on London, "Our House." This book, delightful in itself, is especially interesting to me by reason of the personal inscription of its charming and witty writer: "To A.E.N., a welcome visitor to 'Our House,' from Elizabeth Robins Pennell."

Continuing along Holborn citywards, one comes to (and usually passes) the Great Turnstile, a narrow

court leading into Lincoln's Inn Fields. Here is another bookshop that I frequent,—Hollings's,—not
for the rarest things, but for the choice little bits
which seem almost commonplace when you are buying them, and give so much pleasure when you get
them safely on your shelves at home. I never spend
a few hours with Mr. Redway, the manager, without
thinking of the saying of one of our most delightful
essayists, Augustine Birrell, who, to our loss, seems
to have forsaken literature for politics: "Second-hand
booksellers are a race of men for whom I have the
greatest respect; . . . their catalogues are the true
textbooks of literature."

One sometimes has the pleasure of running across
some reference in a catalogue to a book of which one
has a better or more interesting copy at half the price.
For example, I saw quoted in a catalogue the other
day at eighty pounds a "Set of the Life of the Prince
Consort, in *five* volumes, with an inscription in each
volume in the autograph of Her Majesty Queen Victoria. The first volume being published before Her
Majesty was proclaimed Empress of India, she signed
as Queen; the other four volumes Her Majesty signed
as Queen-Empress."

In my collection there are *seven* volumes, the five
mentioned above and two additional volumes, the
"Speeches and Addresses" and the "Biography of
the Prince Consort." My copies also are signed, but
note: the volume of "Speeches and Addresses" has
this intensely personal inscription:—

To Major General, the Hon. A. Gordon, in recollection of his great, & good master from the beloved Prince's broken hearted Widow   VICTORIA R.

OSBORNE
    Jan : 12. 1863.

The "Biography" has this : —

To Major General, The Hon. Alexander Gordon, C.B. in recollection of his dear Master from the great Prince's affectionate and sorrowing Widow,   VICTORIA R.

April, 1867.

Volume one of the "Life" is inscribed : —

To Lieutenant General, The Hon. Sir Alexander Gordon, K.C.B., in recollection of his dear Master, from
            VICTORIA R.
January 1875.

Volume two : —

To Lieut. General, The Hon. Sir Alexander Hamilton Gordon, K.C.B., from   VICTORIA R.

Dec. 1876.

Volume three : —

To General, The Hon. Sir Alex. H. Gordon, K.C.B., from   VICTORIA R.I.

Dec. 1877.

The inscriptions in the last three volumes are identical, except for the dates. All are written in the large, flowing hand with which we are familiar, and indicate a declining scale of grief. Time heals all wounds, and as these volumes appear at intervals, grief is finally assuaged and Majesty asserts itself.

To

Major General the
Hon. A. Gordon

In recollection of
his great, & good Master

from

his beloved Friend's

broken hearted

Widow

Victoria

Osborne
Jan: 12. 1863.

II

BOOK-COLLECTING AT HOME

IN the preceding chapter I wrote of the amenities of book-collecting in London, of my adventures in the shops of Bond Street and Piccadilly, of Holborn and the Strand — almost as though this paradise of the book-collector were his only happy hunting-ground. But all the good hunting is not found in London: New York has a number of attractive shops, Philadelphia at least two, while there are several in Chicago and in unexpected places in the West.

Where in all the world will you find so free a buyer, always ready to take a chance to turn a volume at a profit, as George D. Smith? He holds the record for having paid the highest price ever paid for a book at auction: fifty thousand dollars for a copy of the Gutenberg Bible, purchased for Mr. Henry E. Huntington at the Hoe sale; and not only did he pay the highest price — he also bought more than any other purchaser of the fine books disposed of at that sale.

I have heard Smith's rivals complain that he is not a bookseller in the proper sense of the word — that he buys without discretion and without exact knowledge. Such criticism, I take it, is simply the natural result of jealousy. George D. Smith has sold more fine books than perhaps any two of his rivals.

GEORGE D. SMITH

"G. D. S." as he is known in the New York Auction Rooms. Like "G. B. S." of London, he
is something of an enigma. What are the qualities which have made him, as he undoubtedly is,
the greatest bookseller in the world?

From a photograph by Arnold Genthe

There is no affectation of dignity or of knowledge
about him, and it is well that there is not. No one
knows all there is to know about books; a man might
know much more than he — such men there are —
and yet lack the qualities which have enabled him to
secure and retain the confidence and commissions of
his patrons. He is practically the main support of the
auction-rooms in this country, and I have frequently
seen him leave a sale at which he had purchased every
important book that came up. He had knowledge and
confidence enough for that, and I cannot see why his
frankness and lack of affectation should be counted
against him. It takes all kinds of men to make a
world, and George is several kinds in himself.

Twenty-five years ago, in London, early in my
book-collecting days, I came across a bundle of dusty
volumes in an old book-shop in the Strand, — the
shop and that part of the Strand have long since disappeared, — and bought the lot for, as I remember,
two guineas. Subsequently, upon going through the
contents carefully, I found that I had acquired what
appeared to be quite a valuable little parcel. There
were the following: —

"Tales from Shakespeare": Baldwin and Cradock, fifth
  edition, 1831.
Lamb's "Prose Works": 3 volumes, Moxon, 1836.
"The Letters of Charles Lamb": 2 volumes, Moxon, 1837;
  with the inscription, "To J. P. Collier, Esq. from his
  friend H. C. Robinson."
Talfourd's "Final Memorials of Charles Lamb": 2 volumes,
  Moxon, 1848.

By the way, the last was Wordsworth's copy, with his signature on the title-page of each volume; and I observed for the first time that the book was dedicated to him. Loosely inserted in several of the volumes were newspaper clippings, a number of pages of manuscript in John Payne Collier's handwriting, a part of a letter from Mary Lamb addressed to Jane Collier, his mother, and in several of the volumes were notes in Collier's handwriting referring to matters in the text: as where, against a reference to Lamb's "Essay on Roast Pig," Collier says, in pencil, "My mother sent the pig to Lamb." Again, where Talfourd, referring to an evening with Lamb, says, "We mounted to the top story and were soon seated beside a cheerful fire: hot water and its better adjuncts were soon before us," Collier writes, "Both Lamb and Talfourd died of the 'Better Adjuncts.'"

There was a large number of such pencil notes. The pages of manuscript in Collier's heavy and, as he calls it, "infirm" hand begin: —

In relation to C. Lamb and Southey, Mr. Cosens possesses as interesting a MS. as I know. It is bound as a small quarto, but the writing of Lamb, and chiefly by Southey is post 8vo. They seem to have been contributions to an "Annual Anthology" published by Cottle of Bristol.

The MS. begins with an "Advertisement" in the handwriting of Southey, and it is followed immediately by a poem in Lamb's handwriting headed "Elegy on a Quid of Tobacco," in ten stanzas rhiming alternately thus: —

> It lay before me on the close grazed grass
> Beside my path, an old tobacco quid:

And shall I by the mute adviser pass
Without one serious thought? now Heaven forbid! [1]

The next day, Collier copied more of the poem, for on another sheet he remarks, "As my hand is steadier to-day I have copied the remaining stanzas."

On still another sheet, referring to the Cosens MS., Collier writes: —

The whole consists of about sixty leaves chiefly in the handwriting of Southey and it contains . . . productions by Lamb, one a sort of *jeu d'esprit* called "The Rhedycinian Barbers" on the hair-dressing of twelve young men of Christ Church College, and the other headed, "Dirge for Him Who Shall Deserve It." This has no signature but the whole is in Lamb's clear young hand, and it shows very plainly that he partook not only of the poetical but of the political feeling of the time.

The signatures are various, Erthuryo, Ryalto, Walter, and so forth, and at the end are four Love Elegies and a serious poem by Charles Lamb, entitled, "Living without God in the World."

How many of these were printed elsewhere, or in Cottle's "Anthology," I do not know. I would willingly copy more did not my hand fail me.

J. P. C.

Twenty years later, in New York one day, George D. Smith asked me if I would care to buy an interesting volume of Southey MSS., and to my great surprise handed me the identical little quarto which

[1] The facsimile is from the original manuscript by Charles Lamb. First published in 1799 in what is usually referred to as Cottle's "Annual Anthology." The poem is generally attributed to Southey, but it sounds like Lamb, who liked tobacco, whereas Southey did not. The MS., in ten stanzas, is undoubtedly in Lamb's handwriting.

Elegy

On a Quid of Tobacco.

It lay before me on the close-grazed grass
 Beside my path, an old Tobacco quid:
And shall I by the mute adviser pass
 Without one serious thought? now Heaven forbids

perhaps some idle drunkard threw thee there.
 Some husband, spendthrift of his weekly hoar,
One who for wife and children takes no care
 But sits and tipples by the alehouse fire.

Ah luckless was the day he learnt to chew!
 Embryo of ills the Quid that pleased him first!
Thirsty from that unhappy Quid he grew,
 Then to the alehouse went to quench his thirst

So great events from causes small arise,
 The forest oak was once an acorn seed,
And many a wretch from drunkenness who dies
 Owes all his evils to the Indian weed.

Let not temptation mortal, ere come nigh—
 Suspect some ambush in the parsley hid,—
From the first kiss of Love, ye maidens fly!
 Ye youths avoid the first Tobacco Quid.

Collier had many years before found so interesting that he had made excerpts from it. It might not have made such instant appeal to my recollection of my purchase in London had it not been for an inserted note, almost identical with the one on the loose slip in my Lamb volume, obviously in Collier's "infirm" hand, repeating briefly what he had said on the loose sheets in my volumes at home.

Mr. Cosens, the former owner of the manuscripts, had added a note: "In 1798 or 1799 Charles Lamb contributed to the 'Annual Anthology' which a Mr. Cottle, a bookseller of Bristol, published jointly with Coleridge and Southey. This manuscript is partly in the handwriting of Southey and was formerly the property of Cottle of Bristol."

Upon investigation I ascertained that the little volume of manuscript verse had passed from Mr. Cosens's possession into that of Augustin Daly, at whose sale it had been catalogued as a Southey MS., with small reference to its Lamb interest. Although the price was high, the temptation to buy was too strong to be resisted; so after many years the small quarto of original poems by Lamb, Southey, and others, and Collier's description of it, stand side by side in my library. For me the three poems by Lamb outweigh in interest and value all others. The volume is labeled, "Southey Manuscripts, a long time since the property of a Mr. Cottle of Bristol."

The most scholarly bookseller in this country today is Dr. Rosenbach — "Rosy" as we who know him well call him. It was not his original intention to deal in rare books, but to become a professor of English, a calling for which few have a finer appreciation; but mere scholars abound. He must have felt that we collectors needed some one to guide our tastes and deplete our bank accounts. In both he is unequaled.

His spacious second-floor room in Walnut Street is filled with the rarest volumes. "Ask and it shall be given you" — with a bill at the end of the month. It is a delightful place to spend a rainy morning, and you are certain to depart a wiser if a poorer man. I once spent some hours with the doctor in company with my friend Tinker — not the great Tinker who plays ball for a bank president's wage, but the less famous Tinker, Professor of English at Yale. We had been looking at Shakespeare folios and quartos, and Spenser's and Herrick's and Milton's priceless volumes of the sixteenth and seventeenth centuries, when, looking out of the window, Rosy remarked, "There goes John G. Johnson." "Oh!" said my friend, "I thought you were going to say John Dryden. It would not have surprised me in the least."

Don't expect ever to "discover" anything at Rosenbach's, except how ignorant you are. Rosy does all the discovering himself, as when, a few years ago, he found in a volume of old pamphlets a copy of the first edition of Dr. Johnson's famous "Prologue Spoken at the Opening of the Theatre in Drury Lane." It will be remembered that this Prologue contains several of the Doctor's most famous lines: criticisms

DR. A. S. W. ROSENBACH

Photograph by Arnold Genthe

of the stage, as true to-day as when they were uttered; as where he says, —

> The Drama's Laws, the Drama's patrons give,
> For we that live to please, must please to live.

It has also the line in which, speaking of Shakespeare, he says, "And panting Time toil'd after him in vain." Garrick having criticized this line, Johnson remarked, "Sir, Garrick is a prosaical rogue. The next time I write I will make both Time and Space pant."

The discovery by Dr. Rosenbach of this Prologue shows that the days of romance in book-hunting are not over. It is not to be found in the British Museum. So far as we know, it is the only copy in existence. Rosy has declined to sell it, though tempting offers have been made, for he is a booklover as well as a bookseller.

That he is a rare judge of human nature, too, is evidenced by a little card over his desk on which is printed the text, —

"It is naught, it is naught, saith the buyer; but when he hath gone his way then he boasteth." — PROVERBS XX. 14.

That is exactly what I did when I secured from him my "Robinson Crusoe," the first edition in two volumes, with the third, which may not be Defoe's. It lacks one "point" perhaps: the word "apply," the last word on page 1 of the preface, is correctly spelled, not spelled "apyly," as in some copies I have seen. The matter, I believe, is not clear. The type may have been correctly set at first and have become corrupted in process of printing, or a few copies may have been so printed before the error, being noted, was corrected.[1] After page 304, of Volume 1, the paper is of thinner and poorer quality than in the pages preceding it. The three volumes are clean, the binding contemporary calf, the folding maps immaculate, and the first two volumes were once the property of "Mr. William Congreve." Altogether it is a book of which this collector "boasteth."

For some unexplained reason I have never been able to buy as many books from Walter Hill of Chicago as I should like. He is one of the most amiable and reliable men in the business. His catalogues issued from time to time are delightful. He once put me under an obligation which I have not yet repaid and which I want to record.

Several years ago I met him in the streets of Philadelphia and said to him, "Hello! what are you doing here? Are you buying or selling?"

"Both," said he; "I bought some nice books only a few minutes ago at Sessler's."

"Don't tell me," I cried, "that 'Oliver Twist,' that presentation copy to Macready, was among them."

"It was," said he; "why, did you want it?"

"Want it!" said I; "I have just been waiting for my bank account to recover from a capital operation, to buy it."

[1] See Professor Trent's remarks on this "point," in chapter III, p. 100.

THE
LIFE
AND
Strange Surprizing
ADVENTURES
OF
ROBINSON CRUSOE,
Of *YORK,* Mariner:

Who lived Eight and Twenty Years,
all alone in an un-inhabited Island on the
Coaſt of AMERICA, near the Mouth of
the Great River of OROONOQUE:

Having been caſt on Shore by Shipwreck, wherein all the Men periſhed but himſelf.

WITH

An Account how he was at laſt as ſtrangely deliver'd by PYRATES.

Written by Himſelf.

L O N D O N;
Printed for W. TAYLOR at the *Ship in Pater-Noſter-
Row.* MDCCXIX.

"All right," said he, "I'll turn it over at just what I paid for it, and you can send me your check when you are ready."

I was mean enough to accept his offer, and the book is to-day worth at least twice what I paid.

Yet, come to think of it, several nice volumes, "collated and perfect," came from him. There is my "Vicar," not the first edition, with the misprints in volume 2, page 159, paged 165; and page 95, "Waekc-field" for "Wakefield," — that came from North, — but the one with Rowlandson plates. And "Eve-lina," *embellished with engravings*, and wretchedly printed on vile paper; and "She Stoops to Conquer," with all the errors just as they should be — a printer's carnival; and I have no doubt there are many more.

Sessler has some unexpectedly fine things from time to time. He goes abroad every year with his pocket full of money, and comes back with a lot of things that quickly empty ours. Dickens is one of his specialties, and from him I have secured at least five of the twenty-one presentation Dickenses that I boast of. A few years ago quite a number came on the market at prices which to-day seem very low. In my last book-hunting experience in London I saw only one presentation Dickens; but as the price was about three times what I had accustomed myself to pay Sessler, I let it pass.

Sessler studies his customer's weaknesses — that's where his strength lies. When I came back from Europe some years ago, I discovered that he had bought

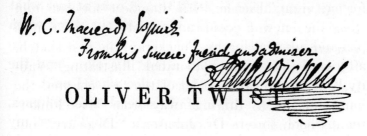

OLIVER TWIST.

BY

CHARLES DICKENS.

AUTHOR OF " THE PICKWICK PAPERS."

IN THREE VOLUMES.

VOL. I.

LONDON:

RICHARD BENTLEY, NEW BURLINGTON STREET.

1838.

for me, in my absence, at the Lambert sale, one item
which he knew I could not resist. It was a little
pen-and-ink drawing by Thackeray, the first sketch,
afterwards more fully elaborated, illustrating "Vanity Fair," where, at the end of the first chapter, the
immortal Becky, driving away from Miss Pinkerton's school, throws Dr. Johnson's "Dixonary" out
of the window of the carriage as it drives off.

I think that all who knew him will agree with me
that Luther S. Livingston was too much of a gentleman, too much of a scholar, — perhaps I should add,
too much of an invalid, — to take high rank as a
bookseller.

His knowledge was profound. He was an appreciative bibliographer, witness the work he did on
Lamb for Mr. J. A. Spoor of Chicago; but I always
felt a trifle embarrassed when I asked him the *price* of
anything he had to sell; one could ask him anything
else, but to offer money to Livingston seemed rather
like offering money to your host after an excellent
dinner.

He enjoyed the love and respect of all book-collectors and we all congratulated him when he graduated from the bookshop to the library. For many
years in charge of the rare-book department of
Dodd, Mead & Company, and subsequently a partner of Robert Dodd, he was the first custodian of
the choice collection of books formed by the late
Harry Elkins Widener and bequeathed by the latter's mother to Harvard. A more admirable selec-

BECKY SHARP THROWING DR. JOHNSON'S "DIXONARY" OUT OF THE CARRIAGE WINDOW, AS SHE LEAVES MISS PINKERTON'S SCHOOL

From the first pen-and-ink sketch, by Thackeray, afterwards elaborated

tion could not have been made. A scholar and a
gentleman, he brought to that position just the qualities needed for a post of such distinction, but, un-
happily, he lived hardly long enough to take possession of it. He died at Christmas, 1914, after a long
and painful illness.

James F. Drake, in New York, specializes in association books and in first editions of nineteenth-cen-
tury authors. His stock I have frequently laid under
contribution. My Surtees and many other colored-
plate books came from him, and first editions innumerable of authors now becoming "collected."

I know of no bibliography of George Moore, but
my set is, I think, complete. Many are presentation
copies. George Moore's many admirers will remember that his volume, " Memoirs of My Dead Life," is
much sought in the first English edition. I have the
proof sheets of the entire volume, showing many corrections, as in the specimen on page 50. My "Literature at Nurse," — a pamphlet attacking the censor-
ship of the novel established by Mudie,—which was
published at threepence, and now commands forty
dollars, is inscribed to Willie Wilde; while "Pagan
Poems" was a suitable gift "To Oscar Wilde with
the author's compliments."

There is no halt in the constantly advancing value
of first editions of Oscar Wilde. That interest in the
man still continues, is evidenced by the steady stream
of books about him. Ransome's "Oscar Wilde," immediately suppressed; "Oscar Wilde Three Times

same tone as the sky. And what did I feel? Soft perfumed airs moving everywhere. And what was the image that rose up in my mind? The sensuous gratification of a vision of a woman bathing at the edge of a summer wood, the intoxication of the odour of her breasts. . . . Why should I think of a woman bathing at the edge of a summer wood? Because the morning seemed the very one that Venus should choose to rise from the sea and come into one's bedroom. Forgive my sensuousness, dear reader; remember that it was the first time I breathed the soft Southern air, the first time I saw orange trees; remember that I am a poet, a modern Jason in search of a golden fleece. 'Is this the garden of the Hesperides?' I asked myself, for nothing seemed more unreal than the golden fruit hanging like balls of yellow worsted among dark and sleek leaves; it reminded me of the fruit I used to see when I was a child under glass shades in lodging-houses, but I knew, nevertheless, that I was looking upon orange trees, and that the golden fruit growing amid the green leaves was the fruit I used to pick from the barrows when I was a boy; the fruit of which I ate so much in boyhood that I cannot eat it any longer; the fruit whose smell we associate with the pit of a theatre; the fruit that women never grow weary of, high and low. It seemed to me a wonderful thing that at last I should see oranges growing on trees ~~; I so happy, so singularly happy, that I am nearly sure that happiness is, after all, no more than a faculty for being surprised. Since I was a boy I~~

, and I felt so happy that morning that I could not but wonder at my happiness, and seeking for a cause for it I stumbled on the reflection that perhaps after all happiness is no more than a faculty for being surprised.

Tried," and "The First Stone," privately printed by
the "Unspeakable Scot," already difficult to procure,
are among the
latest.

For books of the
moment, published
in small editions
which almost im-
mediately become
scarce, Drake's shop
in Fortieth Street is
headquarters; and
as my club in New
York is near by,
I find myself fre-
quently dropping
in for a book and
a bit of gossip.

There are draw-
backs as well as
compensations to
living in the coun-
try. "Gossip about
Book Collecting " has its charms, as William Loring
Andrews has taught us. It is sometimes difficult to
get it, living as I do "twelve miles from a lemon";
and so, when I am in New York and have absorbed
what I can at Drake's, who is very exact in the information he imparts, I usually call on Gabriel Wells.
How Wells receives you with open arms and a good

cigar, in his lofty rooms on the Avenue overlooking
the Library, is known to most collectors. Books in
sets are, — perhaps I should say, were, — his spe-
cialty; recently he has gone in for very choice items,
which, when offered, must be secured, or anguish is
one's portion thereafter. My last interview with him
resulted in my separating myself from a bunch of
Liberty Bonds, which I had intended as a solace for
my old age; but a few words from Wells convinced
me that Dr. Johnson was right when he said, "It is
better to live rich than die rich"; and so I walked
away with a copy of Blake's "Marriage of Heaven
and Hell," which is about as rare a book as one can
hope to find at the end of a busy day.

It was, if I remember correctly, Ernest Dressel
North who first aroused my interest in Lamb, bib-
liographically. I had learned to love him in a dumpy
little green cloth volume, "Elia and Eliana," published
by Moxon, which I had picked up at Leary's, and
which bears upon its title-page the glaring inaccu-
racy, — "The Only Complete Edition." I have this
worthless little volume among my first editions; to
me it is one, and it is certainly the last volume of
Lamb I would part with.

It must be all of thirty years ago that I went to
London with a list of books by and about Charles
Lamb — some twenty volumes in all — which North
had prepared for me. I came across this list not long
ago, and was amused at the prices that he suggested
I might safely pay. Guineas where his list gives

shillings would not to-day separate the books from their owners.

It was at this time, too, that I made my first Lamb pilgrimage, going to every place of interest I could find, from Christ's Hospital, then in Newgate Street, where I saw the Blue-Coat boys at dinner, to the neglected grave in Edmonton Churchyard, where Charles and Mary Lamb lie buried side by side. The illustration facing page 54 is made from a negative I procured in 1890, of the house at Enfield in which Lamb lived from October, 1829, until May, 1833.

A good story is told of my friend, Edmund D. Brooks, the bookseller of far-off Minneapolis. Brooks, who knows his way about London and is as much at home with the talent there as any other man, set out one day to make a "quick turn," in stock-market parlance. Armed with a large sum of money, the sinews of book-buying as well as of war, he casually dropped in on Walter Spencer, who was offering for sale the manuscript of Dickens's "Cricket." The price was known to be pretty steep, but Brooks was prepared to pay it. What he did not know was that, in an upper room over Spencer's shop, another bookseller, also with a large sum in pocket, was debating the price of this very item, raising his offer by slow degrees. But it did not take Brooks long to discover that negotiations were progressing and that quick action was necessary. Calling Spencer aside, he inquired the price, paid the money, and took the invaluable manuscript away in a taxi. The whole transaction had occupied only a couple of minutes. Spencer then returned to his first customer, who continued the attack until, to close the argument, Spencer quietly remarked that the manuscript had been sold, paid for, and had passed out of his possession.

It reminds one of the story of how the late A. J. Cassatt, the master mind of the railroad presidents of his time, bought the Philadelphia, Wilmington & Baltimore Railway right under the nose of President Garrett of the Baltimore & Ohio. There were loud cries of anguish from the defeated parties on both occasions, but the book-selling story is not over yet, for a few hours later Sabin, the bookseller *de luxe*, had the Dickens manuscript displayed in his shop-window in Bond Street, and Brooks had a sheaf of crisp Bank of England notes in his pocket, with which to advance negotiations in other directions.

I take little or no interest in bindings; I want the book as originally published, in boards uncut, in old sheep, or in cloth, and as clean and fair as may be.

I am not without a sense for color, and the backs of books bound in various colored leathers, suitably gilt, placed with some eye for arrangement on the shelves, are to me as beautiful and suggestive as any picture; yet, as one cannot have everything, I yield the beauty and fragrance of leather for the fascination of the "original state as issued."

Nor am I unmindful how invariably in binding a book, in trimming, be it ever so little, and gilding its

CHARLES LAMB'S HOUSE AT ENFIELD

edges, one lops off no small part of its value. This fact should be pointed out to all young collectors. They should learn to let their books alone, and if they must patronize a binder, have slip-cases or pull-cases made. They serve every purpose. The book will be protected if it is falling apart and unpresentable, and one's craving for color and gilt will be satisfied. As Eckel says in his "Bibliography of Dickens," "The tendency of the modern collector has steadily moved toward books in their original state, — books as they were when created, — and it is doubtful if there will be much deviation from this taste in the future."

Only the very immature book-buyer will deprive himself of the pleasure of "collecting," and buy a complete set of some author he much esteems, in first editions, assembled and bound without care or thought other than to produce a piece of merchandise and sell it for as much as it will fetch. The rich and ignorant buyer should be made to confine his attention to the purchase of "subscription" books. These are produced in quantity especially for his benefit, and he should leave our books alone. The present combination of many rich men and relatively few fine books is slowly working my ruin; I know it is. We live in a law-full age, an age in which it seems to be every one's idea to pass laws. I would have a law for the protection of old books, and our legislators in Washington might do much worse than consider this suggestion.

One other form of book the collector should be

This is the novel which
the late W. G. Henley accepted
for serial in the New Review
on the strength of its first
2 chapters with the remark
to S. S. Pawling

"Tell Conrad that if the rest
is up to Sample it shall
certainly go into the N. R."

Joseph Conrad

By these pages I stand
or fall.

INSCRIPTION IN A COPY OF "THE NIGGER OF THE 'NARCISSUS'"

warned against — the extra-illustrated volume. The extra-illustration of a favorite author is a tedious and expensive method of wasting money, and mutilating other books the while. I confess to having a few, but I have bought them at a very small part of what they cost to produce, and I do not encourage their production.

I know something of the art of inlaying prints. I had a distinguished and venerable teacher, the late Ferdinand J. Dreer of Philadelphia, who formed a priceless collection of autographs, which at his death he bequeathed to the Historical Society of Pennsylvania. Mr. Dreer was a collector of the old school. He was a friend of John Allan, one of the earliest book-collectors in this country, of whom a "Memorial" was published by the Bradford Club in 1864. Mr. Dreer spent the leisure of years and a small fortune in inlaying plates and pages of text of such books as he fancied. I remember well as a lad being allowed to pore over his sumptuous extra-illustrated books, filled with autograph letters, portraits, and views, for hours at a time. Little did I think that these volumes, the object of such loving care, would be sold at auction.

Many years after his death the family decided to dispose of a portion of his library. Stan. Henkels conducted the sale. When the well-known volumes came up, I was all in a tremble. It seemed hardly possible that any of the famous Dreer books were to come within my grasp. But alas! fashions change, as I have said before. A "History of the Bank of North

America," our oldest national bank, which enjoys
the unique distinction of not calling itself a national
bank, went, not to an officer or director of that sound
old Philadelphia institution, but to George D. Smith
of New York, for a song — in a high key, but a song
nevertheless.

An "Oration in Carpenter's Hall" in Philadelphia
brought close to a thousand dollars; but, in addition to
the rare portraits and views, there were fifty-seven
autograph letters in it. Sold separately, they would
have brought several times as much. Smith was the
buyer. Then there came a "History of Christ
Church," full of most interesting material, as "old
Christ Church" is the most beautiful and interesting
colonial church in America. Where was the rector,
where were the wardens and the vestry thereof? No
sign of them. Smith was the buyer.

The books were going and for almost nothing, in
every case to "Smith." At last came the "Memoirs
of Nicholas Biddle," of the famous old Bank of the
United States. Hear! ye Biddles, if any Biddles there
be. There are, in plenty, but not here. Smith, having
bought all the rest, stopped when he saw me bidding;
the hammer fell, and I was the owner of the most
interesting volume in the whole Dreer collection, —
the volume I had so often coveted as a boy, with
the letters and portraits of Penn, Franklin, Adams,
Jefferson, Madison, Marshall, and so forth, — in all
twenty-eight of them, and mine for ten dollars
apiece, book, portraits, and binding thrown in. It

is painful to witness the slaughter of another's possessions; it makes one wonder — But that is not what
we collect books for.

In the last analysis pretty much everything, including poetry, is merchandise, and every important
book sooner or later turns up in the auction rooms.
The dozen or fifty men present represent the bookbuyers of the world — you are buying against them.
When you sell a book at auction the whole world is
your market. This refers, of course, only to important
sales. At other times books are frequently disposed
of at much less than their real value. These sales it
pays the book-collector to attend, personally, if he
can; or, better still, to entrust his bid to the auctioneer
or to some representative in whom he has confidence.
Most profitable of all for the buyer are the sales
where furniture, pictures, and rugs are disposed of,
with, finally, a few books knocked down by one who
knows nothing of their value.

Many are the volumes in my library which have
been picked up on such occasions for a very few dollars, and which are worth infinitely more than I paid
for them. I have in mind my copy of the first edition
of Boswell's "Corsica," in fine old calf, with the inscription "To the Right Honourable, the Earl Maris-
chal of Scotland, as a mark of sincere regard and
affection, from the Author, James Boswell." This
stands me only a few dollars. In London I should
have been asked — and would have paid — twenty
pounds for it.

Some men haunt the auction rooms all the time. I do not. I have a living to make and I am not quick in making it; moreover, the spirit of competition invariably leads me astray, and I never come away without finding myself the owner of at least one book, usually a large one, which should properly be entitled, "What Will He Do With It?"

No book-collector should be without a book-plate, and a book-plate once inserted in a volume should never be removed. When the plate is that of a good collector, it constitutes an indorsement, and adds a certain interest and value to the volume.

I was once going through the collection of a friend, and observing the absence of a book-plate, I asked him why it was. He replied, "The selection of a book-plate is such a serious matter." It is; and I should never have been able to get one to suit me entirely had not my good friend, Osgood of Princeton, come to my rescue.

He was working in my library some years ago on an exquisite appreciation of Johnson, when, noticing on my writing-table a pen-and-ink sketch, he asked, "What's this?" I replied with a sigh that it was a suggestion for a book-plate which I had just received from London. I had described in a letter exactly what I wanted — an association plate strictly in eighteenth-century style. Fleet Street was to be indicated, with Temple Bar in the background. It was to be plain and dignified in treatment. What came was indeed

I — 9 — O — 9

A. EDWARD NEWTON

EX LIBRIS

OAK KNOLL

Hill's *Boswell* II 238

" Sir, the biographical part of literature
is what I love moft."

The book-plate illustrates an incident described in Boswell. Johnson and Goldsmith were walking one day in the Poets' Corner of Westminster Abbey. Looking
at the graves, Johnson solemnly repeated a line from a Latin poet, which might
be freely translated, " Perchance some day our *names* will mingle with these."
As they strolled home through the Strand, Goldsmith's eye lighted upon the heads
of two traitors rotting on the spikes over Temple Bar. Remembering that Johnson and he were rather Jacobitic in sentiment, pointing to the heads and giving
Johnson's quotation a twist, Goldsmith remarked, " Perhaps some day our *heads*
will mingle with those."

a sketch of Fleet Street and very much more.   There
were scrolls and flourishes, eggs and darts and *fleurs-
de-lis* — a little of everything.   In a word it was impossible.   "Let me see what I can do," said Osgood.

When I returned home that evening there was waiting for me an exquisite pencil sketch, every detail
faultless: Fleet Street with its tavern signs, in the
background Temple Bar with Johnson and Goldsmith, the latter pointing to it and remarking slyly,
"*Forsitan et nomen nostrum miscebitur istis.*"   I was
delighted, as I had reason to be.   In due course, after
discussions as to the selection of a suitable motto, we
finally agreed on a line out of Boswell: "Sir, the biographical part of literature is what I love most"; and
the sketch went off to Sidney Smith of Boston, the
distinguished book-plate engraver.

I have a fondness for college professors.   I must
have inherited it from a rich old uncle, from whom I
unluckily inherited nothing else, who had a similar
weakness for preachers.   Let a man, however stupid,
once get a license to wear his collar backwards, and
the door was flung wide and the table spread.   I have
often thought what an ecstasy of delight he would
have been thrown into had he met a churchman whose
rank permitted him to wear his entire ecclesiastical
panoply backwards.

My weakness for scholars is just such a whimsy.   As
a rule they are not so indulgent to collectors as they
should be.   They write books that we buy and read
— when we can.   My lifelong friend, Felix Schelling

(in England he would be Sir Felix) is more lenient than most. My copy of his "Elizabethan Drama," which has made him famous among students, is uncut and, I am afraid, to some extent unopened. Frankly, it is too scholarly to read with enjoyment. Indeed, I sometimes think that it was my protest that led him to adopt the easier and smoother style apparent in his later books, "English Literature during the Lifetime of Shakespeare," and "The English Lyric." Be this as it may, he has shown that he can use the scholarly and the familiar style with equal facility; and when he chooses, he can turn a compliment like one of his own sixteenth-century courtiers.

I had always doubted that famous book-index story, "Mill, J. S., 'On Liberty'; Ditto, 'On the Floss,'" until one day my friend Tinker sent me a dedication copy of his "Dr. Johnson and Fanny Burney," in which I read — and knew that he was poking fun at me for my bookish weakness — this: —

This copy is a genuine specimen of the first edition, uncut and unopened, signed and certified by the editor.
CHAUNCEY BREWSTER TINKER.

No copy is now known to exist of the suppressed first state of the first edition — that in which, instead of the present entry in the index, under Pope, Alexander, page 111, occurred the words, "Pope Alexander 111."

How much more valuable this copy would have been if this blunder — "point," the judicious would call it — had not been corrected until the second edition!

The work of my office was interrupted one summer morning several years ago by the receipt of a cable from London, apparently in code, which, I was advised, would not translate. Upon its being submitted to me I found that it did not require translating, but I was not surprised that it was somewhat bewildering to others. It read, "*Johnson Piazza Dictionary Pounds Forty Hut*." To me it was perfectly clear that Mrs. Thrale-Piozzi's copy of Johnson's Dictionary in two volumes folio was to be had from my friend Hutt for forty pounds. I dispatched the money and in due course received the volumes. Inserted in one of them was a long holograph letter to the Thrales, giving them some excellent advice on the management of their affairs.

I think it very probably in your power to lay up eight thousand pounds a year for every year to come, increasing all the time, what needs not be increased, the splendour of all external appearance, and surely such a state is not to be put in yearly hazard for the pleasure of keeping the house full, or the ambition of outbrewing Whitbread. Stop now and you are safe — stop a few years and you may go safely on thereafter, if to go on shall seem worth the while.

Johnson's letters, like his talks, are compact with wisdom, and many of them are as easy as the proverbial old shoe. Fancy Sam Johnson, the great lexicographer, writing to Mrs. Thrale and telling her to come home and take care of him and, as he says, to

> Come with a whoop, come with a call,
> Come with a good will, or come not at all.

I own thirty or forty Johnson letters, including the one in which he describes what she called his "menagerie" — dependents too old, too poor, or too peevish to find asylum elsewhere. He writes, "We have tolerable concord at home, but no love. Williams hates everybody. Levet hates Desmoulines, and does not love Williams. Desmoulines hates them both. Poll loves none of them."

But I must be careful. I had firmly resolved not to say anything which would lead any one to suspect that I am Johnson-mad, but I admit that such is the case. I am never without a copy of Boswell. What edition? Any edition. I have them all — the first in boards uncut, for my personal satisfaction; an extra-illustrated copy of the same, for display; Birkbeck Hill's, for reference, and the cheap old Bohn copy which thirty years ago I first read, because I know it by heart. Yes, I can truly say with Leslie Stephen, "My enjoyment of books began and will end with Boswell's 'Life of Johnson.'"

> "Thou fool! to seek companions in a crowd!
> Into thy room, and there upon thy knees,
> Before thy bookshelves, humbly thank thy God,
> That thou hast friends like these!"

III

OLD CATALOGUES AND NEW PRICES

THE true book-lover is usually loath to destroy an old book-catalogue. It would not be easy to give a reason for this, unless it is that no sooner has he done so than he has occasion to refer to it. Such catalogues reach me by almost every mail, and I while away many hours in turning over their leaves. Anatole France in his charming story, "The Crime of Sylvestre Bonnard," makes his dear old book-collector say, "There is no reading more easy, more fascinating, and more delightful than that of a catalogue"; and it is so, for the most part; but some catalogues annoy me exceedingly: those which contain long lists of books that are not books; genealogies; county (and especially town) histories, illustrated with portraits; obsolete medical and scientific books; books on agriculture and diseases of the horse. How it is that any one can make a living by vending such merchandise is beyond me — but so are most things.

Living, however, in the country, and going to town every day, I spend much time on the trains, and must have something to read besides newspapers, — who was it who said that reading newspapers is a nervous habit? — and it is not always convenient to carry a book; so I usually have a few catalogues which I mark industriously, thus presenting a fine imitation of a

busy man. One check means a book that I own, and
I note with interest the prices; another, a book that
I would like to have; while yet another indicates a
book to which under no circumstances would I give
a place on my shelves. When my library calls for a
ridding up, these slim pamphlets are not discarded
as they should be, but are stored in a closet, to be referred to when needed, until at last something must
be done to make room for those that came to-day and
those that will come to-morrow.

On one of these occasional house-clearings I came
across a bundle of old catalogues which I have never
had it in me to destroy. One of them was published
in 1886, by a man I knew well years ago, Charles
Hutt, of Clement's Inn Gateway, Strand. Hutt himself has long since passed away; so has his shop, the
Gateway; and, indeed, the Strand itself — his part of
it, that is. I sometimes think that the best part of
old London has disappeared. Need I say that I refer
to Holywell Street and the Clare Market district
which lay between the Strand and Lincoln's Inn
Fields, which Dickens knew and described so well?
Hutt in his day was a man of considerable importance. He was the first London bookseller to realize
the direction and value of the American market. Had
he lived, my friends Sabin and Spencer and Maggs
would have had a serious rival.

All the old catalogues before me are alike in one
important respect, namely, the uniformly low prices.
From the standpoint of to-day the prices were ab-

surdly low — or are those of to-day absurdly high?
I, for one, do not think so. When a man puts pen to
paper on the subject of the prices of rare books, he
feels — at least I feel — that it is a silly thing to do,
— and yet we collectors have been doing it always,
or almost always, — to point out that prices have
about reached top notch, and that the wise man will
wait for the inevitable decline before he separates
himself from his money.

Now, it is my belief that books, in spite of the high
prices that they are bringing in the shops and at auction, have only just begun their advance, and that
there is no limit to the prices they will bring as time
goes on. The only way to guess the future is to study
the past; and such study as I have been able to make
leads me to believe that for the really great books the
sky is the limit.

"The really great books!" What are they, and
where are they? I am not sure that I know; they do
not often come my way, nor, when they do, am I in
a position to compete for them; but as I can be perfectly happy without an ocean-going yacht, content-
ing myself with a motor-boat, so can I make shift to
get along without a Gutenberg Bible, without a first
folio of Shakespeare, or any of the quartos, in short,
sans any of those books which no millionaire's library can be without. But this I will say, that if I
could afford to buy them, I would pay any price for
the privilege of owning them.

A man may be possessed of relatively small means

and yet indulge himself in all the joys of collecting, if he will deny himself other things not so important to his happiness. It is a problem in selection, as Elia points out in his essay "Old China," when a weighing for and against and a wearing of old clothes is recommended by his sister Bridget, if the twelve or sixteen shillings saved is to enable one to bring home in triumph an old folio. As a book-collector, Lamb would not take high rank; but he was a true book-lover, and the books he liked to read he liked to buy. And just here I may be permitted to record how I came across a little poem, in the manuscript of the author, which exactly voices his sentiments — and mine.

I was visiting Princeton not long ago, that beautiful little city, with its lovely halls and towers; and interested in libraries as I always am, had secured permission to browse at will among the collections formed by the late Laurence Hutton. After an inspection of his "Portraits in Plaster," — a collection of death-masks, unique in this country or elsewhere, — I turned my attention to his association books. It is a difficult lot to classify, and not of overwhelming interest; not to be compared with the Richard Waln Meirs collection of Cruikshank, which has just been bequeathed to the Library; but nothing which is a book is entirely alien to me, and the Hutton books, with their inscriptions from their authors, testifying to their regard for him and to his love of books, are well worth examination.

I had opened many volumes at random, and finally

chanced upon Brander Matthews's "Ballads of
Books," a little anthology of bookish poems, for many
years a favorite of mine. Turning to the inscription,
I found — what I found; but what interested me
particularly was a letter from an English admirer, one
Thomas Hutchinson, inclosing some verses, of which
I made a copy without the permission of any one. I
did not ask the librarian, for he might have referred
the question to the trustees, or something; but I did
turn to a speaking likeness of "Larry" that hung
right over the bookcase and seemed to say, "Why,
sure, fellow book-lover; pass on the torch, print anything you please." And these are the verses: —

BALLADE OF A POOR BOOK-LOVER

I

Though in its stern vagaries Fate
    A poor book-lover me decreed,
Perchance mine is a happy state —
    The books I buy I like to read:
To me dear friends they are indeed,
    But, howe'er enviously I sigh,
Of others take I little heed —
    The books I read I like to buy.

II

My depth of purse is not so great
    Nor yet my bibliophilic greed,
That merely buying doth elate:
    The books I buy I like to read:
Still e'en when dawdling in a mead,
    Beneath a cloudless summer sky,
By bank of Thames, or Tyne, or Tweed,
    The books I read — I like to buy.

III

Some books tho' tooled in style ornate,
Yet worms upon their contents feed,
Some men about their bindings prate —
The books I buy I like to read:
Yet some day may my fancy breed
My ruin — it may now be nigh —
They reap, we know, who sow the seed:
The books I read I like to buy.

ENVOY

Tho' frequently to stall I speed,
The books I buy I like to read;
Yet wealth to me will never hie —
The books I read I like to buy.

Two things there are which go to make the price
of a book — first the book itself, its scarcity, together
with the urgency of the demand for it (a book may
be unique and yet practically valueless, because of
the fact that no one much cares to have it); and
second, the plentifulness of money, or the ease with
which its owner may have acquired his fortune. No
one will suppose that, at the famous auction in London something over a hundred years ago, when Earl
Spencer bid two thousand, two hundred and fifty
pounds for the famous Boccaccio, and the Marquis of
Blandford added, imperturbedly, "ten," and secured
the prize — no one will suppose that either of the
gentlemen had a scanty rent-roll.

In England, the days of the great private libraries
are over. For generations, indeed for centuries, the
English have had the leisure, the inclination, and the

means to gratify their taste. They once searched the
Continent for books and works of art, very much as
we now go to England for them. They formed their
libraries when books were plentiful and prices low.
Moreover, there were fewer collectors than there
are to-day. We are paying big prices, — the English
never sell except at a profit, — but, all things considered, we are not paying more for the books than
they are worth. There are probably now in England
as many collectors as there ever were, but nevertheless the books are coming to this country; and while
we may never be able to rival the treasures of the
British Museum and the Bodleian, outside the great
public libraries the important collections are now in
this country, and will remain here.

And I am not sure how much longer the London
dealers are going to retain their preëminence. We
hear of New York becoming the centre of the financial
world. It will in time become the centre of the book-
selling world as well, the best market in which to
buy and in which to sell. With the possible exception
of Quaritch, George D. Smith has probably sold as
many rare books as any man in the world; while Dr.
Rosenbach, on the second floor of his shop in Philadelphia, has a stock of rare books unequaled by any
other dealer in this country.

Ask any expert where the great books are, and you
will be told, if you do not know already, of the wonders of Mr. Morgan's collections; of how Mr. Huntington has bought one library after another until he

has practically everything obtainable; of Mr. William K. Bixby's manuscripts, of Mr. White's collection of the Elizabethans, and of Mr. Folger's Shakespeares.

There are as many tastes as there are collectors. Caxtons and incunabula of any sort are highly regarded; even the possession of a set of the Shakespeare folios makes a man a marked man, in spite of the fact that Henrietta Bartlett says they are not rare; but then, Miss Bartlett has been browsing on books rarer still, namely, the first quartos, of which there are of "Hamlet" two copies only, one in this country with a title-page, but lacking the last leaf, while the other copy, in the British Museum, has the last leaf but lacks the title-page; and "Venus and Adonis," of the first eight editions of which only thirteen copies are known to exist. All of these are as yet in England, except one copy of the second edition, which is owned by the Elizabethan Club of Yale University. Of "Titus Andronicus" there is only one copy of the first printing, this in the library of H. C. Folger of New York. Surely no one will dispute Miss Bartlett's statement that the quartos are rare indeed.

But why continue? Enough has been said: the point I want to make is that fifty years from now someone will be regretting that he was not present when a faultless first folio could have been had for the trifling sum of twenty-five thousand dollars, at which figure a dealer is now offering one. Or, glancing over a copy of "Book Prices Current" for 1918, bewail the

HENRY E. HUNTINGTON OF NEW YORK

A few years ago he conceived the idea of forming the greatest private library in the world. With the help of " G. D. S." and assisted by a staff of able librarians, he has accomplished what he set out to do.

time when presentation copies of Dickens could have been had for the trifling sum of a thousand dollars. Hush! I feel the spirit of prophecy upon me.

I sat with Harry Widener at Anderson's auction rooms a few years ago, on the evening when George D. Smith, acting for Mr. Huntington, paid fifty thousand dollars for a copy of the Gutenberg Bible. No book had ever sold for so great a price, yet I feel sure that Mr. Huntington secured a bargain, and I told him so; but for the average collector such great books as these are mere names, as far above the ordinary man as the moon; and the wise among us never cry for them; we content ourselves with — something else.

In collecting, as in everything else, experience is the best teacher. Before we can gain our footing we must make our mistakes and have them pointed out to us, or, by reading, discover them for ourselves. I have a confession to make. Forty years ago I thought that I had the makings of a numismatist in me, and was for a time diligent in collecting coins. In order that they might be readily fastened to a panel covered with velvet, I pierced each one with a small hole, and was much chagrined when I was told that I had absolutely ruined the lot, which was worth, perhaps, ten dollars. This was not a high price to pay for the discovery I then made and noted, that it is the height of wisdom to leave alone anything of value which may come my way; to repair, inlay, insert, mount, frame, or bind as little as possible.

This is not to suggest that my library is entirely devoid of books in bindings. A few specimens of the good binders I have, but what I value most is a sound bit of straight-grained crimson morocco covering the "Poems of Mr. Gray" with one of the finest examples of fore-edge painting I have ever seen, representing Stoke Poges Church Yard, the scene of the immortal "Elegy." I was much pleased when I discovered that this binding bore the stamp of Taylor & Hessey, a name I had always associated with first editions of Charles Lamb.

How many people have clipped signatures from old letters and documents, under the mistaken notion that they were collecting autographs. I happen to own the receipt for the copyright of the "Essays of Elia." It was signed by Lamb twice, originally; one signature has been cut away. It is a precious possession as it is, but I could wish that the "collector" in whose hands it once was had not removed one signature for his "scrapbook" — properly so called. Nor is the race yet dead of those who, indulging a vicious taste for subscription books, think that they are forming a library. My coins I have kept as an ever-present reminder of the mistake of my early days. Luckily I escaped the subscription-book stage.

What we collect depends as well upon our taste as upon our means, for, given zeal and intelligence, it is surprising how soon one acquires a collection of — whatever it may be — which becomes a source of re-

STOKE POGES CHURCH

A fine example of fore-edge painting

laxation and instruction; and after a little one becomes, if not exactly expert, at least wise enough to
escape obvious pitfalls. When experience directs our
efforts the chief danger is past. But how much there
is to know! I never leave the company of a man like
Dr. Rosenbach, or A. J. Bowden, or the late Luther
Livingston, without feeling a sense of hopelessness
coming over me. What wonderful memories these
men have! how many minute "points" about books
they must have indexed, so to speak, in their minds!
And there are collectors whose knowledge is equally
bewildering. Mr. White, or Beverly Chew, for example; and Harry Widener, who, had he lived, would
have set a new and, I fear, hopeless standard for us.

Not knowing much myself, I have found it wise not
to try to beat the expert; it is like trying to beat Wall
Street — it cannot be done. How can an outsider
with the corner of his mind compete with one who is
playing the game ever and always? The answer is
simple — he can't; and he will do well not to try. It
is better to confess ignorance and rely upon the word
of a reliable dealer, than to endeavor to put one over
on him. This method may enable a novice to buy a
good horse, although such has not been my experience. I think it was Trollope who remarked that not
even a bishop could sell a horse without forgetting
that he was a bishop. I think I would rather trust a
bookseller than a bishop.

And speaking of booksellers, they should be regarded as Hamlet did his players, as the abstract and

brief chronicles of the time; and it would be well to
remember that their ill report of you while you live is
much worse than a bad epitaph after you are dead.
Their stock in trade consists, not only in the books
they have for sale, but in their knowledge. This may
be at your disposal, if you use them after your own
honor and dignity; but to live, they must sell books
at a profit, and the delightful talk about books which
you so much enjoy must, at least occasionally, result
in a sale. Go to them for information as a possible
customer, and you will find them, as Dr. Johnson
said, generous and liberal-minded men; but use them
solely as walking encyclopædias, and you may come
to grief.

I have on the shelves over yonder a set of Foxe's
"Martyrs" in three ponderous volumes, which I seldom have occasion to refer to; but in one volume is
pasted a clipping from an old newspaper, telling a story
of the elder Quaritch. A young lady once entered his
shop in Piccadilly and requested to see the great man.
She wanted to know all that is to be known of this
once famous book, all about editions and prices and
"points," of which there are many. Finally, after he
had answered questions readily enough for some
time, the old man became wise, and remarked, "Now,
my dear, if you want to know anything else about
this book, my fee will be five guineas." The transaction was at an end. Had Quaritch been a lawyer
and the young lady a stranger, her first question
would have resulted in a request for a retainer.

But I am a long time in coming to my old catalogues. Let me take one at random, and opening it at the first page, pick out the first item which meets my eye. Here it is: —

ALKEN, HENRY — Analysis of the Hunting Field. Woodcuts and colored illustrations. First edition, royal 8vo. original cloth, uncut. Ackerman, 1846. £2.

It was the last work but one of a man who is now "collected" by many who, like myself, would as soon think of riding a zebra as a hunter. My copy cost me $100, while my "Life of Mytton," third edition, I regarded as a bargain at $50. Had I been wise enough to buy it five and thirty years ago, I would have paid about as many shillings for it.

With sporting books in mind it is quite natural to turn to Surtees. His "Jorrocks' Jaunts and Jollities" is missing from this catalogue, but here are a lot of them. "Mr. Sponge's Sporting Tour" in full levant morocco, extra, by Tout, for three guineas, and "Ask Mamma" in cloth, uncut, for £2 15s. "Handley Cross" is priced at fifty shillings, and "Facey Romford's Hounds" at two pounds — all first editions, mind you, and for the most part just as you want them, in the original cloth, uncut. My advice would be to forget these prices of yesteryear, and if you want a set of the best sporting novels ever written (I know a charming woman who has read every one of them) go at once to them that sell.

But while we are thinking of colored-plate books, let us see what it would have cost us to secure a copy of À Beckett's "Comic History of Rome." Here it is, "complete in numbers as originally published," four guineas; while a "Comic History of England," two volumes, bound by Riviere from the original parts, in full red levant morocco, extra, cost five guineas. I have tried to read these histories — it cannot be done. It is like reading the not very funny book of an old-time comic opera (always excepting Gilbert's), which depended for its success on the music and the acting — as these books depend on their illustrations by Leech. It is on account of the humor of their wonderfully caricatured portraits of historic personages, in anachronistic surroundings, that these books live and deserve to live. What could be better than the landing of Julius Cæsar on the shores of Albion, from the deck of a channel steamer of Leech's own time?

Did you observe that the "History of Rome" was bound up from the original parts? This, according to modern notions, is a mistake. Parts should be left alone — severely alone, I should say. I have no love for books "in parts," and as this is admitted heresy, I should perhaps explain. As is well known, some of the most desired of modern books, "Pickwick" and "Vanity Fair" for example, were so published, and particulars as to one will indicate the reason for my prejudice against all books "in parts."

In April, 1916, in New York, the Coggeshall Dickens collection was dispersed, and a copy of "Pickwick" in parts was advertised, no doubt correctly, as the most nearly perfect copy ever offered at a public sale. Two full pages of the catalogue were taken up in a painstaking description of the birthmarks of this famous book. It was, like most of the other great novels, brought out "twenty parts in nineteen," — that is, the last number was a double number, — and with a page of the original manuscript, it brought $5350. When a novel published less than a century ago brings such a price, it must be of extraordinary interest and rarity. Was the price high? Decidedly not! There are said to be not ten such copies in existence. It was in superb condition, and manuscript pages of "Pickwick" do not grow on trees. All the details which go to make up a perfect set can be found in Eckel's "First Editions of Charles Dickens."

Briefly, in order to take high rank it is necessary that each part should be clean and perfect and should have the correct imprint and date; it should have the proper number of illustrations by the right artist; and these plates must be original and not reëtched, and almost every plate has certain peculiarities which will mislead the unwary. But this is not all. Each part carried certain announcements and advertisements. These must be carefully looked to, for they are of the utmost value in determining whether it be an early or a later issue of the first edition. An advertisement of "Rowland and Son's Toilet Preparations" where "Simpson's Pills" should be, might lead to painful discussion.

But it is difficult to say whether the possession of a copy of "Pickwick" like the Coggeshall copy is an asset or a liability. It must be handled with gloves; the pea-green paper wrappers are very tender, and not everyone who insists on seeing your treasures knows how to treat such a pamphlet; and, horror of horrors! a "part" might get stacked up with a pile of "Outlooks" on the library table, or get mislaid altogether. So on the whole I am inclined to leave such books to those whose knowledge of bibliography is more exact than mine, and who would not regard the loss of a "part" as an irretrievable disaster. My preference is to get, when I can, books bound in cloth or boards "as issued." They are sufficiently expensive and can be handled with greater freedom. My library is, in a sense, a circulating library: my books move around with me, and a bound book, in some measure at least, takes care of itself. Having said all of which, I looked upon that Coggeshall "Pickwick," and lusted after it.

There is, however, an even greater copy awaiting a purchaser at Rosenbach's. It is a presentation copy in parts, the only one known to exist. Each of the first fourteen parts has Dickens's autograph inscription, "Mary Hogarth from hers most affectionately," variously signed — in full, "Charles Dickens," with initials, or "The Editor." After the publication of the fourteenth part Miss Hogarth, his sister-in-law, a young girl in her eighteenth year, died suddenly, and the shock of her death was so great that Dickens was obliged to discontinue work upon "Pickwick" for two months. No doubt this is the finest "Pickwick"

"Blake being unable to find a publisher for his songs, Mrs. Blake
went out with half a crown, all the money they had in the world,
and of that laid out 1s. 10d. on the simple materials necessary for
setting in practice the new revelation. Upon that investment
of 1s. 10d. he started what was to prove a principal means of
support through his future life. . . . The poet and his wife did
everything in making the book, — writing, designing, printing,
engraving, everything except manufacturing the paper. The
very ink, or color rather, they did make." — GILCHRIST.

in the world. It has all the "points" and to spare —
and the price, well, only a very rich or a very wise man
could buy it.

But to return to my catalogue. Here is Pierce
Egan's "Boxiana," five volumes, 8vo, as clean as new,
in the original boards, uncut, — that's my style, —
and the price, twelve pounds; three hundred and
fifty dollars would be a fair price to-day. And here is
the "Anecdotes of the Life and Transactions of Mrs.
Margaret Rudd," a notorious woman who just escaped hanging for forgery, of whom Dr. Johnson once
said that he would have gone to see her, but that he
was prevented from such a frolic by his fear that it
would get into the newspapers. I have been looking
for it in vain for years; here it is, in new calf, price
nine shillings, and Sterne's "Sentimental Journey,"
first edition, in contemporary calf, for thirty.

Let us turn to poetry. Arnold, Matthew, not interesting; nothing, it chances, by Blake; his "Poetical Sketches," 1783, has always been excessively rare,
only a dozen or so copies are known, and "Songs of
Innocence and of Experience," while not so scarce, is
much more desired. This lovely book was originally
"Songs of Innocence" only; "Experience" came later,
as it always does. Of all the books I know, this is the
most interesting. It is in very deed "W. Blake, his
book," the author being as well the designer, engraver, printer, and illuminator of it.

To attempt in a paragraph any bibliographical account of the "Songs" is as impossible as to give the

genealogy of a fairy. In the ordinary sense the book was never published. Blake sold it to such of his friends as would buy, at prices ranging from thirty shillings to two guineas. Later, to help him over a difficulty (and his life was full of difficulties), they paid him perhaps as much as twenty pounds and in return got a copy glowing with colors and gold. Hence no two copies are exactly alike. It is one of the few books of which a man fortunate enough to own any copy may say, "I like mine best." The price to-day for an average copy is about two thousand dollars.

I can see clearly now that in order to be up to date there must be a new edition of this book every minute. I had just suggested $2000 as the probable price of the "Songs" when a priced copy of the Linnell Catalogue of his Blake Collection reached me. This, the last and greatest Blake collection in England, was sold at auction on March 15, 1918, and accustomed as I am to high prices I was bewildered as I turned its pages. There were two copies of the "Songs"; each brought £735. The "Poetical Sketches" was conspicuous by its absence, while the "Marriage of Heaven and Hell" was knocked down for £756. The drawings for Dante's "Divina Commedia," sixty-eight in all, brought the amazing price of £7665. And these prices will be materially advanced before the booksellers are done with them, as we shall see when their catalogues arrive. We come back to earth with a thud after this lofty flight, in the course

"A LEAF FROM AN UNOPENED VOLUME"

An unpublished manuscript in the autograph of Charlotte Brontë, written in microscopical characters on sixteen pages measuring 3½ by 4½ inches ; in a wrapper of druggist's blue paper

of which we seem to have been seeing visions and
dreaming dreams, much as Blake himself did.

Continuing to "beat the track of the alphabet,"
we reach Brontë and note that now scarce item,
"Poems by Currer, Ellis and Acton Bell," the genuine first edition printed by Hasler in 1846, for
Aylott & Jones, before the title-page bore the Smith-
Elder imprint; price two pounds five. Walter Hill's
last catalogue has a Smith-Elder copy at $12.50,
but the right imprint now makes a difference of
several hundred dollars. About a year ago Edmund
D. Brooks, of Minneapolis, was offering Charlotte
Brontë's own copy of the book, with the Aylott and
Jones imprint, with some manuscript notes which
made it especially interesting to Brontë collectors,
the most important of whom, by the way, is my life-
long friend, H. H. Bonnell of Philadelphia, whose
unrivaled Brontë collection is not unworthy of an
honored place in the Brontë Museum at Haworth. I
called his attention to it, but he already had a presentation copy to Ebenezer Elliott, the Corn-Law rhymer.

Burns: the first Edinburgh edition, for a song; no
Kilmarnock edition — that fine old item which every
collector wants has always been excessively scarce;
and in this connection let me disinter a good story of
how one collector secured a copy. The story is told of
John Allan, from whom, as a collector, I am descended
by the process of clasping hands. My old friend,
Ferdinand Dreer, for more than sixty years a distinguished collector in Philadelphia, was an intimate

friend of Allan's, and passed on to me the collecting legends he had received from him. Allan was an old Scotchman, living in New York when the story begins, who by his industry had acquired a small fortune, much of which he spent in the purchase of books. He collected the books of his period and extra-illustrated them. Lives of Mary Queen of Scots, and Byron; Dibdin, of course, and Americana; but Burns was his ruling passion. He had the first Edinburgh edition, and longed for the Kilmarnock — as who does not? He had a standing order for a copy up to seven guineas, which in those days was considered a fair price, and finally one was reported to him from London at eight. He ordered it out, but it was sold before his letter arrived, and he was greatly disappointed. Some time afterward a friend from the old country visited him, and as he was sailing, asked if he could do anything for him at home. "Yes," said Allan, "get me, if you possibly can, the Kilmarnock edition of Burns." His friend was instructed as to its scarcity and the price he might have to pay for it. On his return his friend, engaged as usual in his affairs, discovered that one of his workmen was drunk. In those days it was not considered good form to get drunk except on Saturday night. How could he get drunk in the middle of the week? Where did he get the money? The answer was that by pawning some books ten shillings had been raised. "And what books had you?" "Oh, Burns and some others; every Scotchman has a copy of Burns." Then, suddenly

POEMS,

CHIEFLY IN THE

SCOTTISH DIALECT,

BY

ROBERT BURNS.

THE Simple Bard, unbroke by rules of Art,
He pours the wild effusions of the heart:
And if inspir'd, 'tis Nature's pow'rs inspire;
Her's all the melting thrill, and her's the kindling fire.

ANONYMOUS.

KILMARNOCK:

PRINTED BY JOHN WILSON.

M,DCC,LXXXVI.

remembering his old friend in New York, he asked, "What sort of a copy was it?" "The old Kilmarnock," was the reply. Not to make the story too long, the pawn-ticket was secured for a guinea, the books redeemed, and the Kilmarnock Burns passed into Allan's possession.

After his death his books were sold at auction (1864). This was during our Civil War, and several times the sale was suspended owing to the noise of a passing regiment in the street. Notwithstanding that times were not propitious for book-sales, his friends were astonished at the prices realized: the Burns fetched $106. It was probably a poor copy. A generation or two ago not as much care was paid to condition as now. Very few uncut copies are known. One is owned by a man as should n't. Another is in the Burns Museum in Ayrshire, which cost the Museum Trustees a thousand pounds; the Canfield, which was purchased by Harry Widener for six thousand dollars, and the Van Antwerp copy, which, at the sale of his collection in London in 1907, brought seven hundred pounds; but much bibliographical water has gone over the dam since 1907, and for some reason the Van Antwerp books, with the exception of one or two items, did not bring as good prices as they should have done. They were sold at an unfortunate moment and perhaps at the wrong place. In Walter Hill's current catalogue there is a Kilmarnock Burns, in an old binding, which looks very cheap to me at $2600. At the Allan sale an Eliot Bible brought the then enormous sum of $825. Supposing an Eliot Bible were obtainable to-day, it would bring, no doubt, five thousand dollars, perhaps more.

This is a long digression. There are other desired volumes besides Burns. Here is a "Paradise Lost," perhaps not so fine a copy as Sabin is now offering for four hundred pounds; but the price is only thirty pounds; and this reminds me that in Beverly Chew's copy, an exceptionally fine one, as all the books of that fastidious collector are, there is an interesting note made by a former owner to this effect: "This is the first edition of this book and has the first title-page. It is worth nearly ten pounds and is rising in value. 1857."

Alphabetically speaking, it is only a step from Milton to Moore, George. Here is his "Flowers of Passion," for which I paid fifteen dollars ten or more years ago — priced at half a crown.

But let us take up another catalogue, one which issued from the world-famous shop in Piccadilly, Quaritch's. Forty years ago Quaritch thought it almost beneath his dignity as a bookseller to offer for sale any except the very rarest books in English; very much as, up to within the last few years, the Universities of Oxford and Cambridge did not think it worth their while to refer more than casually to the glories of English literature. When we open an old Quaritch catalogue, we step out of this age into another, which leads me to observe how remarkable is the change in taste which has come over the collecting world in the last fifty years. Formerly it was the fashion to collect extensively books of which few among us now know anything: books in learned or painful languages, on Philosophy or Religion, as well as those which, for the want of a better name, we call "Classics"; books frequently spoken of, but seldom read.

Such books, unless very valuable indeed, no longer find ready buyers. We have come into our great inheritance. We now dip deep in our "well of English undefyled"; Aldines and Elzevirs have gone out of fashion. Even one of the rarest of them, "Le Pastissier François," is not greatly desired; and I take it that the reason for this change is chiefly due to the difference in the type of men who are prominent among the buyers of fine books to-day. Formerly the collector was a man, not necessarily with a liberal education, but with an education entirely different from that which the best educated among us now receive. I doubt if there are in this country to-day half a dozen important bookbuyers who can read Latin with ease, let alone Greek. Of French, German, and Italian some of us have a working knowledge, but most of us prefer to buy books which we can enjoy without constant reference to a dictionary.

The world is the college of the book-collector of to-day. Many of us are busy men of affairs, familiar, it may be, with the price of oil, or steel, or copper, or coal, or cotton, or, it may be, with the price of the "shares" of all of these and more. Books are our relaxation. We make it a rule not to buy what we cannot read. Some of us indulge the vain hope that time will bring us leisure to acquaint ourselves fully with the contents of all our books. We want books written in our own tongue, and most of us have some pet author or group of authors, or period, it may be, in which we love to lose ourselves and forget the cares of the present. One man may have a collection of Pope, another of Goldsmith, another of Lamb, and so on. The drama has its votaries who are never seen in a theatre; but look into their libraries and you will find everything, from "Ralph Roister Doister" to the "Importance of Being Earnest." And note that these collections are formed by men who are not students in the accepted sense of the word, but who, in the course of years, have accumulated an immense amount of learning. Clarence S. Bement is a fine example of the collector of to-day, a man of large affairs with the tastes and learning of a scholar. It has always seemed to me that professors of literature and collectors do not intermingle as they should. They might learn much from each other. I yield to no professor in my passion for English literature. My knowledge is deficient and inexact, but what I lack in learning I make up in love.

But we are neglecting the Quaritch catalogue. Let us open it at random, as old people used to open their Bibles, and govern their conduct by the first text which met their eyes. Here we are: "Grammatica Graeca," Milan, 1476; the first edition of the first book printed in Greek; one of six known copies. So

it is possible for only six busy men to recreate themselves after a hard day's work with a first Greek
Grammar. Too bad! Here is another: Macrobius,
"The Saturnalia" — "a miscellany of criticism and
antiquities, full of erudition and very useful, similar in
their plan to the 'Noctes Atticæ' of Aulus Gellius."
No doubt, but as dead as counterfeit money. Here
is another: Boethius, "De Consolatione Philoso-
phiæ." Boethius! I seem to have heard of him. Who
was he? Not in "Who's Who," obviously. Let us
look elsewhere. Ah! "Famous philosopher and official in the Court of Theodoric, born about 475 A.D.,
put to death without trial about 524." They had a
short way with philosophers in those days. If William the Second to None in Germany had adopted
this method with his philosophers, the world might
not now be in such a plight.

Note : A college professor to whom I was in confidence showing these notes the other day, remarked,
"I suggest that you soft-pedal that Boethius business, my boy." (How we middle-aged men love to
call each other boys; very much as young boys flat-
ter themselves with the phrase, "old man.") "The
'Consolation of Philosophy' was the best seller for a
thousand years or so. Boethius's reputation is not
in the making, as yours is, and when yours is made,
it will in all probability not last as long." I thought
I detected a slight note of sarcasm in this, but I may
have been mistaken.

Let us look further. Here we are: "Coryat's Crudi-

Fifteenth-century English manuscript on vellum, "De Consolatione Philo-
sophiæ." Rubricated throughout. Its chief interest is the contemporary binding, consisting of the usual oak boards covered with pink deerskin, let into
another piece of deerskin which completely surrounds it and terminates in a
large knot. A clasp fastens the outer cover. It was evidently intended to be
worn at the girdle. The British Museum possesses very few bindings of this
character and these service books. Lay books are of even greater rarity.

ties, hastily gobbled up in five Moneths Trauells."
Tom Coryat was a buffoon and a beggar and a brag-
gart, who wrote what has come to be regarded as the
first handbook on travel. Browning thought very
highly of it, as I remember, and Walter Hill is at this
very minute offering his copy of the "Crudities" for
five hundred dollars. The catalogues say there are
very few perfect copies in existence, in which case I
should like to content myself with Browning's imperfect copy. I love these old books, written by frail
human beings for human beings frail as myself.
Clowns are the true philosophers, and all vagabonds
are beloved, most of all, Locke's. Don't confuse my
Locke with the fellow who wrote on the "Human
Understanding," a century or two ago.

Here is the "Ship of Fools," another best seller
of a bygone age. The original work, by Sebastian
Brandt, was published not long after the invention of
printing, in 1494. Edition followed edition, not only
in its original Swabian dialect, but also in Latin,
French, and Dutch. In 1509 an English version, —
it could hardly be called a translation, — by Alexander Barclay, appeared from the press of Pynson —
he who called Caxton "worshipful master." For
quite two hundred years it was the rage of the reading world. In it the vices and weaknesses of all
classes of society were satirized in a manner which
gave great delight; and those who could not read
were able to enjoy the fine, bold woodcuts with
which the work was embellished. No form of folly

escaped. Even the mediæval book-collector is made
to say: —

> Still am I busy bookes assemblynge,
> For to have plentie it is a pleasaunt thynge,
> In my conceyt and to have them ay in hande,
> But what they mene do I not understande.

This is one of the books which can usually be found
in a Quaritch catalogue, if it can be found anywhere.
At the Hoe sale a copy brought $1825; but the aver-
age collector will make shift to get along with an excellent reprint which was published in Edinburgh
forty years or so ago, and which can be had for a few
shillings, when he chances to come across it.

Here is a great book! The first folio of Shakespeare,
the cornerstone of every great Library. What's in a
name? Did Shakespeare of Stratford write the plays?
The late Dr. Furness declined to be led into a discussion of this point, wisely remarking, "We have
the plays; what difference does it make who wrote
them?" But the question will not down. The latest
theory is that Bacon wrote the Psalms of David also,
and to disguise the fact tucked in a cryptogram,
another name. If you have at hand a King James's
version of the Bible, and will turn to the forty-sixth
Psalm and count the words from the beginning to the
forty-sixth word, and will then count the words from
the end until you again come to the forty-sixth word,
you may learn something to your advantage.

But, whoever wrote them, the first folio — the
plays collected by Heming and Condell, and printed

in 1623, at the charges of Isaac Iaggard, and Ed.
Blount — is one of the greatest, if not the greatest,
volume in all literature. In it not less than twenty
dramas, many of which rank among the literary
masterpieces of the world, were brought together for
the first time. Is it any wonder, therefore, that the
first folio of Shakespeare, Shakespeare! "not *our* poet,
but the world's," is so highly regarded? The condition and location of practically every copy in the
world is known and recorded. Originally the price is
supposed to have been a guinea, and a century passed
before collectors and scholars realized that it, like its
author, was not for an age, but for all time. In 1792
a copy brought £30, and in 1818 "an original copy
in a genuine state" changed hands at £121; but what
shall be said of the price it fetches to-day?

When, a few years ago, a Philadelphia collector
paid the record price of almost twenty thousand
dollars, people unlearned in the lore of books expressed amazement that a book should bring so large
a sum; but he secured one of the finest copies in existence, known to collectors as the Locker-Lampson
copy, which had been for a short time in the possession of William C. Van Antwerp, of New York,
who, unluckily for himself and for the book-collecting
world, stopped collecting almost as soon as he began.
This splendid folio has now found a permanent rest-
ing place in the Widener Memorial Library at Harvard. It is no doubt inevitable that these notable
books should at last come to occupy honored niches

in great mausoleums, as public libraries really are, but I cannot escape the conviction that Edmond de Goncourt was right when he said in his will: —

"My wish is that my drawings, my prints, my curiosities, my books — in a word these things of art which have been the joy of my life — shall not be consigned to the cold tomb of a museum, and subjected to the stupid glance of the careless passer-by; but I require that they shall all be dispersed under the hammer of the auctioneer, so that the pleasure which the acquiring of each one of them has given me shall be given again, in each case, to some inheritor of my own tastes."

I wish that my friends, the Pennells, had followed this course when they gave up their London apartments in the Adelphi and disposed of their valuable Whistler collection. But no, with characteristic generosity the whole collection goes to the nation as a gift — the Library of Congress at Washington is to be its resting-place. The demand for Whistler is ever increasing with his fame which, the Pennells say, will live forever. Those who have a lot of Whistler material smile — the value of their collections is enhanced. Those of us who, like the writer, have to be content with two butterflies, or at most three, sigh and turn aside.

Possession is the grave of bliss. No sooner do we own some great book than we want another. The appetite grows by what it feeds on. The Shakespeare folio is a book for show and to be proud of, but we

want a book to love. Here it is: Walton's "Compleat
Angler," beloved by gentle men, such as all collectors
are. We welcome the peace and contentment which
it suggests, "especially," as its author says, "in such
days and times as I have laid aside business and gone
a-fishing."

Therein lies the charm of this book, for those of us
who are wise enough occasionally to lay aside business
and go a-fishing or a-hunting, albeit only book-hunting; for it is the spirit of sport rather than the sport
itself that is important. Old Isaak Walton counted
fishermen as honest men. I wonder did he call them
truthful? If so, there has been a sad falling off since
his day, for I seem to remember words to this effect:
"The fisherman riseth up early in the morning and
disturbeth the whole household. Mighty are his preparations. He goeth forth full of hope. When the day
is far spent, he returneth, smelling of strong drink, and
the truth is not in him."

I wish that some day I might discover an "Angler,"
not on the banks of a stream, but all unsuspected on
some book-stall. It is most unlikely; those days are
past. I shall never own a first "Angler." This little
book has been thumbed out of existence almost, by
generations of readers with coarse, wet hands who
carried the book in their pockets or left it lying by the
river in the excitement of landing a trout. Five impressions, all rare, were made before the author died
in his "neintyeth" year, and was buried in the South
Transept of the Cathedral of William of Wykeham.

But Walton wrote of Fishers of Men as well as of fishing. His lives of John Donne, the Dean of St. Paul's; of Richard Hooker, the "Judicious," as he is usually called, when called at all; of George Herbert, and several other men, honorable in their generation, are quaint and charming. These lives, published originally at intervals of many years, are not rare, nor is the volume of 1670, the first collected edition of the Lives, unless it is a presentation copy. Such a copy sold twenty years ago for fifteen pounds. Some years ago I paid just three times this sum for a copy inscribed by Walton to the Lord Bishop of Oxford. I did not then know that the Bishop of Oxford was also the famous Dr. John Fell, the hero of the well-known epigram: —

> I do not like you Dr. Fell,
> The reason why I cannot tell;
> But this I know and know full well,
> I do not like you Dr. Fell, —

or I would willingly have paid more for it.

But I am wandering from my text. To return to the "Angler." Fifty pounds was a fair price for a fine copy fifty years ago. George D. Smith sold a copy a few weeks since for five thousand dollars, and the Heckscher copy a few years ago brought thirty-nine hundred dollars; but the record price appears to have been paid for the Van Antwerp copy, which is generally believed to be the finest in existence. It is bound in original sheepskin, and was formerly in the library of Frederick Locker-Lampson. It was sold in London

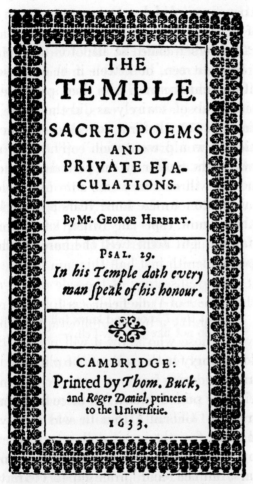

THE TEMPLE.

SACRED POEMS
AND
PRIVATE EJA-
CULATIONS.

By Mr. GEORGE HERBERT.

PSAL. 29.

*In his Temple doth every
man speak of his honour.*

CAMBRIDGE:
Printed by *Thom. Buck,*
and *Roger Daniel,* printers
to the Universitie.
1633.

The rare first edition, and, according to Mr. Livingston
in "The Bibliophile," the earlier issue of the two printed
in that year. A very large copy. From the Hagen collection. Said to be the finest copy in existence. It is bound
in contemporary vellum, and measures 3¼ × 6¼ inches.

some ten years ago and was purchased by Quaritch for "an American," which was a sort of *nom de guerre* of the late J. P. Morgan, for £1290.

When "Anglers" could be had for fifty pounds, "Vicars" brought ten, or fifteen if in exceptionally fine condition, and the man who then spent this sum for a "Vicar" chose as wisely as did the Vicar's wife her wedding gown, "not for a fine glossy surface, but for qualities as would wear well." These two little volumes, with the Salisbury imprint and a required blunder or two, will soon be worth a thousand dollars. When I paid £120 for mine some years ago, I felt that I was courting ruin, especially when I recalled that Dr. Johnson thought rather well of himself for having secured for Goldsmith just half this sum for the copyright of it. Boswell's story of the sale of the manuscript of the "Vicar of Wakefield," as Johnson related it to him, is as pretty a bit of bibliographical history as we have. Those who know it will pardon the intrusion of the story for the sake of the pleasure it may give others.

"I received," said Johnson, "one morning a message from poor Goldsmith that he was in great distress, and as it was not in his power to come to me, begged that I would come to him as soon as possible. I sent him a guinea, and promised to come to him directly. I accordingly went as soon as I was drest, and found that his landlady had arrested him for his rent, at which he was in a violent passion. I perceived that he had already changed my guinea, and had got

a bottle of Madeira and a glass before him. I put the
cork into the bottle, desired he would be calm, and
began to talk to him of the means by which he might
be extricated. He then told me that he had a novel
ready for the press, which he produced to me. I
looked into it and saw its merit; told the landlady I
should soon return, and having gone to a bookseller,
sold it for sixty pounds. I brought Goldsmith the
money, and he discharged his rent, not without rating
his landlady in a high tone for having used him so
ill . . . and Sir," continued Johnson, "it was a sufficient price, too, when it was sold; for then the fame
of Goldsmith had not been elevated, as it afterwards
was by his 'Traveller'; and the bookseller had such
faint hopes of profit by his bargain, that he kept the
manuscript by him a long time, and did not publish
it till after 'The Traveller' had appeared. Then, to
be sure, it was accidentally worth more money."

Here we have a characteristic sketch of the two
men — the excitable, amiable, and improvident Goldy,
and the wise and kindly Johnson, instantly corking
the bottle and getting down to brass tacks, as we
should say.

The first edition of "Robinson Crusoe" is another
favorite book with collectors; as why should it not
be? Here is a copy in two volumes (there should be
three) in red morocco, super extra, gilt edges, by
Bedford. It should be in contemporary calf, but the
price was only £46. Turning to a bookseller's catalogue published a year or two ago, there is a copy

"3 vols. 8vo. with map and 2 plates, in original calf binding," and the price is twenty-five hundred dollars.

A note in one of Stan. Henkel's recent auction catalogues, and there are none better, clears up a point which has always troubled me, and which I will quote at length for the benefit of other collectors who may not have seen it.

The supposed "points," signifying the first issues of this famous book, are stumbling-blocks to all bibliographers.

Professor W. P. Trent, of Columbia University, undoubtedly the foremost authority on Defoe, after extended research and the comparison of many copies, states that he is of the opinion that any purchaser entering Taylor's shop at the sign of the Ship, in Pater Noster Row on April 25th, 1719 (usually taken as the date of issue), might have been handed a copy falling under any of the following categories: —

With "apply" in the preface, and "Pilot," on page 343, line 2.

With "apply" in the preface, and "Pilate" on page 343.

With "apyly" in the preface, and "Pilate" on page 343.

With "apyly" in the preface, and "Pilot" on page 343.

It is unquestionably wrong, in his opinion, to call any one of these "first issue." Prof. Trent sees no reason to believe that there was a re-issue with "apyly" corrected in the preface. Both these mistakes were quite probably corrected while the sheets were passing through the press, and it depends on how the sheets were collated by the binder what category of the four given any special copy belongs to.

This is a great relief to me, as my copy, which was once Congreve's, while leaving nothing to be desired in the matter of condition, binding, and plates, has the word "apply" in the preface and "pilot" on page 343; but it is perfectly clear, having in mind the spacing of the types, that the longer word has given way to the shorter.

There is, however, another edition of "Robinson Crusoe" which, for rarity, puts all first editions in the shade. So immediate was the success of this wonderful romance that it was issued in a newspaper, very much as popular novels are now run. It was published in the "Original London Post," or "Heathcot's Intelligence," numbers from 125 to 289, October 7, 1719, to October 19, 1720. This was publication in parts with a vengeance. Of the entire series of 165 leaves, only one is in facsimile. I see that I have not yet said that I own this copy. There is a copy in the British Museum, but I am told that it is very imperfect, and I know of no other.

I was, a few evenings ago, looking over Arnold's "First Report of a Book-Collector." I had just given an old-time year's salary for a manuscript poem by Keats, and I was utterly bewildered by reading this: "Only a few months after I began collecting, more than one hundred pages of original manuscripts of Keats that were just then offered for sale came in my way and were secured at one-fifth of their value." If the price I paid for one page is any criterion as to the value of one hundred pages, Mr. Arnold is by now a very rich man; and elsewhere in his "Report" he gives a list of books sold at Sotheby's in 1896 at prices which make one's mouth water.

Chapman's Homer, 1616, £15;
Chaucer's Works, 1542, £15 10;
"Robinson Crusoe," 1719–20, £75;
Goldsmith's "Vicar," 1766, £65;
Goldsmith's "Deserted Village," 1770, £25;
Herrick's "Hesperides," 1648, £38.
Milton's "Paradise Lost," 1667, £90.

But why continue? The point of it all is his comment: "If the beginner is alarmed by these prices, let him remember that such are paid only for well-known and highly prized rarities"; and remember, too, that this is the comment of an astute collector upon the prices of only twenty years ago.

But twenty years ago was the last century and seems to make a century's difference in auction prices. In May, 1918, there was sold at the Anderson Galleries in New York City the library of the late Winston H. Hagen. Beverly Chew wrote a brief introduction in the sale catalogue, the closing paragraph of which I must quote. "If I were asked what is the scarcest item in this sale, I should unhesitatingly say that charming little volume containing four of the poems of John Skelton, Poet Laureate to King Henry VII. . . . but why point out the gems? . . . One who followed with some apprehension Mr. Hagen's continual investment in books said he thought he would do better to purchase good bonds. 'No,' said Hagen, 'my books are worth more than your bonds.' Let us hope he was right; and recent events in the stock market would seem to confirm his judgment."

This was written before the event. What happened?

THE ORIGINAL LONDON POST,
OR
Heathcot's Intelligence;

Being a Collection of the

Fresheft Advices Foreign and Domeftick.

Wednefday October 7. 1719.

The Life and ftrange Adventures of *Robinfon Crufoe* of *York*, Mariner : Who lived Eight and Twenty Years alone in an uninhabited Ifland on the Coaft of *America*, near the Mouth of the Great River *Oroonoque* ; having been caft on Shore by Shipwreck, wherein all the Men perifhed but himfelf. With an Account how he was at laft ftrangely delivered by Pyrates. Written by himfelf.

The PREFACE.

I F ever the Story of any private Man's Adventures in the World were worth making Publick, and were acceptable when Publifhed, the Editor of this Account thinks this will be fo.

The Wonders of this Man's Life exceed all that (he thinks) is to be found Extant ; the Life of one Man being fcarce capable of a greater Variety.

The Story is told with Modefty, with Serioufnefs, and with a religious Application of Events to the Ufe to which wife Men always apply them, viz. to the Inftruction of others by this Example, and to juftify and honour the Wifdom of Providence in all the variety of our Circumftances, let them happen how they will.

The Editor believes the thing to be a juft Hiftory of Fact ; neither is there any Appearance of Fiction in it : And however thinks, becaufe all fuch things are difpatched, that the Improvement of it, as well to the Diverfion, as to the Inftruction of the Reader, will be the fame ; and as fuch he thinks, without further Compliment to the World, he does them a great Service in the Publication.

The

We know what has happened in the bond market.
Bonds have gone down, I am told by those who own
them, an average of twenty points. I was present
when the books were sold, and saw Beverly Chew's
hope confirmed. The books were very choice, it must
be admitted, and there was that atmosphere of good-
humor and good-fellowship which Mitchell Kennerley
tries so successfully to disseminate, and which is so
important in the auction-room.

Listen to a few of the prices. The Skelton brought
$9700; but let me tabulate a few other prices.

Browning's "Pauline," first edition (1833), $1610.
Kilmarnock Burns (1786), $2750.
Goldsmith's "She Stoops to Conquer" (1773), $305.
Gray's "Elegy" (1751), $4350.

(Note that Gray's Elegy must be "*Wrote* in a Country Church Yard." When it becomes "*Written*," it
brings only $111 although published in the same year.)

Herrick's "Hesperides" (1648), $1075.
Milton's "Lycidas" (1638), $3500.
Milton's "Paradise Lost" (1667); first edition, first title
    page, $1510.

And there is not the slightest doubt that in twenty
years from now these prices will look as cheap as Mr.
Arnold's now look to me.

Returning for a moment to Mr. Arnold and his contributions to bibliography, he did the booksellers a
good turn and helped collectors justify their extravagance to their wives by publishing some years ago
"A Record of Books and Letters." Mr. Arnold de-

voted the leisure of six years to forming a collection of books with perseverance and intelligence; then he suddenly stopped and turned over to Bangs & Company, the auctioneers, the greater part of his collection, and awaited the result with interest. I say "with interest" advisedly, for the result fully justified his judgment. In his "Record" he gives the date of acquisition, together with the cost of each item, in one column, and in another the selling price. He also states whether the item was bought of a bookseller or a collector, or at auction. He had spent a trifle over ten thousand dollars, and his profit almost exactly equalled his outlay. I said his profit, but I have used the wrong word. His profit was the pleasure he received in discovering, buying, and owning the treasures which for a time were in his possession. The difference in actual money between what he paid and what he received, some ten thousand dollars, was the reward for his industry and courage in paying what doubtless many people supposed to be extravagant prices for his books.

Let us examine one only. It is certainly not a fair example, but it happens to interest me. He had a copy of Keats's "Poems," 1817, with an inscription in the poet's handwriting: "My dear Giovanni, I hope your eyes will soon be well enough to read this with pleasure and ease." There were some other inscriptions in Keats's hand, and for this treasure Arnold paid a bookseller, in 1895, seventy-one dollars. At the auction in 1901 it brought five hundred dollars,

To the Misses M—— at Hastings

What though while the wonders of Nature exploring,
  I cannot your light, mazy footsteps, attend;
Nor listen to accents that almost adoring
  Bless Cynthia's face the Enthusiast's friend.

Yet over the steep whence the Mountain Stream gushes,
  With your kindest friends in idea I muse:
Mark the clear tumbling crystal, its passionate gushes,
  Inspray that the wild flower kindly bedews.

Why linger you so, the wild Labyrinth strolling?
  Why breathless, unable your bliss to declare?
Ah! you list to the Nightingale's tender condoling
  Responsive to Sylphs in the moon beamy air!

'Tis Morn, and the flowers with dew are yet drooping,
  I see you are treading the verge of the Sea:
And now! Ah! I see it—you just now are stooping
  To pick up the Keepsake intended for me!

If a Cherub on Pinions of silver descending,
  Had brought me a Gem from the feet mark of heaven,
And smiles with his Star cheering voice sweetly blending,
  The Blessings of Tighe had melodiously given;
It had not created a warmer emotion,
  Than the present, fair Nymphs, I was blest with from you,
Than the shell from the bright golden sands of the Ocean,
  Which the Emerald waves at your feet gladly threw.

For indeed 'tis a sweet and peculiar Pleasure,
  (And blissful to he who such Happiness finds!)
To possess but a sam in the hour of leisure
  Of elegant, pure and aerial Minds! 1815

and it subsequently passed into the Van Antwerp collection, finally going back to London, where it was sold in 1907 for ninety pounds, being bought by Quaritch. Finally it passed into the possession of the late W. H. Hagen and, at the sale of his library, in May, 1918, was knocked down to "G.D.S." for $1950. From him I tried to secure it, but was "too late."[1]

My copy of the Poems has, alas, no inscription, but it cost me in excess of five hundred dollars; and a well-known collector has just paid Rosenbach nine thousand dollars for Keats's three slender volumes, each with inscriptions in the poet's hand. Three into nine is a simple problem: even I can do it; but the volume of "Poems" is much rarer than "Endymion" or "Lamia."

[1] The facsimile on page 105 is from the original manuscript of John Keats's "To some Ladies," published in Keats's first volume (1817). The ladies were the sisters of George Felton Mathew, to whom Keats also addressed a poem. It will be observed that in the second verse he used the word "gushes" at the end of the third as well as the first line. This error does not occur in the printed text. On the other hand the MS. shows a correction which has never been made in the printed text, where the word "rove" is corrected to "muse." There is an interesting communication in the Athenæum, April 16, 1904, by H. Buxton Forman, anent this holograph.

To Algernon Swinburne
with all affection
DG Rossetti 1879

IV

"ASSOCIATION" BOOKS AND FIRST EDITIONS

No books have appreciated more in value than presentation or association volumes, and the reason is not far to seek. Of any given copy there can hardly be a duplicate. For the most part presentation copies are first editions — *plus*. Frequently there is a note or a comment which sheds biographical light on the author. In the slightest inscription there is the record of a friendship by means of which we get back of the book to the writer. And speaking of association books, every one will remember the story that General Wolfe, in an open boat on the St. Lawrence as he was being rowed down the stream to a point just below Quebec, recited the lines from Gray's "Elegy," —

"The boast of heraldry, the pomp of pow'r,
    And all that beauty, all that wealth, e'er gave
Await alike the inevitable hour.
    The paths of glory lead but to the grave," —

adding, "I would rather be the author of that piece than have the honor of beating the French to-morrow." When Wolfe left England he carried with him a copy of the "Elegy," the gift of his fiancée, Miss Katherine Lowther. He learned the poem by heart, he underscored his favorite lines, among them the passage quoted; he filled the book with his notes.

After his death the book and a miniature of the lady were returned to her, and only a few days ago this book, a priceless volume of unique association interest, was offered for sale. The first man who saw it bought it. He had never bought a fine book before, but he could not resist this one. When I heard of the transaction I was grieved and delighted — grieved that so wonderful a volume had escaped me, delighted that I had not been subjected to so terrible a temptation. What was the price of it? Only the seller and the buyer know, but I fancy some gilt-edged securities had to be parted with.

How the prices of these books go a-soaring is shown by the continuous advance in the price of a copy of Shelley's "Queen Mab." It is a notable copy, referred to in Dowden's "Life of Shelley." On the fly leaf is an inscription in Shelley's hand, "Mary Wollstonecraft Godwin, from P.B.S."; inside of the back cover Shelley has written in pencil, "You see, Mary, I have not forgotten you"; and elsewhere in the book in Mary's hand, we read, "This book is sacred to me, and as no other creature shall ever look into it, I may write in it what I please. Yet what shall I write? That I love the author beyond all powers of expression and that I am parted from him"; and much more to the same effect. At the Ives sale in 1891 this volume of supreme interest brought $190; in 1897, at the Frederickson sale, it brought $615; and a year ago a dealer sold it for $7500; and cheap at that, I say, for where will you find another?

I have before me a copy of Stevenson's "Inland Voyage." Pamphlets aside, which, by reason of their manner of publication, are now rare, it may be said to be the author's first book. It has an inscription, "My dear Cummy: If you had not taken so much trouble with me all the years of my childhood, this little book would never have been written. Many a long night

My dear Cummy,
If you had not taken so much trouble with me all the years of my childhood, this little book would never have been written. Many a long night you sat up with me when I was ill. I wish I could hope, by way of return, to amuse a single evening for you with my little book! But whatever you may think of it, I know you will continue to think kindly of
The Author

you sat up with me when I was ill; I wish I could hope by way of return to amuse a single evening for you with my little book! But whatever you may think of it, I know you will continue to think kindly of the Author." I thought, when I gave four hundred dollars for it, that I was paying a fabulous price; but as I have since been offered twice that sum, Rosenbach evidently let me have a bargain. He tells me that it is good business sometimes to sell a book for less than it is worth. He regards it as bait. He angles for you very skilfully, does Rosy, and lands you — me — every time.

"A Child's Garden of Verses" is another book which has doubled in value two or three times in the

last few years. Gabriel Wells is now offering a copy,
with a brief inscription, for three hundred dollars, having sold me not long ago, for twice this sum, a copy in
which Stevenson's writing is mingled with the type
of the title-page so that it reads:—

ROBERT LOUIS STEVENSON
his copy of
A CHILD'S GARDEN OF
VERSES
and if it is [in] the hands of any one
else, explain it who can!
but not by the gift of
ROBERT LOUIS STEVENSON

That Stevenson afterward changed his mind and
gave it to "E. F. Russell, with hearty good will," is
shown by another inscription. This copy was purchased at the sale for the British Red Cross in London, shortly after the outbreak of the war. It may be
some time before it is worth what I paid for it, or the
price may look cheap to-morrow — who shall say?

Watching the quotations of the first editions of
Stevenson is rather like looking at the quotations
of stocks you have n't got, as they recover from a
panic. A point or two a day is added to their prices;
but Stevenson's move five or ten points at a time, and
there has been no reaction — as yet. Only a year or
two ago I paid Drake fifty dollars for a copy of "The
New Arabian Nights"; and a few days ago I saw in
the papers that a copy had just been sold for fifty
pounds in a London auction room.[1]

[1] In Walter Hill's recent catalogue a copy is priced at $350.

Robert Louis Stevenson
his copy of

A CHILD'S GARDEN

OF VERSES

and if it is the hands of any one
else, explain it who can!

BY
but not by
the gift of
ROBERT LOUIS STEVENSON

LONDON
LONGMANS, GREEN, AND CO.
1885

I cannot quite understand Stevenson's immense
vogue. Perhaps it is the rare personality of the man.
Try as we may, it is impossible to separate the personality of a man from his work. Why is one author
"collected" and another not? I do not know. Practically no one collects Scott, or George Eliot, or
Trollope; but Trollope collectors there will be, and
"The Macdermots of Ballycloran" and "The Kellys
and the O'Kellys" will bring fabulous prices some of
these days — five hundred dollars each; more, a
thousand, I should say; and when you pay this sum,
look well for the errors in pagination and see that
Mortimer Street is spelt Morimer on the title-page
of volume three of the former. And remember, too,
that this book is so rare that there is no copy of it in
the British Museum — at least so I am told; but you
will find one on my shelves, in the corner over there,
together with everything else this great Victorian
has written — of all novelists my favorite. Trollope
proved the correctness of Johnson's remark, "A man
may write at any time if he will set himself doggedly
at it." This we know Trollope did, we have his word
for it. His personality was too sane, too matter of
fact, to be attractive; but his books are delightful.
One does n't read Trollope as Coleridge did Shakespeare — by flashes of lighting (this is n't right, but it
expresses the idea); but there is a good, steady glow
emanating from the author himself, which, once you
get accustomed to it, will enable you to see a whole
group of mid-Victorian characters so perfectly that

you come to know them as well as the members of your own family, and, I sometimes think, understand them better.

But for one collector who expresses a mild interest in Trollope, there are a thousand who regard the brave invalid, who, little more than twenty years ago, passed away on that lonely Samoan island in the Pacific, as one of the greatest of the moderns, as certain of immortality as Charles Lamb. They may be right. His little toy books and leaflets, those which

> The author and the printer
> With various kinds of skill
> Concocted in the Winter
> At Davos on the Hill,

and elsewhere, are simply invaluable. The author and the printer were one and the same — R. L. S., assisted, or perhaps hindered, by S. L. O., Mrs. Stevenson's son, then a lad. Of these Stevensons, "Penny Whistles" is the rarest. But two copies are known. One is in a private collection in England; the other was bought at the Borden sale in 1913 by Mrs. Widener, for twenty-five hundred dollars, in order to complete, as far as might be, the Stevenson collection now in the Widener Memorial Library. It was a privately printed forerunner of "A Child's Garden of Verses," published several years later.

It is a far cry from these bijoux to Stevenson's regularly published volumes; but when it is remembered that these latter were printed in fairly large editions and relatively only a few years ago, it will be seen that no other author of yesterday fetches such high prices as Stevenson.

In recent years there have been published a number of bibliographies without which no collector can be expected to keep house. We are indebted to the Grolier Club for some of the best of these. Its members have the books and are most generous in exhibiting them, and it must indeed be a churlish scholar who cannot freely secure access to the collections of its members.

Aside from the three volumes entitled "Contributions to English Bibliography," published and sold by the Club, the handbooks of the exhibitions held from time to time are much sought, for the wealth of information they contain. The Club's librarian, Miss Ruth S. Granniss, working in coöperation with the members, is largely responsible for the skill and intelligence with which these little catalogues are compiled. The time and amount of painstaking research which enter into the making of them is simply enormous. Indeed, no one quite understands the many questions which arise to vex the bibliographer unless they have attempted to make for themselves even the simplest form of catalogue. Over the door of the room in which they work should be inscribed the text, "Be sure your sin will find you out." Some blunders are redeemed by the laughter they arouse. Here is a famous one: —

Shelley — Prometheus — unbound, etc.
    "   — Prometheus — bound in olive morocco, etc.

But for the most part the lot of the bibliographer, as Dr. Johnson said of the dictionary-maker, is to be exposed to censure without hope of praise.

That Oscar Wilde continues to interest the collector is proved, if proof were necessary, by the splendid bibliography by Stuart Mason, in two large volumes. Its editor tells us that it was the work of ten years, which I can readily believe; and Robert Ross, Wilde's literary executor, says in the introduction, that, in turning over the proof for ten minutes, he learned more about Wilde's writings than Wilde himself ever knew. It gave me some pleasure, when I first took the book up, to see that Mason had used for his frontispiece the caricature of Wilde by Aubrey Beardsley, the original of which now hangs on the wall near my writing-table, together with a letter from Ross in which he says, "From a technical point of view this drawing is interesting as showing the artistic development of what afterwards was called his Japanese method in the 'Salome' drawings. Here it is only in embryo, but this is the earliest drawing I remember in which the use of dotted lines, a peculiarity of Beardsley, can be traced."[1]

Another favorite bibliography is that of Dickens, by John C. Eckel. His "First Editions of Charles Dickens" is a book which no lover of Dickens — and who is not? — can do without. It is a book to be read, as well as a book of reference. In it Mr. Eckel does one thing, however, which is, from its very nature,

[1] See *infra*, page 319.

THE NEW BUILDING OF THE GROLIER CLUB
47 EAST SIXTIETH ST., NEW YORK

hopeless and discouraging. He attempts to indicate
the prices at which first editions of his favorite author
can be secured at auction, or from the dealers in London and this country. Alas, alas! while waiting to secure prizes at Eckel's prices I have seen them soar-
ing to figures undreamed of a few years ago. In his
chapter on "Presentation Copies," he refers to a copy
of "Bleak House" given by Dickens to Dudley Cos-
tello. "Some years ago," he says, "it sold for $150.00.
Eighteen months later the collector resold the book to
the dealer for $380.00, who made a quick turn and
sold the book for ten per cent advance, or $418.00."
These figures Mr. Eckel considers astonishing. I now
own the book, but it came into my possession at a
figure considerably in excess of that named.

A copy of "American Notes," with an inscription,
"Thomas Carlyle from Charles Dickens, Nineteenth
October, 1842," gives an excellent idea of the rise in
the price of a book, interesting itself and on account
of its inscription. At auction, in London, in 1902, it
sold for £45. After passing through the hands of several dealers it was purchased by W. E. Allis, of Mil-
waukee; and at the sale of his books in New York, in
1912, it was bought by George D. Smith for $1050.
Smith passed the book on to Edwin W. Coggeshall;
but its history is not yet at an end, for at his sale, on
April 25, 1916, it was bought by the firm of Dutton
for $1850, and by them passed on, the story goes, to
a discriminating collector in Detroit, a man who can
call all the parts of an automobile by name. For-

tunately, while this book was in full flight, I secured a copy with an inscription, "W. C. Macready from his friend Charles Dickens, Eighteenth October, 1842." Now, what is my copy worth?

Seven years ago I paid Charles Sessler nine hundred dollars for three books: a presentation "Carol," to Tom Beard, a "Cricket," to Macready, and a "Haunted Man," to Maclise. At the Coggeshall sale a dealer paid a thousand dollars for a "Carol," while

I gave Smith ten per cent advance on a thousand dollars for a "Chimes," with an inscription, "Charles Dickens, Junior, from his affectionate father, Charles Dickens." This copy at the Allis sale had brought seven hundred and seventy-five dollars, at which time I was prepared to pay five hundred dollars for it.

AN ILLUSTRATION, "THE LAST OF THE SPIRITS," BY JOHN LEECH,
FOR DICKENS'S "CHRISTMAS CAROL"

From the original water-color drawing

I always return from these all-star performances depressed in spirit and shattered in pocket. "Where will it stop?" I say to myself. "When will you stop?" my wife says to me. And both questions remain unanswered; certainly not, while presentation Dickenses can be had and are lacking from my collection. I now possess twenty-one, and it is with presentation Dickenses as with elephants — a good many go to the dozen; but I lack and sadly want — Shall I give a list? No, the prices are going up fast enough without stimulation from me. Wait until my "wants" are complete; then let joy be unconfined.

A final word on Dickens: the prices are skyrocketing because everyone loves him. Age cannot wither nor custom stale his infinite variety. As a great creative genius he ranks with Shakespeare. He has given pleasure to millions; he has been translated into all the languages of Europe. "Pickwick," it is said, stands fourth in circulation among English printed books, being exceeded only by the Bible, Shakespeare, and the English Prayer-Book; and the marvel is that when Dickens is spoken of, it is difficult to arrive at an agreement as to which is his greatest book.

But this paper is supposed to relate to prices rather than to books themselves. Other seductive arguments having failed, one sometimes hears a vendor of rare books add, in his most convincing manner, "And you couldn't possibly make a better investment." The idea, I suppose, is calculated to enable a man to meet his wife's reproachful glance, or something

Dedication
To J. P. Harley Esqre

My dear Sir.

My dramatic banterlings are no sooner born, than you foster them. You have made my strayed gentleman exclusively your own; you have adopted Martin Stokes with equal readiness; and you still profess your willingness to do the same kind office for all future sons of the same stock, no matter how numerous they may be or how quickly they may follow in succession.

I dedicate to you the first play I ever published and you made for me, the first play I ever wrote. The balance is in your favor, and I am afraid it will remain so.

That you may long contribute to the amusement of the Public, and long be spared to shed a lustre, by the honor and integrity of your private life on the profession which for many years you have done so much to uphold, is the sincere and earnest wish of

My dear Sir
Yours most Faithfully
Boz.

December 1836

DEDICATION TO "THE VILLAGE COQUETTES," BY CHARLES DICKENS

From the manuscript formerly in the Coggeshall collection, much reduced in size

worse, as he returns home with a book under his arm. But when one is about to commit some piece of extravagance, such as buying a book of which one already has several copies, one will grasp at any straw, the more so as there may be some truth in the statement.

There are, however, so many good reasons why we should buy rare books, that it seems a pity ever to refer to the least of them. I am not sure that I am called on to give any judgment in the matter; but my belief is that the one best and sufficient reason for a man to buy a book is because he thinks he will be happier with it than without it. I always question myself on this point, and another which presses it closely — can I pay for it? I confess that I do not always listen so attentively for the answer to this second question; but I try so to live as to be able to look my bookseller in the eye and tell him where to go. I govern myself by few rules, but this is one of them — never to allow a book to enter my library as a creditor.

"Un livre est un ami qui ne change jamais"; I want to enjoy my friends whenever I am with them. One would get very tired of a friend if, every time one met him, he should suggest a touch for fifty or five hundred dollars. On the shelves in my office are some books that are mine, some in which there is at the moment a joint ownership, and some which will be mine in the near future, I hope — and doubtless in this hope I am not alone; but the books on the shelves

around the room in which I write are mine, all of
them.

The advice given by "Punch" to those about to
marry — "Don't" — seems, then, to be the best advice to a man who is tempted to buy by the hope of
making a profit out of his books; but I observe that
this short and ugly word deters very few from following their inclinations in the matter of marriage,
and this advice may fall, as advice usually falls, on
deaf ears. Only when a man is safely ensconced in
six feet of earth, with several tons of enlauding granite
upon his chest, is he in a position to give advice with
any certainty, and then he is silent; but it will nevertheless be understood that I do not recommend the
purchase of rare books as an investment, and this in
spite of the fact that many collectors have made
handsome profits out of the books they have sold.
While a man may do much worse with his money than
buy rare books, he cannot be certain that he can dispose of them at a profit, nor is it necessary that he
should do so. He should be satisfied to eat his cake
and have it; books selected with any judgment will
almost certainly afford this satisfaction, and of what
other hobby can this be said with the same assurance?

The possession of rare books is a delight best understood by the owners of them. They are not called
upon to explain. The gentle will understand, and
the savage may be disregarded. It is the scholar
whose sword is usually brandished against collectors;
and I would not have him think that, in addition

MODERN LOVE

AND

POEMS OF THE ENGLISH ROADSIDE,

WITH

Poems and Ballads.

BY

GEORGE MEREDITH,

AUTHOR OF 'THE SHAVING OF SHAGPAT,' 'THE ORDEAL OF RICHARD
FEVEREL,' ETC.

LONDON:

CHAPMAN & HALL, 193, PICCADILLY.

1862.

to our being ignorant of our books, we are specula-
tors in them also. Let him remember that we have
our uses.

> Unlearned men of books assume the care,
> As eunuchs are the guardians of the fair.

It may as well be admitted that we do not buy expensive books to read. We may say that it is a delight to us to look upon the very page on which appeared for the first time such a sonnet as "On First
Looking into Chapman's Homer," or to read that
bit of realism unsurpassed, where Robinson Crusoe
one day, about noon, discovered the print of a man's
naked foot upon the sand; but when we sit down with
a copy of Keats, we do not ask for a first edition;
much less when we want to live over again the joys
of our childhood, do we pick up a copy of Defoe
which would be a find at a thousand dollars. But
first editions of Keats's Poems, 1817, in boards, with
the paper label if possible, and a Defoe unwashed, in
a sound old calf binding, are good things to have.
They are indeed a joy forever, and will never pass into
nothingness. I cannot see why the possession of fine
books is more reprehensible than the possession of
valuable property of any other sort.

In speaking of books as an investment, one implies
first editions. First editions are scarce; tenth editions, as Charles Lamb stutteringly suggested, are
scarcer, but there is no demand for them. Why, then,
first editions? The question is usually dodged; the

truth may as well be stated. There is a joy in mere ownership. It may be silly, or it may be selfish; but it is a joy, akin to that of possessing land, which seems to need no defense. We do not walk over our property every day; we frequently do not see it; but when the fancy takes us, we love to forget our cares and responsibilities in a ramble over our fields. In like manner, and for the same reason, we browse with delight in a corner of our library in which we have placed our most precious books. We should buy our books as we buy our clothes, not only to cover our nakedness, but to embellish us; and we should buy more books and fewer clothes.

I am told that, in proportion to our numbers and our wealth, less money is spent on books now than was spent fifty years ago. I suppose our growing love of sport is to some extent responsible. Golf has taken the place of books. I know that it takes time and costs money. I do not play the game myself, but I have a son who does. Perhaps when I am his age, I shall feel that I can afford it. My sport is book-hunting. I look upon it as a game, a game requiring skill, some money, and luck. The pleasure that comes from seeing some book in a catalogue priced at two or three times what I may have paid for a copy, is a pleasure due to vindicated judgment. I do not wish to rush into the market and sell and secure my profit. What is profit if I lose my book? Moreover, if one thinks of profit rather than of books, there is an interest charge to be considered. A book for which I

paid a thousand dollars a few years ago, no longer
stands me at a thousand dollars, but at a considerably greater sum. A man neat at figures could tell
with mathematical accuracy just the actual cost of
that book down to any given minute. I neither know
nor want to know.

There is another class of collector with whom I am
not in keen sympathy, and that is the men who spe-
cialize in the first published volumes of some given
group of authors. These works are usually of relatively little merit, but they are scarce and expensive:
scarce, because published in small editions and at
first neglected; expensive, because they are desired to
complete sets of first editions. Anthony Trollope's
first two novels have a greater money value than all
the rest of his books put together — but they are
hard to read. In like manner, a sensational novel,
"Desperate Remedies," by Hardy, his first venture
in fiction, is worth perhaps as much as fifty copies of
his "Woodlanders," one of the best novels of the last
half century. George Gissing, when he was walking
our streets penniless and in rags, could never have
supposed that a few years later his first novel, "Work-
ers in the Dawn," would sell for one hundred and
fifty dollars, but it has done so. I have a friend who
has just paid this price.

Just here I would like to remark that for several
years I have been seeking, without success, a copy
of the first edition of that very remarkable book,
Samuel Butler's "The Way of All Flesh." Book-

sellers who jauntily advertise, "Any book got," will
please make a note of this one.

Nor do I think it necessary to have every scrap,
every waif and stray, of any author, however much
I may esteem him. My collection of Johnson is fairly
complete, but I have no copy of Father Lobo's
"Abyssinia." It was
an early piece of hack-
work, a translation
from the French, for
which Johnson re-
ceived five pounds.
It is not scarce; one
would hardly want to
read it. It was the

*To Mrs Percy
from the author
Sam: Johnson.*

IN A COPY OF "RASSELAS"

recollection of this book, doubtless, that suggested
the "Prince of Abissinia" to Johnson years later,
when he wanted to write "fiction," as the dear old
ladies in "Cranford" called "Rasselas"; but it has
never seemed necessary to my happiness to have a
copy of "Lobo." On the other hand I have "stocked"
"Rasselas" pretty considerably, and could supply
any reasonable demand. Such are the vagaries of
collectors.

Only once, I think, have I been guilty of buying a
book I did not particularly want, because of its spec-
ulative value — that was when I stumbled across a
copy of Woodrow Wilson's "Constitutional Government in the United States" with a long inscription
in its author's cursive hand. Even in this case I

think it was my imagination rather than avarice that led me to pay a fancy price for a book which some day when I am not "among those present" will fetch

The Constitution of the United States, like the Constitution of every living State, grows and is altered by force of circum-stance and changes in affairs. The effect of a written Constitution is only to render the growth more subtle, more studious, more conservative, more a thing of carefully, almost unconsciously, wrought sequences. Our statesmen must, in the midst of origination, have the spirit of lawyers.

Woodrow Wilson

Princeton, 18 Oct., '09.

as many thousands as I paid hundreds. In 1909, when the inscription was written, its author was a relatively unimportant man — to-day he is known throughout the world and is in a position to influence its destinies as no other man has ever been.

No paper dealing with the prices of books would be complete without the remark that condition is everything. Any rare book is immensely more valuable if in very fine condition. Imagine for a moment a book worth, say, six hundred dollars in good condition, — for example, the "Vicar of Wakefield," — and then imagine — if you can — a copy of this same book in boards uncut. Would twenty-five hundred dollars be too high a price for such a copy? I think not.

Another point to be remembered is that the price of a book depends, not only on its scarcity, but also on the universality of the demand for it. And once again I may take the "Vicar" as an example of what I mean. The "Vicar" is not a scarce book. For from six to eight hundred dollars, dependent upon condition, one could, I think, lay his hands on as many as ten copies in as many weeks. It is what the trade call a bread-and-butter book — a staple. There is always a demand for it and always a supply at a price; but try to get a copy of Fanny Burney's "Evelina," and you may have to wait a year or more for it. It was the first book of an unknown young lady; the first edition was very small, it was printed on poor paper, proved to be immensely popular, and was immediately worn out in the reading; but there is no persistent demand for it as there is for the "Vicar," and it costs only half as much.

In reading over whatever I have written on the subject of the prices of rare books, I am aware that my remarks may sound to some like a whistle — a whistle to keep up my courage at the thought of the prices I am paying. But so long as the "knockout" does not get a foothold in this country, — and it would immediately be the subject of investigation if it did, and be stopped, as other abuses have been, — the prices of really great books will always average higher and higher. "Of the making of many books there is no end," nor is there an end to the prices men will be willing to pay for them.

This first book of my writings is dearest to my soul,
Because all of 'em's bought called "The Old Swimmin'-Hole."

Ever thine,

Benj. F. Johnson, Boone Co., Ind. —
James Whitcomb Riley

For —
Wallace H. Cathcart, Cleveland, Ohio.

Indianapolis, Jan. 23
1899

V

"WHAT MIGHT HAVE BEEN"

On a cold, raw day in December, 1882, there was laid
to rest in Brompton Cemetery, in London, an old
lady, — an actress, — whose name, Frances Maria
Kelly, meant little to the generation of theatre-goers,
then busy with the rising reputation of Henry Irving
and Ellen Terry. She was a very old lady when she
died — ninety-two, to be exact; she had outlived her
fame and her friends, and few followed her to her
grave.

I have said that the day was cold and raw. I do
not know certainly that it was so; I was not there;
but for my sins I have passed many Decembers in
London, and take the right, in Charles Lamb's phrase,
to damn the weather at a venture.

Fanny Kelly, as she was called by the generations
that knew her, came of a theatrical family, and most
of her long life had been passed on the stage. She
was only seven when she made her first appearance at
Drury Lane, at which theatre she acted for some
thirty-six years, when she retired; subsequently she
established a school of dramatic art and gave from
time to time what she termed "Entertainments," in
which she sometimes took as many as fourteen different parts in a single evening. With her death the
last link connecting us with the age of Johnson was

broken. She had acted with John Philip Kemble and
with Mrs. Siddons. By her sprightliness and grace
she had charmed Fox and Sheridan and the generations which followed, down to Charles Dickens, who
had acted with her in private theatricals at her own
private theatre in Dean Street, — now the Royalty,
— taking the part of Captain Bobadil in *Every Man
in his Humor*.

Nothing is more evanescent than the reputation of
an actor. Every age lingers lovingly over the greatness of the actors of its own youth; thus it was that
the theatre-goer of the eighteen-eighties only yawned
when told of the grace of Miss Kelly's Ophelia, of the
charm of her Lydia Languish, or of her bewitch-
ingness in "breeches parts." To some she was the
old actress for whom the government was being so-
licited to do something; a few thought of her as the
old maiden lady who was obsessed with the idea
that Charles Lamb had once made her an offer of
marriage.

It was well known that, half a century before,
Lamb had been one of her greatest admirers. Every
reader of his dramatic criticisms and his letters knew
that; they knew, too, that in one of his daintiest
essays, perhaps the most exquisite essay in the language, "Dream Children, A Reverie," Lamb, speaking apparently more autobiographically than usual
even for him, says: —

"Then I told how, for seven long years, in hope
sometimes, sometimes in despair, yet persisting ever,

Charles Lamb,

I courted the fair Alice W——n; and, as much as children could understand, I explained to them what coyness, and difficulty, and denial meant to maidens — when suddenly, turning to Alice, the soul of the first Alice looked out at her eyes with such a reality of re-presentment, that I became in doubt which of them stood there before me, or whose that bright hair was; and while I stood gazing, both the children gradually grew fainter to my view, receding and still receding, till nothing at last but two mournful features were seen in the uttermost distance, which, without speech, strangely impressed upon me the effects of speech: —

" 'We are not of Alice, nor of thee, nor are we children at all. The children of Alice call Bartrum father. We are nothing; less than nothing, and dreams. We are only what might have been.' "

I am quoting, not from the printed text, but from the original manuscript, which is my most cherished literary possession; and this lovely peroration, if such it may be called, is the only part of the essay which has been much interlineated or recast. It appears to have occasioned Lamb considerable difficulty; there was obviously some searching for the right word; a part of it, indeed, was entirely rewritten.

The coyness, the difficulty, and the denial of Alice: was it not immortally written into the record by Lamb himself? Miss Kelly's rejection of an offer of marriage from him must be a figment of the imagination of an old lady, who, as her years approached a century, had her dream-children, too — children who called Lamb father.

There the matter rested. Fanny Kelly was by way of being forgotten; all the facts of Lamb's life were known, apparently, and he had lain in a curiously neglected grave in Edmonton Churchyard for seventy years. Innumerable sketches and lives and memorials of him, "final" and otherwise, had been written and read. His letters — not complete, perhaps, but volumes of them — had been published and read by the constantly increasing number of his admirers, and no one suspected that Lamb had had a serious love-affair — the world accepting without reserve the statement of one of his biographers that "Lamb at the bidding of duty remained single, wedding himself to the sad fortunes of his sister."

Then, quite unexpectedly, in 1903, John Hollingshead, the former manager of the Gaiety Theatre, discovered and published two letters of Charles Lamb written on the same day, July 20, 1819. One, a long letter in Lamb's most serious vein, in which he formally offers his hand, and in a way his sister's, to Miss Kelly, and the other a whimsical, elfish letter, in which he tries to disguise the fact that in her refusal of him he has received a hard blow.

By reason of this important discovery, every line that Lamb had written in regard to Fanny Kelly was read with new interest, and an admirable biography of him by his latest and most sympathetic critic, Edward Verrall Lucas, appearing shortly afterwards,

Miss Frances Maria Kelly

was carefully studied to see what, if any, further light
could be thrown upon this interesting subject. But
it appears that the whole story has been told in the
letters, and students of Lamb were thrown back upon
the already published references.

In the Works of Lamb, published in 1818, he had
addressed to Miss Kelly a sonnet: —

> You are not, Kelly, of the common strain,
> That stoop their pride and female honor down
> To please that many-headed beast, the town,
> And vend their lavish smiles and tricks for gain;
> By fortune thrown amid the actor's train,
> You keep your native dignity of thought;
> The plaudits that attend you come unsought,
> As tributes due unto your natural vein.
> Your tears have passion in them, and a grace
> Of genuine freshness, which our hearts avow;
> Your smiles are winds whose ways we cannot trace,
> That vanish and return we know not how —
> And please the better from a pensive face,
> And thoughtful eye, and a reflecting brow.

And early in the following year he had printed in a
provincial journal an appreciation of her acting, comparing her, not unfavorably, with Mrs. Jordan, who,
in her day, then over, is said to have had no rival in
comedy parts.

Lamb's earliest reference to Miss Kelly, however,
appears to be in a letter to the Wordsworths, in which
he says that he can keep the accounts of his office,
comparing sum with sum, writing "Paid" against
one and "Unpaid" against t'other (this was long
before the days of scientific bookkeeping and much-

vaunted efficiency), and still reserve a corner of his mind for the memory of some passage from a book, or "the gleam of Fanny Kelly's divine plain face." This is an always quoted reference and seems correctly to describe the lady, who is spoken of by others as an unaffected, sensible, clear-headed, warm-hearted woman, plain but engaging, with none of the vanities or arrogance of the actress about her. It will be recalled that Lamb had no love for blue-stocking women, and speaking of one, said, "If she belonged to me I would lock her up and feed her on bread and water till she left off writing poetry. A female poet, or female author of any kind, ranks below an actress, I think." This shortest way with minor poets has, perhaps, much to recommend it.

It was Lamb's whim in his essays to be frequently misleading, setting his signals at full speed ahead when they should have been set at danger, or, at least, at caution. Thus in his charming essay "Barbara S——" (how unconsciously one invariably uses this adjective in speaking of anything Lamb wrote), after telling the story of a poor little stage waif receiving by mistake a whole sovereign instead of the half a one justly due for a week's pay, and how she was tempted to keep it, but did not, he adds, "I had the anecdote from the mouth of the late Mrs. Crawford." Here seemed to be plain sailing, and grave editors pointed out who Mrs. Crawford was: they told her maiden name, and for good measure threw in the names of her several husbands. But Lamb, in a letter to Bernard Barton in 1825, speaking of these essays, said: "Tell me how you like 'Barbara S——.' I never saw Mrs. Crawford in my life, nevertheless 't is all true of somebody." And some years later, not long before he died, to another correspondent he wrote: "As Miss Kelly is just now in notoriety," — she was then giving an entertainment called "Dramatic Recollections" at the Strand Theatre, — "it may amuse you to know that 'Barbara S——' is all of it true of her, being all communicated to me from her own mouth. Can we not contrive to make up a party to see her?"

There is another reference to Miss Kelly, which, in the light of our subsequent knowledge, is as dainty a suggestion of marriage with her as can be found in the annals of courtship. It appeared in "The Examiner" just a fortnight before Lamb's proposal. In a criticism of her acting as Rachel in "The Jovial Crew," now forgotten, Lamb was, he says, interrupted in the enjoyment of the play by a stranger who sat beside him remarking of Miss Kelly, "What a lass that were to go a gypsying through the world with!"

Knowing how frequently Lamb addressed Elia, his other self, and Elia, Lamb, may we not suppose that on this occasion the voice of the stranger was the voice of Elia? Was it unlikely that Miss Kelly, who would see the criticism, would hear the voice and recognize it as Lamb's? I love to linger over these delicate incidents of Lamb's courtship, which was all too brief.

But what of Mary? I think she cannot but have contemplated the likelihood of her brother's marriage and determined upon the line she would take in that event. Years before she had written, "You will smile when I tell you I think myself the only woman in the world who could live with a brother's wife, and make a real friend of her, partly from early observations of the unhappy example I have just given you, and partly from a knack I know I have of looking into people's real character, and never expecting them to act out of it — never expecting another to do as I would in the same case."

Mary Lamb was an exceptional woman; and even though her brother might have thought he kept the secret of his love to himself, she would know and, I fancy, approve. Was it not agreed between them that she was to die first? and when she was gone, who would be left to care for Charles?

Before I come to the little drama — tragedy one could hardly call it — of Lamb's love-affair as told in his own way by his letters, I may be permitted to refer to two letters of his to Miss Kelly, one of them relatively unimportant, the other a few lines only, both unpublished, which form a part of my own Lamb collection. These letters, before they fell from high estate, formed a part of the "Sentimental Library" of Harry B. Smith, to whom I am indebted for much information concerning them. It will be seen that both these letters work themselves into the story of Lamb's love-affair, which I am trying to tell. So

F. B.? from &c.?

MISS KELLY in the VARIOUS CHARACTERS of her ENTERTAINMENT

far as is known, four letters are all that he ever addressed to the lady: the two above referred to, and the proposal and its sequel, in the collection of Mr. Huntington of New York, where I saw them not long ago. I have held valuable letters in my hand before, but these letters of Lamb! I confess to an emotional feeling with which the mere book-collector is rarely credited.

The earlier and briefer letter is pasted into a copy of the first edition of the "Works of Charles Lamb,"

Mr Lamb having taken the liberty of addressing a slight compliment to Miss Kelly in his first volume, respectfully requests her acceptance of the collection.

7th June 1818

1818, "in boards, shaken," which occupies a place of honor on my shelves. It reads: "Mr. Lamb having taken the liberty of addressing a slight compliment to Miss Kelly in his first volume, respectfully requests her acceptance of the collection. 7th June, 1818." The compliment, of course, is the sonnet already quoted.

The second letter was written just ten days before Lamb asked Miss Kelly to marry him. The bones playfully referred to were small ivory discs, about the size of a two-shilling piece, which were allotted to leading performers for the use of their friends, giving admission to the pit. On one side was the name of the theatre; on the other the name of the actor or actress to whom they were allotted. The letter reads:

DEAR MISS KELLY, —

If your Bones are not engaged on Monday night, will you favor us with the use of them? I know, if you can oblige us, you will make no bones of it; if you cannot, it shall break none betwixt us. We might ask somebody else; but we do not like the bones of any strange animal. We should be welcome to dear Mrs. Liston's, but then she is so plump, there is no getting at them. I should prefer Miss Iver's — they must be ivory I take it for granted — but she is married to Mr. ——, and become bone of his bone, consequently can have none of her own to dispose of. Well, it all comes to this, — if you can let us have them, you will, I dare say; if you cannot, God rest your bones. I am almost at the end of my bon-mots.

C. LAMB.

9th *July*, 1819.

This characteristic note in Lamb's best punning manner ("I fancy I succeed best in epistles of mere fun; puns and that nonsense") may be regarded as a prologue to the drama played ten days later, the whole occupying but the space of a single day.

And now the curtain is lifted on the play in which Lamb and Miss Kelly are the chief actors. Lamb is in his lodgings in Great Russell Street, Covent Garden, the individual spot he likes best in all London. Bow Street Police Court can be seen through the window, and Mary Lamb seated thereby, knitting, glances into the busy street as she sees a crowd of people follow in the wake of a constable, conducting a thief to

Dear Miss Kelly,

If your Bones are not engaged on Monday night, will you favor us with the use of them? I know, if you can oblige us, you will make no bones of it; if you cannot, it shall break none betwixt us. We might ask somebody else, but we do not like the bones of any strange animal. We should be welcome to dear Mrs Liston's, but then she is so plump, there is no getting at them. I should prefer Miss Iver's —— they must be ivory I take it for granted —— but she is married to Mr * * * , and become bone of his bone, consequently can have none of her own to dispose of. Well, it all comes to this, — if you can let us have them, you will, I dare say; if you cannot, God rest your bones. I am almost at the end of my bon-mots.

                                            C Lamb

9th July 1819

his examination. Lamb is seated at a table, writing. We, unseen, may glance over his shoulder and see the letter which he has just finished.

DEAR MISS KELLY, —

We had the pleasure, *pain* I might better call it, of seeing you last night in the new Play. It was a most consummate piece of acting, but what a task for you to undergo! at a time when your heart is sore from real sorrow! It has given rise to a train of thinking which I cannot suppress.

Would to God you were released from this way of life; that you could bring your mind to consent to take your lot with us, and throw off forever the whole burden of your Profession. I neither expect nor wish you to take notice of this which I am writing, in your present over-occupied & hurried state. — But to think of it at your pleasure. I have quite income enough, if that were to justify me for making such a proposal, with what I may call even a handsome provision for my survivor. What you possess of your own would naturally be appropriated to those for whose sakes chiefly you have made so many hard sacrifices. I am not so foolish as not to know that I am a most unworthy match for such a one as you, but you have for years been a principal object in my mind. In many a sweet assumed character I have learned to love you, but simply as F. M. Kelly I love you better than them all. Can you quit these shadows of existence, & come & be a reality to us? Can you leave off harassing yourself to please a thankless multitude, who know nothing of you, & begin at last to live to yourself & your friends?

As plainly & frankly as I have seen you give or refuse assent in some feigned scene, so frankly do me the justice to answer me. It is impossible I should feel injured or aggrieved by your telling me at once, that the proposal does not suit you. It is impossible that I should ever think of molesting you with idle importunity and persecution after your mind [is] once firmly spoken — but happier, far happier, could I have leave to hope a time might come when our friends might be your friends; our interests yours; our book-knowledge, if in that inconsiderable particular we have any little advantage, might impart something to you, which you would every day have it in your power ten thousand fold to repay by the added cheerfulness and joy which you could not fail to bring as a dowry into whatever family should have the honor and happiness of receiving *you*, the most welcome accession that could be made to it.

In haste, but with entire respect & deepest affection, I subscribe myself

C. LAMB.

20 *July*, 1819.

No punning or nonsense here. It is the most serious letter Lamb ever wrote — a letter so fine, so manly, so honorable in the man who wrote it, so honoring to the woman to whom it was addressed, that, knowing Lamb as we do, it can hardly be read without a lump in the throat and eyes suffused with tears.

The letter is folded and sealed and sent by a serving-maid to the lady, who lives hard by in Henrietta Street, just the other side of Covent Garden — and the curtain falls.

Before the next act we are at liberty to wonder how Lamb passed the time while Miss Kelly was writing her reply. Did he go off to the "dull drudgery of the desk's dead wood" at East India House, and there busy himself with the prices of silks or tea or indigo, or did he wander about the streets of his beloved London? I fancy the latter. In any event the curtain rises a few hours later, and Lamb and his sister are seen as before. She has laid aside her knitting. It is late afternoon. Lamb is seated at the table endeavoring to read, when a maid enters and hands him a letter; he breaks the seal eagerly. Again we look over his shoulder and read: —

HENRIETTA STREET, July 20th, 1819.

An early & deeply rooted attachment has fixed my heart on one from whom no worldly prospect can well induce me to withdraw it, but while I thus frankly & decidedly decline your proposal, believe me, I am not insensible to the high honour which the preference of such a mind as yours confers upon me — let me, however, hope that all thought upon this subject will end with this letter, & that you henceforth encourage no other sentiment towards me than esteem in my private character and a continuance of that approbation of my humble talents which you have already expressed so much and so often to my advantage and gratification.

Believe me I feel proud to acknowledge myself

Your obliged friend

F. M. KELLY.

Lamb rises from his chair and attempts to walk over to where Mary is sitting; but his feelings overcome him, and he sinks back in his chair again as the curtain falls.

It moves quickly, the action of this little drama. The curtain is down but a moment, suggesting the passage of a single hour. When it is raised, Lamb is alone; he is but forty-five, but looks an old man. The curtains are drawn, lighted candles are on the table. We hear the rain against the windows. Lamb is writing, and for the last time we intrude upon his privacy.

Now poor Charles Lamb, now dear Charles Lamb, "Saint Charles," if you will! Our hearts go out to him; we would comfort him if we could. But read slowly one of the finest letters in all literature: a letter in which he accepts defeat instantly, but with a smile on his face; tears there may have been in his eyes, but she was not to see them. See Lamb in his supreme rôle — *of a man*. How often had he urged his friends to play that difficult part — which no one could play better than he. The letter reads: —

DEAR MISS KELLY, —

Your injunctions shall be obeyed to a tittle. I feel myself in a lackadaisical no-how-ish kind of a humor. I believe it is the rain, or something. I had thought to have written seriously, but I fancy I succeed best in epistles of mere fun; puns & that nonsense. You will be good friends with us, will you not? Let what has past "break no bones" between us. You will not refuse us them next time we send for them?

Yours very truly,   C. L.

P.S. Do you observe the delicacy of not signing my full name?

N.B. Do not paste that last letter of mine into your book.

We sometimes, mistakenly, say that the English are not good losers. To think of Charles Lamb may help us to correct that opinion.

All good plays of the period have an epilogue. By all means this should have one; and ten days later Lamb himself provided it. It appeared in "The Examiner," where, speaking of Fanny Kelly's acting in "The Hypocrite," he said, —

"She is in truth not framed to tease or torment even in jest, but to utter a hearty Yes or No; to yield or refuse assent with a noble sincerity. We have not the pleasure of being acquainted with her, but we have been told that she carries the same cordial manners into private life."

The curtain falls! The play is at an end.

VI

JAMES BOSWELL — HIS BOOK

SITTING one evening with my favorite book and enjoying the company of a crackling wood fire, I was interrupted by a cheerful idiot who, entering unheard, announced himself with the remark, "This is what I call a library." Indifferent to a forced welcome, he looked about him and continued, "I see you are fond of Boswell. I always preferred Macaulay's 'Life of Johnson' to Boswell's — it's so much shorter. I read it in college."

Argument would have been wasted on him. If he had been alone in his opinion, I would have killed him and thus exterminated the species; but he is only one of a large class, who having once read Macaulay's essay, and that years ago, feel that they have received a peculiar insight into the character of Samuel Johnson and have a patent to sneer at his biographer.

Having a case of books by and about the dear old Doctor, I have acquired a reputation that plagues me. People ask to see my collection, not that they know anything about it, or care, but simply to please me, as they think. Climbing to unusual intellectual heights, when safe at the top, where there is said to be always room, they look about and with a knowing leer murmur, "Oh! rare Ben!" I have become quite expert at lowering them from their dangerous position without showing them the depths of their ignorance. This is a feat which demands such skill as can be acquired only by long practice.

Macaulay's essay is anathema to me. If it were a food-product, the authorities would long since have suppressed it on account of its artificial coloring matter; but prep.-school teachers and college professors go on "requiring" its reading from sheer force of habit; and as long as they continue to do so, the true Samuel Johnson and the real James Boswell will both remain unknown.

Out of a thousand who have read this famous essay and remember its wonderfully balanced sentences, which stick in the memory like burrs in the hair, perhaps not more than one will be able to recall the circumstances under which it was written. Purporting to be a review of a new edition of Boswell's "Life of Johnson," edited by John Wilson Croker, it is really a personal attack on a bitter political enemy. Written at a time when political feeling ran high, it begins with a lie. Using the editorial "We," Macaulay opens by saying, "We are sorry to be obliged to say that the merits of Mr. Croker's performance are on a par with those of a certain leg of mutton on which Dr. Johnson dined while travelling from London to Oxford, and which he, with characteristic energy, pronounced to be as bad as could be."

Let us see how sorry Macaulay really was. In a letter written to his sister just before Croker's book appeared he writes: "I am to review Croker's edition

JAMES BOSWELL OF AUCHINLECK, ESQR.

Painted by Sir Joshua Reynolds. Engraved by John Jones

of Bozzy. . . . I detest Croker more than cold boiled
veal. . . . See whether I do not dust the varlet's
jacket in the next number of the 'Edinburgh Review.'" And he did, and the cloud of dust he then
raised obscured Johnson, settled on Boswell, and for
a time almost smothered him.

I suspect that Macaulay prepared himself for writing his smashing article by reading Croker's book
through in half a dozen evenings, pencil in hand,
searching for blemishes. After that, his serious work
began. Blinded by his hatred of the editor, he makes
Johnson grotesque and repulsive, and grossly insults
Boswell. He started with the premise that Boswell
was mean, but that his book was great. Then the
proposition defined itself in his mind something like
this: Boswell was one of the smallest men that ever
lived, yet his "Life of Johnson" is one of the greatest books ever written. Boswell was always laying
himself at the feet of some eminent man, begging to
be spit upon and trampled upon, yet as a biographer
he ranks with Shakespeare as a dramatist; and so he
goes on, until at last, made dizzy by the sweep of his
verbal seesaw and the lilt of his own brutal rhetoric,
he finally reaches the conclusion that, *because* Boswell was a great fool, he was a very great writer.

Absurdity can go no further. Well may we ask
ourselves what Boswell had done to be thus pilloried?
Nothing! except that he had written a book which is
universally admitted to be the best book of its kind
in any language.

What manner of a man was James Boswell? He was, more than most men, a mass of contradictions. It would never, I think, have been easy to answer this question. Since Macaulay answered it, in his cocksure way, and answered it wrongly, to answer it rightly is most difficult. It is so easy to keep ringing the changes on Macaulay. Any fool with a pen can do it. Some time ago, apropos of the effort being made to preserve the house in Great Queen Street, in London, in which Boswell lived when he wrote the biography, some foolish writer in a magazine said, "Boswell shrivels more and more as we look at him. . . . It would be absurd to preserve a memorial to him alone." — "Shrivels!" Impossible! Johnson and Boswell as a partnership have been too long established for either member of the firm to "shrivel." Unconsciously perhaps, but consciously I think, Boswell has so managed it that, when the senior partner is thought of, the junior also comes to mind. Johnson's contribution to the business was experience and unlimited common sense; Boswell made him responsible for output: the product was words, merely spoken words, either of wisdom or of wit. Distribution is quite as important as production — any railroad man will tell you so. Boswell had a genius for packing and delivering the goods so that they are, if anything, improved by time and transportation.

Let me have one more fling at Macaulay. He missed, and for his sins he deserved to miss, two good things without which this world would be a sad place.

He had no wife and he had no sense of humor. Either
would have told him that he was writing sheer nonsense when he said, "The very wife of his [Boswell's]
bosom laughed at his fooleries." What are wives for,
I should like to know, if not to laugh at us?

But reputation is like a pendulum, and it is now
swinging from Macaulay. James Boswell is coming
into his own. The biographer will outlive the essayist, brilliant and wonderful writer though he be; and
I venture the prophecy that, when the traveler from
New Zealand takes his stand on the ruined arch of
London Bridge to sketch the ruins of St. Paul's, he
will have a pocket edition of Boswell with him, in
which to read something of the lives of those strange
people who inhabited that vast solitude when it was
called London.

James Boswell was born in 1740. His father was
a Scottish judge, with the title of Lord Auchinleck.
Auchinleck is in Ayrshire, and the estate had belonged to the Boswells for over two hundred years
when the biographer of Johnson was born. As a
young man, he was rather a trial to his father, and
showed his ability chiefly in circumventing the old
man's wishes. The father destined him for the law;
but he was not a good student, and was fond of society; so the choice of the son was for the army.

We, however, know Boswell better than he knew
himself, and we know that when he fancied that he
heard the call to arms, what he really wanted was

to parade around in a scarlet uniform and make love to the ladies. But even in those early days there must have been something attractive about him, for when he and his father went up to London to solicit the good offices of the Duke of Argyle to secure a commission for him, the duke is reported to have declined, saying, "My Lord, I like your son. The boy must not be shot at for three shillings and six-pence a day."

Boswell was only twenty when he first heard of the greatness of Samuel Johnson and formed a desire to meet him; but it was not until several years later that the great event occurred. What a meeting it was! It seems almost to have been foreordained. A proud, flippant, pushing young particle, irresponsible and practically unknown, meets one of the most distinguished men then living in London, a man more than thirty years his senior and in almost every respect his exact opposite, and so carries himself that, in spite of a rebuff or two at the start, we find Johnson a few days later shaking him by the hand and asking him why he does not come oftener to see him.

The description of the first meeting between Johnson and Boswell, written many years afterwards, is a favorite passage with all good Boswellians. "At last, on Monday, the 16th of May [1] [1763], when I was sitting in Mr. Davies' back parlour, after having

[1] I received a note some time ago from Christopher Morley, saying, " Let us hereafter and forever drink tea together on this date in celebration of this meeting."

PORTRAIT OF DR. JOHNSON BY SIR JOSHUA REYNOLDS, PROBABLY IDEALIZED.
THE DOCTOR IS WEARING A TIE-WIG AND HOLDS A COPY OF "IRENE"

Engraved by Zobel

drunk tea with him and Mrs. Davies, Johnson unexpectedly came into the shop; and Mr. Davies, having
perceived him through the glass-door in the room in
which we were sitting, advancing toward us, — he
announced his aweful approach to me, somewhat in
the manner of an actor in the part of Horatio, when
he addresses Hamlet on the appearance of his father's
ghost, 'Look, my Lord, it comes!'"

This is a good example of Boswell's style. In the
fewest possible words he creates a picture which one
never forgets. We not only hear the talk, we see the
company, and soon come to know every member of it.

Without this meeting the world would have lost
one of the most delightful books ever written, Boswell himself would probably never have been heard
of, and Johnson to-day would be a mere name instead of being, as he is, next to Shakespeare, the most
quoted of English authors. As Augustine Birrell has
pointed out, we have only talk *about* other talkers.
Johnson's is a matter of record. Johnson stamped his
image on his own generation, but it required the genius
of Boswell to make him known to ours, and to all
generations to come. "Great as Johnson is," says
Burke, "he is greater in Boswell's books than in his
own." That we now speak of the "Age of Johnson"
is due rather to Boswell than to the author of the
"Dictionary," "Rasselas," and endless "Ramblers."

Someone has said that the three greatest characters in English literature are Falstaff, Mr. Pickwick,
and Dr. Johnson. Had James Boswell created the

third of this great trio, he would indeed rank with
Shakespeare and with Dickens; but Johnson was his
own creation, and Boswell, posing as an artist, painted
his portrait as mortal man has never been painted
before. In his pages we see the many-sided Johnson,
the great burly philosopher, scholar, wit, and ladies'
man — Boswell makes him a shade too austere —
more clearly than any other man who ever lived.
As a portrait-painter, Boswell is the world's greatest
artist; and he is not simply a portrait-painter — he
is unsurpassed at composition, atmosphere, and color.
His book is like Rembrandt's Night Watch — the
canvas is crowded, the portraits all are faultless and
distinct, but there is one dominating figure standing
out from the rest — one masterly, unsurpassed, and
immortal figure.

Boswell, when he first met Johnson, was twenty-
two years of age. A year later he writes him: "It
shall be my study to do what I can to render your
life happy; and if you die before me, I shall endeavor
to do honor to your memory." He kept his word.
From that hour almost to the time of Johnson's death
(I say almost, for just before the end there seems to
have fallen upon their friendship a shadow, the cause
of which has never been fully explained), they were
unreservedly friends. Superficially they had little in
common, but in essentials, all that was important;
and they supplemented each other as no two men
have ever done before or since. Reading the Life
casually, as it is usually read, one would suppose that

they were very much together; but such is not the case. Birkbeck Hill, Boswell's most painstaking editor, has calculated that, including the time when Boswell and Johnson were together in the Hebrides, they could have seen each other only for 790 days in all; and this on the assumption that Boswell, when in London, was always in Johnson's company, which we know was not the case; moreover, when they were apart there were gaps of years in their correspondence.

Boswell, however, weaves the story of Johnson's life so skillfully that we come to have the feeling that whenever Johnson was going to say anything important, Boswell was at his side. Johnson, in speaking of his Dictionary once said, "Why, Sir, I knew very well how to go about it and have done it very well." Boswell could have said the same of his great work. We had no great biography before his, and in comparison we have had none since. The combination of so great a subject for portraiture and so great an artist had never occurred before and may never occur again. Geniuses ordinarily do not run in couples.

Boswell hoped that his book would bring him fame. Over it he labored at a time when labor was especially difficult for him. For it he was prepared to sacrifice himself, his friends, anything. Whatever would add to his book's value he would include, at whatever cost. A more careful and exact biographer never lived. Reynolds said of him that he wrote as if he were under oath; and we all remember the reply he made to Hannah More, who, when she heard he was

engaged in writing the life of her revered friend, urged
him to mitigate somewhat the asperities of his disposition: "No, madam, I will not cut his claws or
make my tiger a cat to please anyone."

And for writing this book Boswell has been held
up to almost universal scorn. His defenders have
been few and faint-hearted. I have never derived
much satisfaction from Boswell's rescue (the word
is Lowell's) by Carlyle. That unhappy old dyspeptic,
unable to enjoy a good dinner himself, could not forgive Boswell his gusto for the good things of life.

What were Boswell's faults above those of other
men, that stones should be thrown at him? He drank
too much! True, but what of it? Who in his day did
not? Johnson records that many of the most respectable people in his cathedral city of Lichfield
went nightly to bed drunk.

He was an unfaithful husband! Admitted; but
Mrs. Boswell forgave him, and why should not we?

He was proud! He was, but the pride of race is not
unheard of in the scion of an old family; nor did he
allow his pride to prevent his attaching himself to an
old man who admitted that he hardly knew who was
his grandfather.

He had a taste for knowing people highly placed!
He had, and he came to number among his friends
the greatest scholar, the greatest poet, the greatest
painter, the greatest actor, the greatest historian,
and most of the great statesmen of his day; and these
men, though they laughed with him frequently, and

at him sometimes, did not think him altogether a fool.

He was vain and foolish! Yes, and inquisitive; yet while neither wise nor witty himself, he had an exquisite appreciation of wit in others. He carried repartees and arguments with accuracy. Mrs. Thrale very cleverly said that his long-head was better than short-hand; yet, as some one has pointed out, to follow the hum of conversation with so much intelligence required unusual quickness of apprehension and cannot be reconciled with the opinion that he was simply endowed with memory.

He lived beyond his means and got into debt! I seem to have heard something of this of other men whose fathers were not enjoying a comfortable estate and whose children were not adequately provided for.

Let there be an end to a discussion of the weaknesses of Boswell. They have been sufficiently advertised and his good qualities overlooked. If a man is a genius, let his personal shortcomings be absorbed in the greatness of his work. The worst that can be fairly said of Boswell is that he was vain, inquisitive, and foolish. Let us forget the silly questions he sometimes put to Johnson, and remember how often he started something which made the old Doctor perform at his unrivaled best.

The difficulty is that Boswell told on himself. As he was speaking to Johnson one day of his weaknesses, the old man admitted that he had them, too, but added, "I don't tell of them. A man should be careful not to tell tales of himself to his own dis-advantage." It would have been well if Boswell could have remembered this excellent bit of advice; but Johnson's advice, whether sought or unsought, was too frequently disregarded.

One of his most intimate friends, Sir Joshua Rey-nolds, has testified to his truthfulness, and even a casual reader of the Life will admit that he was cou-rageous. Tossed and gored by Johnson, as he fre-quently was, he always came back; and, much as he respected the old man, he was never overawed by him. He differed with him on the wisdom of taxing the American Colonies, on the merits of the novels of Fielding, on the poetry of Gray, and on many other subjects. To differ with Johnson required courage and conversational ability of no common order. Indeed, it may be doubted whether, next to Johnson himself, Boswell was not the best talker in the circle — and Johnson's circle included the most brilliant men of his time. He was sometimes very happy in his refer-ence to himself: as where, having brought Paoli and Johnson together, he compares himself to an isthmus connecting two great continents. Indeed, the great work is so famous as a biography of Johnson that few people realize to what an extent and how subtly Bos-well has made it his own autobiography.

Johnson once said, "Sir, the biographical part of literature is what I love best." I am inclined to think that it is so with most of us. It would have been impossible for Boswell, the biographer *par excellence,*

not to have told in one way or another the story of
his own life. He told it in his account of the island
of Corsica, and in his letters to his life-long friend,
Temple. These deserve to be better known than they
are. They are indeed just such letters as Samuel
Pepys might have written in cipher to his closest
friend, whom he had already provided with a key.

The first letter of this correspondence is dated
Edinburgh, 29 July, 1758, when Boswell was eighteen
years of age; and the last was on his writing-desk in
London when the shadow of death fell upon him,
thirty-seven years later.

The manner in which these letters came to be published is interesting. An English clergyman touring
in France, having occasion to make some small purchases at a shop in Boulogne, observed that the paper
in which they were wrapped was a fragment of an
English letter. Upon inspection a date and some well-
known names were observed, and further investigation showed that the piece of paper was part of a
correspondence carried on nearly a century before
between Boswell and a friend, the Reverend William
Johnson Temple. On making inquiry, it was ascertained that this piece of paper had been taken from
a large parcel recently purchased from a hawker, who
was in the habit of passing through Boulogne once
or twice a year, for the purpose of supplying the different shops with paper. Beyond this no further information could be obtained. The whole contents of
the parcel were immediately secured.

At the death of the purchaser of these letters they passed into the hands of a nephew, from whom they were obtained, and published in 1857, after such editing and expurgating as was then fashionable. Who did the work has never been discovered, nor does it matter, as the letters fortunately passed into the collection of J. P. Morgan, and are now, finally, being edited, together with such other letters as are available, by Professor Tinker of Yale. Students of eighteenth-century literature have good reason for believing that a volume of supreme interest is in preparation for them; for such self-revealing letters, such human documents as those of James Boswell, could have been written only by their author, or by Samuel Pepys. As these letters are little known, let me give a few excerpts from them as originally published. On one of his journeys to London, Boswell writes: —

I have thought of making a good acquaintance in each town on the road. No man has been more successful in making acquaintances easily than I have been; I even bring people quickly on to a degree of cordiality . . . but I know not if I last sufficiently, though surely, my dear Temple, there is always a warm place for you.

Further along on the road he writes again: —

I am in charming health and spirits. There is a handsome maid at this inn, who interrupts me by coming sometimes into the room. I have no confession to make, my priest; so be not curious.

On his way back to Edinburgh he goes somewhat out of his way to stop again at this inn and have

another look at the handsome chambermaid, — her
name was Matty, — and finds that she has disappeared, as handsome chambermaids have a way of
doing; but Boswell comforts himself by reflecting

James Boswell.

Inner Temple, London 1763. —

*A present from my worthy
friend — Temple.*

INSCRIPTION IN BOSWELL'S COPY OF MASON'S "ELFRIDA"

that he can find mistresses wherever he goes. He
remembers also that he had promised Dr. Johnson to
accept a chest of books of the moralist's own selection, and to "read more and drink less."

Again he writes from Edinburgh: —

I have talked a great deal of my sweet little mistress;
I am, however, uneasy about her. Furnishing a house and
maintaining her with a maid will cost me a great deal of
money, and it is too like marriage, or too much a settled
plan of licentiousness; but what can I do? I have already
taken the house, and the lady has agreed to go in at Whit-
suntide; I cannot in honour draw back. . . . Nor am I
tormented because my charmer has formerly loved others.
Besides she is ill-bred, quite a rompish girl. She debases my
dignity: she has no refinement, but she is very handsome
and very lively. What is it to me that she has formerly
loved? So have I.

Temple's letters to Boswell have not been pre-

served, but he appears to have warned him of the
danger of his course, for Boswell comes back with, —

I have a dear infidel, as you say; but don't think her unfaithful. I could not love her if she was. There is a base-
ness in all deceit which my soul is virtuous enough to
abhor, and therefore I look with horror on adultery. But
my amiable mistress is no longer bound to him who was
her husband: he has used her shockingly ill; he has deserted her, he lives with another. Is she not then free?
She is, it is clear, and no arguments can disguise it. She
is now mine, and were she to be unfaithful to me she ought
to be pierced with a Corsican poniard; but I believe she
loves me sincerely. She has done everything to please
me; she is perfectly generous, and would not hear of any
present.

Boswell seemed to enjoy equally two very different
things, namely, going to church and getting drunk.
On Easter Sunday he "attends the solemn service at
St. Paul's," and next day informs Mr. Temple that
he had "received the holy sacrament, and was exalted in piety." But in the same letter he reports that
he is enjoying "the metropolis to the full," and that
he has had "too much dissipation."

He resolves to do better when his book on Corsica
appears, and he has the reputation of a literary man
to support. Meanwhile, he confesses: —

I last night unwarily exceeded my one bottle of old
Hock; and having once broke over the pale, I run wild, but
I did not get drunk. I was, however, intoxicated, and very
ill next day. I ask your forgiveness, and I shall be more
cautious for the future. The drunken manners of this
country are very bad.

Boswell's affairs with chambermaids, grass widows, and women of the town moved along simultaneously with efforts to land an heiress. He asks Temple to help him in an affair with a Miss Blair. Temple did his best and failed. He reported his failure and Boswell was deeply dejected for five minutes; then he writes:

My dear friend, suppose what you please; suppose her affections changed, as those of women too often are; suppose her offended at my *Spanish stateliness* [italics mine]; suppose her to have resolved to be more reserved and coy in order to make me more in love.

Then he felt that he must have a change of scene, and off he was to London.

I got into the fly at Buckden [he says], and had a very good journey. An agreeable young widow nursed me, and supported my lame foot on her knee. Am I not fortunate in having something about me that interests most people at first sight in my favour?

In a letter to Mrs. Thrale, Johnson once wrote: "It has become so much the fashion to publish letters that in order to avoid it, I put as little into mine as I can." Boswell was not afraid of publication. His fear, as he said, was that letters, like sermons, would not continue to attract public curiosity, so he spiced his highly. Did he do or say a foolish thing, he at once sat down and told Temple all about it, usually adding that in the near future he intended to amend. His comment on his contemporaries is characteristic. "Hume," he says, "told me that he would give me half-a-crown for every page of Johnson's Dictionary in which he could not find an absurdity, if I would give him half-a-crown for every page in which he could find one.

He announces Adam Smith's election to membership in the famous literary club by saying: "Smith is now of our club — it has lost its select merit." Of Gibbon he says: "I hear nothing of the publication of his second volume. He is an ugly, affected, disgusting fellow, and poisons our literary club to me."

As he grows older and considers how unsuccessful his life has been, how he had failed at the bar both in Scotland and in London, he begins to complain. He can get no clients; he fears that, even were he entrusted with cases, he would fail utterly.

I am afraid [he says], that, were I to be tried, I should be found so deficient in the forms, the quirks and the quiddities, which early habit acquires, that I should expose myself. Yet the delusion of Westminster Hall, of brilliant reputation and splendid fortune as a barrister, still weighs upon my imagination. I must be seen in the Courts, and must hope for some happy openings in causes of importance. The Chancellor, as you observe, has not done as I expected; but why did I expect it? I am going to put him to the test. Could I be satisfied with being Baron of Auchinleck, with a good income for a gentleman in Scotland, I might, no doubt, be independent. What can be done to deaden the ambition which has ever raged in my veins like a fever?

But the highest spirits will sometimes flag. Boswell, the friendly, obliging, generous roué, was getting old. He begins to speak of the past.

Do you remember when you and I sat up all night at Cambridge, and read Gray with a noble enthusiasm; when we first used to read Mason's "Elfrida," and when we talked of that elegant knot of worthies, Gray, Mason and Walpole?

"Elfrida" calls itself on the title-page, "A Dra-matic Poem written on the model of the Ancient Greek Tra-gedy." I happen to own and value highly the very copy of this once famous poem, which Boswell and Temple read together; on the fly leaf, un-der Boswell's signa-ture, is a character-istic note in his bold, clear hand: "A pres-ent from my worthy friend Temple."

He becomes more than ever before the butt of his acquaint-ance. He tells his old

> ELFRIDA,
>
> A
>
> Dramatic Poem.
>
> Written on the MODEL of
>
> The Ancient GREEK Tragedy.
>
> By Mr MASON.
>
> The SIXTH EDITION, Corrected.
>
> LONDON:
> Printed for J. KNAPTON in Ludgate-Street.
> MDCCLIX.

friend of a trick which has been played on him — only one of many. He was staying at a great house crowded with guests.

I and two other gentlemen were laid in one room. On Thursday morning my wig was missing; a strict search was made, all in vain. I was obliged to go all day in my nightcap, and absent myself from a party of ladies and gentlemen who went and dined with an Earl on the banks of the lake, a piece of amusement which I was glad to shun, as well as a dance which they had at night. But I was in a ludicrous situation. I suspect a wanton trick, which some people think witty; but I thought it very ill-timed to one in my situation.

When his father dies and he comes into his estates, he is deeply in debt; he hates Scotland, he longs to be in London, to enjoy the Club, to see Johnson, to whom he writes of his difficulties, asking his advice. Johnson gives him just such advice as might be expected.

To come hither with such expectations at the expense of borrowed money, which I find you know not where to borrow, can hardly be considered prudent. I am sorry to find, what your solicitations seem to imply, that you have already gone the length of your credit. This is to set the quiet of your whole life at hazard. If you anticipate your inheritance, you can at last inherit nothing; all that you receive must pay for the past. You must get a place, or pine in penury, with the empty name of a great estate. Poverty, my dear friend, is so great an evil, that I cannot but earnestly enjoin you to avoid it. Live on what you have; live, if you can, on less; do not borrow either for vanity or pleasure; the vanity will end in shame, and the pleasure in regret; stay therefore at home till you have saved money for your journey hither.

His wife dies and Johnson dies. One by one the props are pulled from under him; he drinks, constantly gets drunk; is, in this condition, knocked down in the streets and robbed, and thinks with horror of giving up his soul, intoxicated, to his Maker. "Oh, Temple, Temple!" he writes, "is this realizing any of the towering hopes which have so often been the subject of our conversation and letters?" At last he begins a letter which he is never to finish. "I would fain write you in my own hand but really cannot." These were the last words poor Boswell ever wrote.

But Boswell's life is chiefly interesting where it impinges upon that of his great friend. A few months after the famous meeting in Davies's book-shop, he started for the Continent, with the idea, following the fashion of the time, of studying law at Utrecht, Johnson accompanying him on his way as far as Harwich.

After a short time at the University, during which he could have learned nothing, we find him wandering about Europe in search of celebrities, — big game, — the hunting of which was to be the chief interest of his life. He succeeded in bagging Voltaire and Rousseau, — there was none bigger, — and after a short stay in Rome he turned North, sailing from Leghorn to Corsica, where he met Paoli, the patriot, and finally returned home, escorting Thérèse Levasseur, Rousseau's mistress, as far as London. Hume at this time speaks of him as "a friend of mine, very good-humored, very agreeable and very mad."

Meanwhile his father, Lord Auchinleck, who had borne with admirable patience such stories as had reached him of his son's wild ways, insisted that it was time for him to settle down; but Boswell was too full of his adventures in the island of Corsica and his meeting with Paoli, to begin drudgery at the law. His accounts of his travels made him a welcome guest at London dinner-parties, and he had finally decided to write a book of his experiences.

At last the father, by a threat to cut off supplies, secured his son's return; but his desire to publish a book had not abated, and while he finally was admitted to the Scotch bar, we find him corresponding with his friend Mr. Dilly, the publisher, in regard to the book upon which he was busily employed. From an unpublished letter, which I was fortunate enough to secure quite recently from a book-seller in New York, Gabriel Wells, we may follow Boswell in his negotiations.

EDINBURGH, 6 *August*, 1767.

SIR

I have received your letter agreeing to pay me One Hundred Guineas for the Copy-Right of my Account of Corsica, &c., the money to be due three months after the publication of the work in London, and also agreeing that the first Edition shall be printed in Scotland, under my direction, and a map of Corsica be engraved for the work at your Expence.

In return to which, I do hereby agree that you shall have the sole Property of the said work. Our Bargain therefore is now concluded and I heartily wish that it may be of advantage to you.

I am Sir   Your most humble Servant

JAMES BOSWELL.

To MR. DILLY,
    Bookseller, London.

Sir

Edinburgh
6 August 1767

     I have received your letter
agreeing to pay me one Hundred Guineas
for the Copy-right of my Account of
Corsica & the money to be due three
months after the publication of the
Work in London, and also agreeing
that the first Edition shall be
printed in Scotland under my direction
and a map of Corsica engraved for
the work at your Expence

     In return to which, I do hereby agree
that you shall have the sole Property
of the said Work. Our Bargain therefore
is now concluded, and I heartily wish
that it may be of advantage to you
To Mr. Dilly, Bookseller   I am Sir your most humble Servant
    London   James Boswell

COPY OF JAMES BOSWELL'S AGREEMENT WITH MR. DILLY, RECITING THE TERMS AGREED ON FOR THE PUBLICATION OF "CORSICA"

Through the kindness of my fellow collector and generous friend, Judge Patterson of Philadelphia, I own an interesting fragment of a brief in Boswell's hand, written at about this period. It appears therefrom that Boswell had been retained to secure the return of a stocking-frame of the value of a few shillings, which had been forcibly carried off. The outcome of the litigation is not known, but the paper bears the interesting indorsement, "This was the first Paper drawn by me as an Advocate. James Boswell."

But I am allowing my collector's passion to carry me too far afield. The preface of Boswell's "Account of Corsica" closes with an interesting bit of self-revelation. He says, characteristically, —

For my part I should be proud to be known as an author; I have an ardent ambition for literary fame; for of all possessions I should imagine literary fame to be the most valuable. A man who has been able to furnish a book which has been approved by the world has established himself as a respectable character in distant society, without any danger of having that character lessened by the observation of his weaknesses. To preserve a uniform dignity among those who see us every day is hardly possible; and to aim at it must put us under the fetters of a perpetual restraint. The author of an approved book may allow his natural disposition an easy play, and yet indulge the pride of superior genius, when he considers that by those who know him only as an author he never ceases to be respected. Such an author in his hours of gloom and discontent may have the consolation to think that his writings are at that very time giving pleasure to numbers, and such an author may cherish the hope of being remembered after death, which has been a great object of the noblest minds in all ages.

A brief contemporary criticism sums up the merits of "Corsica" in a paragraph. "There is a deal about the Island and its dimensions that one does n't care a straw about, but that part which relates to Paoli is amusing and interesting. The author has a rage for knowing anybody that was ever talked of."

Boswell thought that he was the first, but he proved to be the second Englishman (the first was an Englishwoman) who had ever set foot upon the island. He visited Paoli, and his accounts of his reception by the great patriot and his conversation with the people are amusing in the extreme. To his great satisfaction it was generally believed that he was on a public mission.

The more I disclaimed any such thing, the more they persevered in affirming it; and I was considered as a very

close young man. I therefore just allowed them to make
a minister of me, till time should undeceive them. . . . The
Ambasciadore Inglese — as the good peasants and soldiers
used to call me — became a great favorite among them.
I got a Corsican dress made, in which I walked about with
an air of true satisfaction.

On another occasion: —

When I rode out I was mounted on Paoli's own horse,
with rich furniture of crimson velvet, with broad gold lace,
and had my guard marching along with me. I allowed
myself to indulge a momentary pride in this parade, as I
was curious to experience what should really be the pleasure of state and distinction with which mankind are so
strangely intoxicated.

The success of this publication led Boswell into
some absurd extravagances which he thought were
necessary to support his position as a distinguished
English author. Praise for his work he skillfully extracted from most of his friends, but Johnson proved
obdurate. He had expressed a qualified approval of
the book when it appeared; but when Boswell in a
letter sought more than this, the old Doctor charged
him to empty his head of "Corsica," which he said he
thought had filled it rather too long.

Boswell wrote at least two of what we should to-
day call press notices of himself. One is reminded of
the story of the man in a hired dress-suit at a charity
ball rushing about inquiring the whereabouts of the
man who puts your name in the paper. To such an
one Boswell presented this brief account of himself
on the occasion of the famous Shakespeare Jubilee.

One of the most remarkable masks upon this occasion was James Boswell, Esq., in the dress of an armed Corsican Chief. He entered the amphitheatre about twelve o'clock. He wore a short dark-coloured coat of coarse cloth, scarlet waistcoat and breeches, and black spatterdashes; his cap or bonnet was of black cloth; on the front of it was embroidered in gold letters, "Viva la Liberta," and on one side of it was a handsome blue feather and cockade, so that it had an elegant as well as a warlike appearance. On the breast of his coat was sewed a Moor's head, the crest of Corsica, surrounded with branches of laurel. He had also a cartridge-pouch into which was stuck a stiletto, and on his left side a pistol was hung upon the belt of his cartridge-pouch. He had a fusee slung across his shoulder, wore no powder in his hair, but had it plaited at full length with a knot of blue ribbon at the end of it. He had, by way of staff, a very curious vine all of one piece, with a bird finely carved upon it emblematical of the sweet bard of Avon. He wore no mask, saying that it was not proper for a gallant Corsican. So soon as he came into the room he drew universal attention. The novelty of the Corsican dress, its becoming appearance, and the character of that brave nation concurred to distinguish the armed Corsican Chief.

May we not suppose that several bottles of "Old Hock" contributed to his enjoyment of this occasion? Here is the other one: —

Boswell, the author, is a most excellent man: he is of an ancient family in the West of Scotland, upon which he values himself not a little. At his nativity there appeared omens of his future greatness. His parts are bright, and his education has been good. He has travelled in post-chaises miles without number. He is fond of seeing much of the world. He eats of every good dish, especially apple pie. He drinks Old Hock. He has a very fine temper. He is somewhat of a humorist and a little tinctured with pride. He has a good manly countenance, and he owns himself to be amorous. He has infinite vivacity, yet is observed at times to have a melancholy cast. He is rather fat than lean, rather short than tall, rather young than old. His shoes are neatly made, and he never wears spectacles.

The success of "Corsica" was not very great, but it sufficed to turn Boswell's head completely. He spent as much time in London as he could contrive to, and led there the life of a dissipated man of fashion. He quarreled with his father, and after a series of escapades with women of the town and love-affairs with heiresses, he finally married his cousin, Margaret Montgomerie, a girl without a fortune. Much to Boswell's disgust, his father, on the very same day, married for the second time, and married his cousin.

For a time after marriage he seemed to take his profession seriously, but he deceived neither his father nor his clients. The old man said that Jamie was simply taking a toot on a new horn. Meanwhile Boswell never allowed his interest in Johnson to cool for a moment. When he was in London, — and he went there on one excuse or another as often as his means permitted, — he was much with Johnson; and when he was at home, he was constantly worrying Johnson for some evidence of his affection for him. Finally Johnson writes, "My regard for you is greater almost than I have words to express" (this from the maker of a dictionary); "but I do not chuse to be always repeating it; write it down in the first leaf of your pocketbook, and never doubt of it again."

Neither wife nor father could understand the feeling of reverence and affection which their Jamie had for Johnson. I always delight in the story of his father saying to an old friend, "There's nae hope for Jamie, mon. Jamie is gaen clean gyte. What do you think, mon? He's done wi' Paoli — he's off wi' the land-louping scoundrel of a Corsican; and whose tail do you think he has pinned himself to now, mon? A dominie, mon — an auld dominie: he keeped a schule, and ca'd it an academy."

Mrs. Boswell, a sensible, cold, rather shadowy person, saw but little of Johnson, and was satisfied that it should be so. There is one good story to her credit. Unaccustomed to the ways of genius, she caught Johnson, who was nearsighted, one evening burnishing a lighted candle on her carpet to make it burn more brightly, and remarked, "I have seen many a bear led by a man, but never before have I seen a man led by a bear." Boswell was just the fellow to appreciate this, and promptly repeated it to Johnson, who failed to see the humor of it.

In 1782 his father died and he came into the estate, but by his improvident management he soon found himself in financial difficulties. Johnson's death two years later removed a restraining influence that he much needed. He tried to practice law, but he was unsuccessful. Never an abstemious man, he now drank heavily and constantly, and as constantly resolved to turn over a new leaf.

Shortly after Johnson's death, Boswell published

his "Journal of the Tour of the Hebrides," which reached a third edition within the year and established his reputation as a writer of a new kind, in which anecdotes and conversation are woven into a narrative with a fidelity and skill which were as easy to him as they were impossible to others.

The great success of this book encouraged him to begin, and continue to work upon, the great biography of Johnson on which his fame so securely rests. Others had published before him. Mrs. Piozzi's "Anecdotes of the Late Samuel Johnson" had sold well, and Hawkins, the "unclubable Knight," as Johnson called him, had been commissioned by the booksellers of London to write a formal biography, which appeared in 1787; while of lesser publications there was seemingly no end; nevertheless, Boswell persevered, and wrote his friend Temple that his

mode of biography which gives not only a history of Johnson's visible progress through the world, and of his publications, but a view of his mind in his letters and conversations, is the most perfect that can be conceived, and will be more of a life than any work that has yet appeared.

He had been preparing for the task for more than twenty years; he had, in season and out, been taking notes of Johnson's conversations, and Johnson himself had supplied him with much of the material. Thus in poverty, interrupted by periods of dissipation, amid the sneers of many, he continued his work. While it was in progress his wife died, and he, poor fellow, justly upbraided himself for his neglect of her.

DR. JOHNSON IN TRAVELING DRESS, AS DESCRIBED
IN BOSWELL'S TOUR

Engraved by Trotter

Meanwhile, a "new horn" was presented to him. He had, or thought he had, a chance of being elected to Parliament, or at least of securing a place under government; but in all this he was destined to be disappointed. It would be difficult to imagine conditions more unfavorable to sustained effort than those under which Boswell labored. He was desperately hard up. Always subject to fits of the blues, which amounted almost to melancholia, he many a time thought of giving up the task from which he hoped to derive fame and profit. He considered selling his rights in the publication for a thousand pounds. But it would go to his heart, he said, to accept such a sum; and again, "I am in such bad spirits that I have fear concerning it — I may get no profit, nay, may lose — the public may be disappointed and think I have done it poorly — I may make enemies, and even have quarrels." Then the depression would pass and he could write: "It will be, without exception, the most entertaining book you ever read." When his friends heard that the Life would make two large volumes quarto, and that the price was two guineas, they shook their heads and Boswell's fears began again.

At last, on May 16, 1791, the book appeared, with the imprint of Charles Dilly, in the Poultry; and so successful was it that by August twelve hundred copies had been disposed of, and the entire edition was exhausted before the end of the year. The writer confesses to such a passion for this book that of this edition he owns at present four copies in various states, the one he prizes most having an inscription in Boswell's hand: "To James Boswell, Esquire, Junior, from his affectionate father, the Authour." Of other editions — but why display one's weakness?

"Should there," in Boswell's phrase, "be any cold-blooded and morose mortals who really dislike it," I

To James Boswell Esq: Junior from his affectionate Father The Authour.

am sorry for them. To me it has for thirty years been a never-ending source of profit — and pleasure, which is as important. It is a book to ramble in — and with. I have never, I think, read it through from cover to cover, as the saying is, but some day I will; meanwhile let me make a confession. There are parts of it which are deadly dull; the judicious reader will skip these without hint from me. I have, indeed, always had a certain sympathy with George Henry Lewes, who for years threatened to publish an abridgment of it. It could be done: indeed, the work could be either expanded or contracted at will; but every good Boswellian will wish to do this for himself; tampering with a classic is somewhat like tampering with a will — it is good form not to.

What is really needed is a complete index to the sayings of Johnson — his *dicta*, spoken or written. It would be an heroic task, but heroic tasks are constantly being undertaken. My friend Osgood, of

Princeton, a ripe scholar and an ardent Johnsonian, has been devoting the scanty leisure of years to a concordance of Spenser. No one less competent than he should undertake to supervise such a labor of love.

It will be remembered that the Bible is not lacking in quotations, nor is Shakespeare; but these sources of wisdom aside, Boswell, quoting Johnson, supplies us more frequently with quotations than any other author whatever. Could the irascible old Doctor come to earth again, and with that wonderful memory of his call to mind the purely casual remarks which he chanced to make to Boswell, he would surely be amazed to hear himself quoted, and to learn that his *obiter dicta* had become fixed in the minds of countless thousands who perhaps have never heard his name.

I chanced the other day to stop at my broker's office to see how much I had lost in an unexpected drop in the market, and to beguile the time, picked up a market letter in which this sentence met my eye: "The unexpected and perpendicular decline in the stock of Golden Rod mining shares has left many investors sadder if not wiser. When will the public learn that investors in securities of this class are only indulging themselves in proving the correctness of Franklin's [*sic*] adage, that the expectation of making a profit in such securities is simply *the triumph of hope over experience?*" Good Boswellians will hardly need to be reminded that this is Dr. Johnson on marriage. He had something equally wise to say, too, on the subject of "shares"; but in this instance he was speaking of a man's second venture into matrimony, his first having proved very unhappy.

Most men, when they write a book of memoirs in which hundreds of living people are mentioned, discreetly postpone publication until after they and the chief personages of the narrative are dead. Johnson refers to Bolingbroke as a "cowardly scoundrel" for writing a book (charging a blunderbuss, he called it) and leaving half a crown to a beggarly Scotchman to pull the trigger after his death. Boswell spent some years in charging his blunderbuss; he filled it with shot, great and small, and then, taking careful aim, pulled the trigger.

Cries of rage, anguish, and delight instantly arose from all over the kingdom. A vast number of living people were mentioned, and their merits or failings discussed with an *abandon* which is one of the great charms of the book to-day, but which, when it appeared, stirred up a veritable hornets' nest. As some one very cleverly said, "Boswell has invented a new kind of libel." "A man who is dead once told me so and so" — what redress have you in law? None! The only thing to do is to punch his head.

Fortunately Boswell escaped personal chastisement, but he made many enemies and alienated some friends. Mrs. Thrale, by this time Mrs. Piozzi, quite naturally felt enraged at Boswell's contemptuous remarks about her, and at his references to what Johnson

said of her while he was enjoying the hospitality of
Streatham. The best of us like to criticize our friends
behind their backs; and Johnson could be frank, and
indeed brutal, on occasion. Mrs. Boscawen, the wife
of the admiral, on the other hand, had no reason to
be displeased when she read: "If it is not presumptu-
ous in me to praise her, I would say that her manners
are the best of any lady with whom I ever had the
happiness to be acquainted."

Bishop Percy, shrewdly suspecting that Boswell's
judgment was not to be trusted, when he complied
with his request for some material for the Life, desired that his name might not be mentioned in the
work; to which Boswell replied that it was his intention to introduce as many names of eminent persons
as he could, adding, "Believe me, my Lord, you are
not the only Bishop to grace my pages." We may
suspect that he, like many another, took up the book
with fear and trembling, and put it down in a rage.

Wilkes, too, got a touch of tar, but little he cared;
the best beloved and the best hated man in England,
he probably laughed, properly thinking that Boswell
could do little damage to his reputation. But what
shall we say of Lady Diana Beauclerk's feelings when
she read the stout old English epithet which Johnson had applied to her. Johnson's authorized biographer, Sir John Hawkins, dead and buried "without his shoes and stawkin's," as the old jingle goes,
had sneered at Boswell and passed on; verily he hath
his reward. Boswell accused him of stupidity, inac-

curacy, and writing fatiguing and disgusting "rig-marole." His daughter came to the rescue of his fame, and Boswell and she had a lively exchange of letters; indeed Boswell, at all times, seemed to court that which most men shrink from, a discussion of questions of veracity with a woman.

But on the whole the book was well received, and over his success Boswell exulted, as well he might; he had achieved his ambition, he had written his name among the immortals. With its publication his work was done. He became more and more dissipated. His sober hours he devoted to schemes for self-reform and a revision of the text for future editions. He was engaged on a third printing when death overtook him. The last words he wrote — the unfinished letter to his old friend Temple — have already been quoted. The pen which he laid down was taken up by his son, who finished the letter. From him we learn the sad details of his death. He passed away on May 19, 1795, in his fifty-fifth year.

Like many another man, Boswell was always intending to reform, and never did. His practice was ever at total variance with his principles. In opinions he was a moralist; in conduct he was — otherwise. Let it be remembered, however, that he was of a generous, open-hearted, and loving disposition. A clause in his will, written in his own hand, sheds important light upon his character. "I do beseech succeeding heirs of entail to be kind to the tenants, and not to turn out old possessors to get a little more rent."

What were the contemporary opinions of Boswell? Walpole did not like him, but Walpole liked few. Paoli was his friend; with Goldsmith and with Garrick he had been intimate. Mrs. Thrale and he did not get along well together; he could not bear the thought that she saw more of Johnson than he, and he was jealous of her influence over him. Fanny Burney did not like him, and declined to give him some information which he very naturally wanted for his book, because she wanted to use it herself. Gibbon thought him terribly indiscreet, which, compared with Gibbon, he certainly was. Reynolds and he were firm friends — the great book is dedicated to Sir Joshua.

Of Boswell, Johnson wrote during their journey in Scotland, "There is no house where he is not received with kindness and respect"; and elsewhere, "He never left a house without leaving a wish for his return"; also, "He was a man who finds himself welcome wherever he goes and makes friends faster than he can want them"; and "He was the best traveling companion in the world." If there is a greater test than this, I do not know it. It is summering and wintering with a man in a month. Burke said of him that "good humor was so natural to him as to be scarcely a virtue to him." I know many admirable men of whom this cannot be said.

Several years ago, being in Ayrshire, I found myself not far from Auchinleck; and although I knew that Boswell's greatest editor, Birkbeck Hill, had experi-

enced a rebuff upon his attempt to visit the old estate
which Johnson had described as "very magnificent
and very convenient," I determined, out of loyalty to
James Boswell, to make the attempt. I thought that
perhaps American nerve would succeed where English
scholarship had failed.

We had spent the night at Ayr, and early next
morning I inquired the cost of a motor-trip to take
my small party over to Auchinleck; and I was careful
to pronounce the word as though spelled Afflek, as
Boswell tells us to.

"To where, sir?"

"Afflek," I repeated.

The man seemed dazed. Finally I spelled it for
him, "A-U-C-H-I-N-L-E-C-K."

"Ah, sir, Auchinleck," — in gutturals the types will
not reproduce, — "that would be two guineas, sir."

"Very good," I said; "pronounce it your own way,
but let me have the motor."

We were soon rolling over a road which Boswell
must have taken many times, but certainly never so
rapidly or luxuriously. How Dr. Johnson would have
enjoyed the journey! I recalled his remark, "Sir, if I
had no duties and no reference to futurity, I would
spend my life driving briskly in a post-chaise with a
pretty woman." Futurity was not bothering me and I
had a pretty woman, my wife, by my side. Moreover,
to complete the Doctor's remark, she was "one who
could understand me and add something to the conversation." We set out in high spirits.

As we approached the house by a fine avenue bordered by venerable trees, — no doubt those planted by the old laird, who delighted in such work, — my courage almost failed me; but I had gone too far to retire. To the servant who responded to my ring I stated my business, which seemed trivial enough.

I might as well have addressed a graven image. At last it spoke. "The family are away. The instructions are that no one is to be admitted to the house under pain of instant dismissal."

Means elsewhere successful failed me here.

"You can walk in the park."

"Thanks, but I did not come to Scotland to walk in a park. Perhaps you can direct me to the church where Boswell is buried."

"You will find the tomb in the kirk in the village."

Coal has been discovered on the estate, and the village, a mile or two away, is ugly, and, to judge from the number of places where beer and spirits could be had, their consumption would seem to be the chief occupation of the population. I found the kirk, with door securely locked. Would I try for the key at the minister's? I would; but the minister was away for the day. Would I try the sexton? I would; but he, too, was away, and I found myself in the midst of a crowd of barefooted children who embarrassed me by their profitless attentions. It was cold and it began to rain. I remembered that we were not far from Greenock where "when it does not rain, it snaws."

My visit had not been a success. I cannot recommend a Boswell pilgrimage. I wished that I was in London, and bethought me of Johnson's remark that "the noblest prospect in Scotland is the high-road that leads to England." On that high-road my party made no objection to setting out.

I once heard an eminent college professor speak disparagingly of Boswell's "Life of Johnson," saying that it was a mere literary slop-pail into which Boswell dropped scraps of all kinds — gossip, anecdotes and scandal, literary and biographical refuse generally. I stood aghast for a moment; then my commercial instinct awakened. I endeavored to secure this nugget of criticism in writing, with permission to publish it over the author's name. In vain I offered a rate per word that would have aroused the envy of a Kipling. My friend pleaded "writer's cramp," or made some other excuse, and it finally appeared that, after all, this was only one of the cases where I had neglected, in Boswell's phrase, to distinguish between talk for the sake of victory and talk with the desire to inform and illustrate. Against this opinion there is a perfect chorus of praise rendered by a full choir.[1]

[1] The original of the portrait opposite was owned by Boswell, who used the engraving as the frontispiece of his "Life of Johnson." Now in the Johnson collection of Robert B. Adam, Esq., of Buffalo. There is a proof plate with an inscription in Boswell's hand: "This is the first impression of the Plate after Mr. Heath the engraver thought it was finished. He went with me to Sir Joshua Reynolds who suggested that the countenance was too young and not thoughtful enough. Mr. Heath thereupon altered it so much to its advantage that Sir Joshua was quite satisfied and Heath then saw such a difference that he said he would not for a hundred pounds have had it remain as it was."

SAMUEL JOHNSON

Painted by Sir J. Reynolds. Engraved by Heath

The great scholar Jowett confessed that he had read the book fifty times. Carlyle said, "Boswell has given more pleasure than any other man of this time, and perhaps, two or three excepted, has done the world greater service." Lowell refers to the "Life" as a perfect granary of discussion and conversation. Leslie Stephen says that his fondness for reading began and would end with Boswell's "Life of Johnson." Robert Louis Stevenson wrote: "I am taking a little of Boswell daily by way of a Bible. I mean to read him now until the day I die." It is one of the few classics which is not merely talked about and taken as read, but is constantly being read; and I love to think that perhaps not a day goes by when some one, somewhere, does not open the book for the first time and become a confirmed Boswellian.

"What a wonderful thing your English literature is!" a learned Hungarian once said to me. "You have the greatest drama, the greatest poetry, and the greatest fiction in the world, and you are the only nation that has any biography." The great English epic is Boswell's "Life of Johnson."

The Right Honourable
Edmund Burke
from the Authour

VII

A LIGHT–BLUE STOCKING

SOMETIME, when seated in your library, as it becomes too dark to read and is yet too light, — to ring for candles, I was going to say, but nowadays we simply touch a button, — let your thoughts wander over the long list of women who have made for themselves a place in English literature, and see if you do not agree with me that the woman you would like most to meet in the flesh, were it possible, would be Mrs. Piozzi, born Hester Lynch Salusbury, but best known to us as Mrs. Thrale.

Let us argue the matter. It may at first seem almost absurd to mention the wife of the successful London brewer, Henry Thrale, in a list which would include the names of Fanny Burney, Jane Austen, George Eliot, the Brontës, and Mrs. Browning; but the woman I have in mind should unite feminine charm with literary gifts: she should be a woman whom you would honestly enjoy meeting and whom you would be glad to find yourself seated next to at dinner.

The men of the Johnsonian circle affected to love "little Burney," but was it not for the pleasure her "Evelina" gave them rather than for anything in the author herself? According to her own account, she was so easily embarrassed as to be always "retir-

Engraved by Ridley from a Miniature by Barber.

Mrs Piozzi

ing in confusion," or "on the verge of swooning." It is possible that we would find this rather limp young lady a trifle tiresome.

Jane Austen was actually as shy and retiring as Fanny Burney affected to be. She could hardly have presided gracefully in a drawing-room in a cathedral city; much less would she have been at home among the wits in a salon in London.

Of George Eliot one would be inclined to say, as Dr. Johnson said of Burke when he was ill, "If I should meet Burke now it would kill me." Perhaps it would not kill one to meet George Eliot, but I suspect few men would care for an hour's tête-à-tête with her without a preliminary oiling of their mental machinery — a hateful task.

The Brontës were geniuses undoubtedly, particularly Emily, but one would hardly select the author of "Wuthering Heights" as a companion for a social evening.

Mrs. Browning, with her placid smile and tiresome ringlets, was too deeply in love with her husband. After all, the woman one enjoys meeting must be something of a woman of the world. She need not necessarily be a good wife or mother. We are provided with the best of wives and at the moment are not on the lookout for a good mother.

It may at once be admitted that as a mother Mrs. Thrale was not a conspicuous success; but she was a woman of charm, with a sound mind in a sound body. Although she could be brilliant in conversation, she

would let you take the lead if you were able to; but
she was quite prepared to take it herself rather than
let the conversation flag; and she must have been
a very exceptional woman, to steady, as she did, a
somewhat roving husband, to call Dr. Johnson to
order, and upon occasion to reprove Burke, even while
entertaining the most brilliant society of which London at the period could boast.

At the time when we first make her acquaintance,
she was young and pretty, the mistress of a luxurious
establishment; and if she was not possessed of literary gifts herself, it may fairly be said that she was
the cause of literature in others.

In these days, when women, having everything
else, want the vote also (and I would give it to them
promptly and end the discussion), it may be suggested that to shine by a reflected light is to shine
not at all. Frankly, Mrs. Thrale owes her position in
English letters, not to anything important that she
herself did or was capable of doing, but to the eminence of those she gathered about her. But her position is not the less secure; she was a charming and
fluffy person; and as firmly as I believe that women
have come to stay, so firmly am I of the opinion that,
in spite of all the well-meaning efforts of some of their
sex to prevent it, a certain, and, thank God, sufficient
number of women will stay charming and fluffy to the
end of the chapter.

On one subject only could Mrs. Thrale be tedious
— her pedigree. I have it before me, written in her

own bold hand, and I confess that it seems very exalted indeed. She would not have been herself had she not stopped in transcribing it to relate how one of her ancestors, Katherine Tudor de Berayne, cousin and ward of Queen Elizabeth and a famous heiress, as she was returning from the grave of her first husband, Sir John Salusbury, was asked in marriage by Maurice Wynne of Gwydir, who was amazed to learn that he was too late, as she had already engaged herself to Sir Richard Clough. "But," added the lady, "if in the providence of God I am unfortunate enough to survive him, I consent to be the lady of Gwydir." Nor does the tale end here, for she married yet another, and having sons by all four husbands, she came to be called "Mam y Cymry," — Mother of Wales, — and no doubt she deserved the appellation.

With such marrying blood in her veins it is easily understood that, as soon as Thrale's halter was off her neck, — this sporting phrase, I regret to say, is Dr. Johnson's, — she should think of marrying again; and that having the first time married to please her family, she should, at the second venture, marry to please herself. But this chapter is moving too rapidly — the lady is not yet born.

Hester Lynch Salusbury's birthplace was Bodvel, in Wales, and the year, 1741. She was an only child, very precocious, with a retentive memory. She soon became the plaything of the elderly people around her, who called her "Fiddle." Her father had the reputation of being a scamp, and it fell to her uncle's lot to direct, somewhat, her education. Handed from one relation to another, she quickly adapted herself to her surroundings. Her mother taught her French; a tutor, Latin; Quin, the actor, taught her to recite; Hogarth painted her portrait; and the grooms of her grandmother, whom she visited occasionally, made her an accomplished horsewoman. In those days education for a woman was highly irregular, but judging from the results in the case of Mrs. Thrale and her friends, who shall say that it was ineffective? We have no Elizabeth Carters nowadays, good at translating Epictetus, and — we have it on high authority — better at making a pudding.

Study soon became little Hester's delight. At twelve years she wrote for the newspapers; also, she used to rise at four in the morning to study, which her mother would not have allowed had she known of it. I have a letter written many years afterwards in which she says: "My mother always told me I ruined my Figure and stopt my Growth by sitting too long at a Writing Desk, though ignorant how much Time I spent at it. Dear Madam, was my saucy Answer, —

"Tho' I could reach from Pole to Pole
And grasp the Ocean with my Span,
I would be measur'd by my Soul.
The Mind's the Standard of the Man."

She is quoting Dr. Watts from memory evidently, and improving, perhaps, upon the original.

But little girls grow up and husbands must be

found for them. Henry Thrale, the son of a rich Southwark brewer, was brought forward by her uncle; while
her father, protesting that he would not have his only
child exchanged for a barrel of "bitter," fell into a rage
and died of an apoplexy. Her *dot* was provided by the
uncle; her mother did the courting, with little opposition on the part of the lady and no enthusiasm on the
part of the suitor. So, without love on either side, she

*I ruined my Figure and stopt my Growth by sitting so long at
a Writing Desk, though ignorant how much Time I spent at it.
Dear Madam' was my saucy Answer*

*Tho' I could reach from Pole to Pole
And grasp the Ocean with my Span,
I would be measur'd by my Soul.
The Mind's the Standard of the Man.*

being twenty-two and her husband thirty-five, she
became Mrs. Thrale. "My uncle," she records in her
journal, "went with us to the church, gave me away,
dined with us at Streatham after the ceremony, and
then left me to conciliate as best I could a husband
who had never thrown away five minutes of his time
upon me unwitnessed by company till after the wedding day was done."

More happiness came from this marriage than might
have been expected. Henry Thrale, besides his suburban residence, Streatham, had two other estab-
lishments, one adjoining the brewery in Southwark,
where he lived in winter, and another, an unpreten-
tious villa at the seaside. He also maintained a stable

of horses and a pack of hounds at Croydon; but, although a good horsewoman, Mrs. Thrale was not permitted to join her husband in his equestrian diversions; indeed, her place in her husband's establishment was not unlike that of a woman in a seraglio. She was allowed few pleasures, and but one duty was impressed upon her, namely, that of supplying an heir to the estate; to this duty she devoted herself unremittingly.

In due time a child was born, a daughter; and while this was of course recognized as a mistake, it was believed to be one which could be corrected.

Meanwhile Thrale was surprised to find that his wife could think and talk — that she had a mind of her own. The discovery dawned slowly upon him, as did the idea that the pleasure of living in the country may be enhanced by hospitality. Finally the doors of Streatham Park were thrown open. For a time her husband's bachelor friends and companions were the only company. Included among these was one Arthur Murphy, who had been *un maître de plaisir* to Henry Thrale in the gay days before his marriage, when they had frequented the green rooms and Ranelagh together. It was Murphy who suggested that "Dictionary Johnson" might be secured to enliven a dinner-party, and then followed some discussion as to the excuse which should be given Johnson for inviting him to the table of the rich brewer. It was finally suggested that he be invited to meet a minor celebrity, James Woodhouse, the shoemaker poet.

Johnson rose to the bait, — Johnson rose easily to any bait which would provide him a good dinner and lift him out of himself, — and the dinner passed off successfully. Mrs. Thrale records that they all liked each other so well that a dinner was arranged for the following week, without the shoemaker, who, having served his purpose, disappears from the record.

And now, and for twenty years thereafter, we find Johnson enjoying the hospitality of the Thrales, which opened for him a new world. When he was taken ill, not long after the introduction, Mrs. Thrale called on him in his stuffy lodgings in a court off Fleet Street, and suggested that the air of Streatham would be good for him. Would he come to them? He would. He was not the man to deny himself the care of a young, rich, and charming woman, who would feed him well, understand him, and add to the joys of conversation. From that time on, whether at their residence in Deadman's Place in Southwark, or at Streatham, or at Brighton, even on their journeys, the Thrales and Johnson were constantly together; and when he went on a journey alone, as was sometimes the case, he wrote long letters to his mistress or his master, as he affectionately called his friends.

Who gained most by this intercourse? It would be hard to say. It is a fit subject for a debate, a copy of Boswell's "Life of Johnson" to go to the successful contestant. Johnson summed up his obligations to the lady in the famous letter written just before her second marriage, probably the last he ever wrote her.

"I wish that God may grant you every blessing, that you may be happy in this world . . . and eternally happy in a better state; and whatever I can contribute to your happiness I am ready to repay for that kindness which soothed twenty years of a life radically wretched."

On the other hand, the Thrales secured what, perhaps unconsciously, they most desired, social position and distinction. At Streatham they entertained the best, if not perhaps the very highest, society of the time. Think for a moment of the intimates of this house, whose portraits, painted by Reynolds, hung in the library. There were my Lords Sandys and Westcote, college friends of Thrale; there were Johnson and Goldsmith; Garrick and Burke; Burney, and Reynolds himself, and a number of others, all from the brush of the great master; and could we hear the voices which from time to time might have been heard in the famous room, we should recognize Boswell and Piozzi, Baretti, and a host of others; and would it be necessary for the servant to announce the entrance of the great Mrs. Siddons, or Mrs. Garrick, or Fanny Burney, or Hannah More, or Mrs. Montagu, or any of the other ladies who later formed that famous coterie which came to be known as the Blue-Stockings?

But Johnson was the Thrales' first lion and remained their greatest. He first gave Streatham parties distinction. The master of the house enjoyed having the wits about him, but was not one himself. Johnson said of him that "his mind struck the hours very regularly but did not mark the minutes." It was his wife who, by her sprightliness and her wit and readiness, kept the ball rolling, showing infinite tact and skill in drawing out one and, when necessary, repressing another; asking — when the Doctor was not speaking — for a flash of silence from the company that a newcomer might be heard.

But I am anticipating. All this was not yet. A salon such as she created at Streatham Park is not the work of a month or of a year.

If Mrs. Thrale had ever entertained any illusions as to her husband's regard for her, they must have received a shock when she discovered, as she soon did, that Mr. Thrale had previously offered his hand to several ladies, coupling with his proposal the fact that, in the event of its being accepted, he would expect to live for a portion of each year in his house adjoining the brewery. The famous brewery is now Barclay & Perkins's, and still stands on its original site, where the Globe Theatre once stood, not far from the Surrey end of Southwark Bridge. A more unattractive place of residence it would be hard to imagine, but for some reason Mr. Thrale loved it.

On the other hand, Streatham was delightful. It was a fine estate, something over an hour's drive from Fleet Street in the direction of Croydon. The house, a mansion of white stucco, stood in a park of more than a hundred acres, beautifully wooded. Drives and gravel-walks gave easy access to all parts of the

grounds. There was a lake with a drawbridge, and
conservatories, and glass houses stocked with fine
fruits. Grapes, peaches, and pineapples were grown
in abundance, and Dr. Johnson, whose appetite was
robust, was able for the first time in his life to indulge himself in these things to his heart's content.
In these delightful surroundings the Thrales spent the
greater part of each year, and here assembled about
them a coterie almost, if not quite, as distinguished
as that which made Holland House famous half a
century later.

A few years ago Barrie wrote a delightful play,
"What Every Woman Knows"; and I hasten to say,
for the benefit of those who have not seen this play,
that what every woman knows is how to manage a
husband. In this respect Mrs. Thrale had no superior.
Making due allowance, the play suggests the relationship of the Thrales. A cold, self-contained, and
commonplace man is married to a sprightly and engaging wife. With her to aid him, he is able so to carry
himself that people take him for a man of great ability; without her, he is utterly lost. To give point to
the play, the husband is obliged to make this painful
discovery. Mrs. Thrale, mercifully, never permitted
her husband to discover how commonplace he was.
Could he have looked in her diary he might have
read this description of himself, and, had he read it,
he would probably have made no remark. He spoke
little.

"Mr. Thrale's sobriety, and the decency of his

conversation, being wholly free from all oaths, rib-
aldry and profaneness, make him exceedingly comfortable to live with; while the easiness of his temper and
slowness to take offence add greatly to his value as a
domestic man. Yet I think his servants do not love
him, and I am not sure that his children have much affection for him. With regard to his wife, though little
tender of her person, he is very partial to her understanding; but he is obliging to nobody, and confers
a favor less pleasingly than many a man refuses one."

Elsewhere she refers to him as the handsomest man
in London, by whom she has had thirteen children,
two sons and eleven daughters. Both sons and all
but three of the daughters died either in infancy or
in early childhood. Constantly in that condition in
which ladies wish to be who love their lords, Mrs.
Thrale, by her advice and efforts, once, at least, saved
her husband from bankruptcy, and frequently from
making a fool of himself. She grew to take an intelligent interest in his business affairs, urged him to
enter Parliament, successfully electioneered for him,
and in return was treated with just that degree of
affection that a man might show to an incubator
which, although somewhat erratic in its operations,
might at any time present him with a son.

Such was the household of which Dr. Johnson became a member, and which, to all intents and purposes, became his home. Retaining his lodgings in a
court off Fleet Street, he established in them what

Mrs. Thrale called his menagerie of old women: dependents too poor and wretched to find asylum elsewhere. To them he was at all times considerate, if not courteous. It was his custom to dine with them two or three times each week, thus insuring them an ample dinner; but the library at Streatham was especially devoted to his service. When he could be induced to work on his "Lives of the Poets," it became his study; but for the most part it was his arena, where, in playful converse or in violent discussion, he held his own against all comers.

In due time, under the benign influence of the Thrales, he overcame his repugnance to clean linen. Mr. Thrale suggested silver buckles for his shoes, and he bought them. As he entered the drawing-room, a servant might have been seen clapping on his head a wig which had not been badly singed by a midnight candle as he tore the heart out of a book. The great bear became bearable. One of his most intimate friends, Baretti, a highly cultivated man, was secured as a tutor for the Thrale children, of whom the eldest, nicknamed "Queenie," was Johnson's favorite.

Henry Thrale's table was one of the best in London. By degrees it became known that at Streatham one might always be sure of an excellent dinner and the best conversation in England. Dr. Johnson voiced, not only his own, but the general opinion, that to smile with the wise and to feed with the rich was very close upon human felicity; and he would have admitted, had his attention been called to it, that there was at least one house in London in which people could enjoy themselves as much as at a capital inn.

And people did. For the best description of life at Streatham we must turn to the pages of Fanny Burney (Madame d'Arblay). Her diary is a work of art, but that part of it which pleases most is where the art is so concealed that one feels that the daily entries are intended for no other eye than the writer's. It is its confidential character which is its greatest charm. As the years pass, it loses this quality, and to the extent that it does so it becomes less interesting to us. "Evelina" has just been published

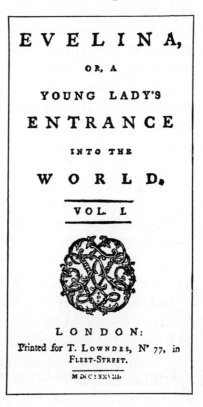

E V E L I N A,

OR, A

YOUNG LADY'S

E N T R A N C E

INTO THE

W O R L D,

VOL. I.

L O N D O N:

Printed for T. LOWNDES, N° 77, in FLEET-STREET.

M DCCLXXVIII.

and Fanny has become a welcome guest at the Thrales' when the record opens. "I have now to write an account of the most consequential day I have spent since my birth; namely, my Streatham visit," is an early entry. Johnson is there and "is very proud to sit by Miss Burney at dinner." Mrs.

Thrale, described as a very pretty woman, gay and agreeable, without a trace of pedantry, repeats some lines in French, and Dr. Johnson quotes Latin which Mrs. Thrale turns into excellent English.

Then the talk is of Garrick, who, some one says, appears to be getting old, on which Johnson remarks that it must be remembered that his face has had more wear and tear than any other man's. Then Mrs. Montagu is mentioned, and the merits of her book on Shakespeare are discussed, and Reynolds and his art, and finally the talk drifts back again to "Evelina," and Dr. Johnson, stimulated by the gayety of an excellent dinner in such surroundings, cries, "Harry Fielding never drew so good a character. . . . There is no character better drawn anywhere — in any book, by any author"; and Fanny pinches herself in delight, under the table, as she had a right to do, for was not the great Cham of literature praising her?

And so with talks and walks and drives and dinners and tea-drinkings unceasing, with news, gossip, and scandal at retail, wholesale, and for exportation, it was contrived that life at Streatham was as delightful as life can be made to be. Occasionally there was work to be done. Dr. Johnson was called on for an introduction to something, or the proof-sheets of "The Lives of the Poets" arrived, and it became Mrs. Thrale's duty to keep the Doctor up to his work — no easy task when a pretty woman was around, and there were always several at Streatham. Breakfast was always served in the library, and tea was pouring

MRS. THRALE'S BREAKFAST-TABLE

incessantly. Thanks to Boswell and to "Little Burney," we know this life better than we know any other
whatever; and what life elsewhere is so intimate and
personal, so well worth knowing?

One morning Mrs. Thrale, entering the library and
finding Johnson there, complained that it was her
birthday, and that no one had sent her any verses.
She admitted to being thirty-five, yet Swift, she said,
fed Stella with them till she was forty-six. Thereupon
Johnson without hesitation began to compose aloud,
and Mrs. Thrale to write at his dictation, —

> "Oft in danger, yet alive,
> We are come to thirty-five;
> Long may better years arrive,
> Better years than thirty-five.
> Could philosophers contrive
> Life to stop at thirty-five,
> Time his hours should never drive
> O'er the bounds of thirty-five.
> High to soar, and deep to dive,
> Nature gives at thirty-five.
> Ladies, stock and tend your hive,
> Trifle not at thirty-five;
> For howe'er we boast and strive,
> Life declines from thirty-five:
> He that ever hopes to thrive
> Must begin by thirty-five;
> And all who wisely wish to wive
> Must look on Thrale at thirty-five," —

adding, as he concluded, "And now, my dear, you
see what it is to come for poetry to a dictionary-
maker. You may observe that the rhymes run in
alphabetical order exactly."

But life is not all cakes and ale. Mr. Thrale's ample

income was constantly in jeopardy from his business speculations. He was led by a charlatan to spend a fortune in the endeavor to brew without hops; this failing, he sought to recoup himself by over-brewing, despite the protests of his wife, seconded by Dr. Johnson, who was becoming an excellent man of affairs. Listen to the man whose boast was that he was bred in idleness and the pride of literature. "The brewhouse must be the scene of action. . . . The first consequence of our late trouble ought to be an endeavor to brew at a cheaper rate, an endeavor not violent and transient, but steady and continual, prosecuted with total contempt of censure or wonder, and animated by resolution not to stop while more can be done. Unless this can be done, nothing can help us; and if this is done we shall not want help. Surely there is something to be saved; there is to be saved whatever is the difference between vigilance and neglect, between parsimony and profusion."

It is proper to observe that it is Dr. Johnson, and not Andrew Carnegie, who is speaking, and in Mrs. Thrale's copy of the Dictionary, which I happen to own, his gift to her, there is pasted in the book a letter in Dr. Johnson's autograph written about this time, one paragraph of which reads, "I think it very probably in your power to lay up eight thousand pounds a year for every year to come, increasing all the time, what needs not be increased, the splendour of all external appearance; and surely such a state is not to be put in yearly hazard for the pleasure of keeping the house full, or the ambition of out-brewing Whitbread. Stop now and you are safe — stop a few years and you may go safely on thereafter, if to go on shall seem worth the while."

Meanwhile, Mr. Thrale was quietly digging his grave with his teeth. Warned by his physician and his friends that he must exercise more and eat less, he snapped his fingers at them, I was going to say; but he did nothing so violent. He simply disregarded their advice and gave orders that the best and earliest of everything should be placed upon his table in profusion. His death was the result, and at forty Mrs. Thrale found herself a widow, wealthy, and with her daughters amply provided for. She, with Dr. Johnson and several others, was an executor of the estate, and promptly began to grapple with the problems of managing a great business. Not long after Thrale's death we find this entry in her journal: "I have now appointed three days a week to attend at the counting-house. If an angel from Heaven had told me twenty years ago that the man I knew by the name of Dictionary Johnson should one day become partner with me in a great trade, and that we should jointly or separately sign notes, drafts, etc., for three or four thousand pounds, of a morning, how unlikely it would have seemed ever to happen! Unlikely is not the word, it would have seemed incredible, neither of us then being worth a groat, and both as immeasurably removed from commerce as birth, literature, and inclination could get us."

The opinion was general that Mrs. Thrale had been a mere sleeping partner, and her friends were amazed at the insight the sparkling little lady showed in the management of a great business. "Such," says Mrs. Montagu, "is the dignity of Mrs. Thrale's virtue, and such her superiority in all situations of life, that nothing now is wanting but an earthquake to show how she will behave on that occasion."

But this state of things was not long to continue. A knot of rich Quakers came along, and purchased the enterprise for a hundred and thirty-five thousand pounds. Dr. Johnson was not quite clear that the property ought to be sold; but when the sale was finally decided upon, he did his share toward securing a good price. Capitalization of earning power has never been more succinctly described than when, in going over the great establishment with the intending purchasers, he made his famous remark, "We are not here to sell a parcel of boilers and vats, but the potentiality of growing rich beyond the dreams of avarice."

For Mrs. Thrale and her daughters the affair was a matter of great moment; excitement ran high. Fanny Burney was staying at Streatham while the business was pending, and it was arranged that on the day the transaction was to be consummated, if all went well, Mrs. Thrale would, on her return from town, wave a white pocket-handkerchief out of the coach window. Dinner was at four; no Mrs. Thrale. Five came, and no Mrs. Thrale. At last the coach appeared and out of the window fluttered a handkerchief.

THE BEST-KNOWN PORTRAIT OF DR. JOHNSON, BY SIR JOSHUA REYNOLDS. ORIGINALLY IN THE LIBRARY AT STREATHAM. SOLD IN 1816 FOR £378. PASSED EVENTUALLY INTO THE NATIONAL GALLERY.

Engraved by Doughty

Mrs. Thrale's own notes are amusing. She was glad to bid adieu to the brewhouse and to the Borough — the business had been a great burden. Her daughters were provided for, and she did not much care for money for herself. By the bargain she had purchased peace, and, as she said, "restoration to her original rank in life"; recording in her journal, "Now that it is all over I'll go to church and give God thanks and forget the frauds, follies and inconveniences of commercial life; as for Dr. Johnson, his honest heart was cured of its incipient passion for trade by letting him into *some* and *only some* of its mysteries."

A final word on the subject of the Thrale brewhouse, which still exists. A year or two ago I spent a morning looking for Deadman's Place, which has disappeared, but the great enterprise dominates the whole district, which is redolent with the odor of malt and hops. Johnson's connection with the business is immortalized by his portrait — the famous one so generally known — being used as its trademark. The original picture is in the National Gallery, but an excellent copy hangs in the directors' room of the brewery. The furnishings of this room are of the simplest. I doubt if they would fetch at auction a five-pound note, were it not for the fact that Johnson's chair and desk are among them. In this room a business running annually into millions is transacted. The English love to leave old things as they are. With them history is always in the making.

These Books written by
Doctor Samuel Johnson
were presented to Mr.
Gabbrielle Piozzi by
Hester = Lynch Thrale

Streatham
Sunday 10: June
1781.

And Twenty Eight Years after that Time
presented again to his Nephew
John Piozzi Salusbury by

Brynbella
1st August 1809.   Hester Lynch Piozzi.

Not many Sundays after Mrs. Thrale's thanksgiving she had a visitor at Streatham — a visitor who, when he left, carried with him as a token of her regard two little calf-bound volumes, in one of which was the inscription, "These books written by Dr. Samuel Johnson were presented to Mr. Gabbrielle Piozzi by Hester-Lynch Thrale. Streatham, Sunday 10 June, 1781"; with a further note in an equally clear and flowing hand: "And Twenty Eight Years after that Time presented again to his Nephew John Piozzi Salusbury by Hester Lynch Piozzi. Brynbella 1st August, 1809."

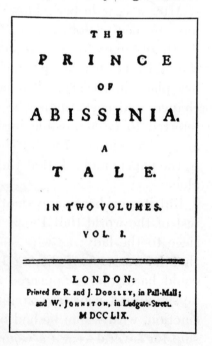

THE

P R I N C E

OF

A B I S S I N I A.

A

T A L E.

IN TWO VOLUMES.

VOL. I.

LONDON:

Printed for R. and J. DODSLEY, in Pall-Mall; and W. JOHNSTON, in Ledgate-Street.

MDCCLIX.

I am able to be exact in this small matter, for the volumes in question were given me not long ago by a friend who understands my passion for such things. The book was the first edition of the "Prince of Abissinia" (it was not known as "Rasselas" until after Dr. Johnson's death), and Mrs. Thrale at the time did not know Piozzi sufficiently well to spell his name correctly; but she was soon to learn, and to learn, too, that she was in love with him and he with her.

She had first met Piozzi about a year before, at a musicale at the house of Dr. Burney, Fanny's father. On this occasion she had taken advantage of his back being turned to mimic him as he sat at the piano. For this she was reprimanded by Dr. Burney, and she must have felt that she deserved the correction, for she took it in good part and behaved with great decorum during the rest of the evening.

After a year in her widow's weeds, — which must have tormented Johnson, for he hated the thought of death and liked to see ladies dressed in gay colors, — she laid aside her severe black and began to resume her place in society. The newspapers marked the change, and every man who entered her house was referred to as a possible husband for the rich and attractive widow. Finally she was obliged to write to the papers and ask that they would let the subject alone.

But it soon became evident to Johnson and to the rest of the world that Piozzi was successfully laying siege to the lady; as why should he not? The fact that he was a Catholic, an Italian, and a musician could hardly have appeared to him as reasons why he should not court a woman of rare charm and distinction, with whom he had been on terms of friendship for several years; a woman who was of suitable age, the mistress of a fine estate and three thousand pounds a year, and whose children were no longer children but young ladies of independent fortune.

That she should marry some one seemed certain. Why not Piozzi? Her daughters protested that their mother was disgracing herself and them, and the world held up its hands in horror at the thought; the co-executors of the estate became actually insulting, and Fanny Burney was so shocked at the idea that she finally gave up visiting Streatham altogether. Society ranged itself for and against the lady — few for, many against.

There were other troubles, too: a lawsuit involving a large sum was decided against her, and Johnson, ill, querulous, and exacting, behaved as an irritable old man would who felt his influence in the family waning. I am a Johnsonian, — Tinker has called me so and Tinker may be depended upon to know a Johnsonian when he sees one, — but I am bound to admit that Johnson had behaved badly and was to behave worse. Johnson was very human and the lady was very human, too. They had come to a parting of the ways.

It was inevitable that the life at Streatham must be terminated. Its glory had departed, and the expense of its upkeep was too great for the lady; so a tenant was secured and Mrs. Thrale and Dr. Johnson prepared to leave the house in which so many happy years had been spent. Dr. Johnson was once more to make his lodgings in Bolt Court, and Mrs. Thrale, after a visit to Brighton, was to go to Bath to repose her purse. The engagement, or understanding, or whatever it was, with Piozzi was broken off, and Italy was proposed as a place of residence for him. Broken hearts there were in plenty.

Life for Mrs. Thrale at Bath proved to be impossible. If concealment did not feed on the damask of her cheek, love did, and at last it became evident, even to the young ladies, that their mother was pining away for Piozzi, and they gave their consent that he be recalled.

He came at once. Mrs. Thrale, on his departure, had sent him a poem which reached him at Dover. She now sent him another which was designed to reach him on his return, at Calais.

> Over mountains, rivers, vallies,
> See my love returns to Calais,
> After all their taunts and malice,
> Ent'ring safe the gates of Calais.
> While Delay'd by winds he dallies,
> Fretting to be kept at Calais,
> Muse, prepare some sprightly sallies
> To divert my dear at Calais;
> Say how every rogue who rallies
> Envies him who waits at Calais
> For her that would disdain a Palace
> Compar'd to Piozzi, Love and Calais.

Pretty poor poetry those who know tell me; but if Piozzi liked it, it served its purpose. And now Mrs. Thrale announced her engagement in a circular letter to her co-executors under the Thrale will, sending, in addition, to Johnson a letter in which she says, "The dread of your disapprobation has given me some anxious moments, and I feel as if acting without a parent's consent till you write kindly to me."

Johnson's reply is historic: —

MADAM, — If I interpret your letter right, you are
ignominiously married: if it is yet undone, let us once more
talk together. If you have abandoned your children and
your religion, God forgive your wickedness; if you have
forfeited your fame and your country, may your folly do
no further mischief. If the last act is yet to do, I who have
loved you, esteemed you, reverenced you, and served you,
I who long thought you the first of womankind, entreat
that, before your fate is irrevocable, I may once more see
you. I was, I once was, Madam, most truly yours,

SAM JOHNSON.

July 2, 1784.

It was a smashing letter, and showed that the mind
which had composed the famous letter to Chesterfield and another, equally forceful, to Macpherson
had not lost its vigor. But those letters had brought
no reply. His letter to Mrs. Thrale did, and one at
once dignified and respectful. The little lady was no
novice in letter-writing, and I can imagine that upon
the arrival of her letter the weary, heartsick old man
wept. Remember that his emotions were seldom completely under his control, and that he had nothing of
the bear about him but its skin.

Sir [she wrote]; I have this morning received from you
so rough a letter in reply to one which was both tenderly
and respectfully written, that I am forced to desire the
conclusion of a correspondence which I can bear to continue no longer. The birth of my second husband is not
meaner than that of my first; his sentiments are not
meaner; his profession is not meaner; and his superiority
in what he professes acknowledged by all mankind. Is

it want of fortune, then, that is ignominious? The character of the man I have chosen has no other claim to such an epithet. The religion to which he has been always a zealous adherent will, I hope, teach him to forgive insults he has not deserved; mine will, I hope, enable me to bear them at once with dignity and patience. To hear that I have forfeited my fame is indeed the greatest insult I ever yet received. My fame is as unsullied as snow, or I should think it unworthy of him who must henceforth protect it.

Johnson, she says, wrote once more, but the letter has never come to light; the correspondence, which had continued over a period of twenty years, was at an end. An interesting letter of Thomas Hardy on this subject came into my possession recently. In it he says, "I am in full sympathy with Mrs. Thrale under the painful opposition to her marriage with Piozzi. The single excuse for Johnson's letter to her on that occasion would be that he was her lover himself, and hoped to win her, otherwise it was simply brutal." I do not think that Johnson was her lover, and I am afraid I must agree that Johnson was brutal. In extenuation I urge that he was a very weary, sick old man.

At the time Mrs. Thrale's detractors were many and her defenders few. Two dates were given as to the time of her marriage, which started some wandering lies, much to her disadvantage. The fact is that both dates were correct, for she was married to Piozzi once by a Catholic and several weeks later by a Church of England ceremony. In her journal she writes under date of July 25, 1784, "I am now the wife of my faithful Piozzi . . . he loves me and will be mine forever. . . . The whole Christian Church, Catholic and Protestant, all are witnesses."

For two years they traveled on the continent. No marriage could have been happier. Piozzi, by comparison with his wife, is a rather shadowy person. He is described as being a handsome man, a few months older than she, with gentle, pleasant, unaffected manners, very eminent in his profession; nor was he, as was so frequently stated, a man without a fortune. The difference in their religious views was the cause of no difficulty. Each respected the religion of the other and kept his or her own. "I would preserve my religious opinions inviolate at Milan as my husband did his at London," is an entry in her journal.

She was staying at Milan when tidings of Johnson's death reached her. All of her correspondents hastened to apprize her of the news. I have a long letter to her from one Henry Johnson, — who he was, I am unable to determine, — written one day after the funeral, describing the procession forming in Bolt Court; the taking of mourning coaches in Fleet Street and "proceeding to Westminster Abbey where the corpse was laid close to the remains of David Garrick, Esquire."

That Madam Piozzi, as we must now call her, was deeply affected, we cannot doubt. Only a few days before the news of his death reached her, we find her writing to a friend, urging him not to neglect Dr. Johnson, saying, "You will never see any other mortal so wise or so good. I keep his picture constantly before me." Before long she heard, too, that several of her old friends had engaged to write his life, and Piozzi urged her to be one of the number. The result was the "Anecdotes of the late Samuel Johnson during the last Twenty Years of his Life." It is not a great work, but considering the circumstances under which it was written, her journals being locked up in England while she was writing at Florence, greater faults than were found in it could have been overlooked. It provided Boswell with some good anecdotes for his great book, and it antedated Hawkins's "Life of Johnson" by about a year.

The public appetite was whetted by the earlier publication of Boswell's "Journal of a Tour of the Hebrides," in which he had given a taste of his quality, and the "Anecdotes" appeared at a time when everything which related to Johnson had a great vogue. The book was published by Cadell, and so great was the demand, that the first edition was exhausted on the day of publication; so that, when the King sent for a copy in the evening, on the day of its publication, the publisher had to beg for one from a friend.

Bozzy and Piozzi thus became rival biographers in the opinion of the public, and the public got what pleasure it could out of numerous caricatures and satires with which the bookshops abounded, many of these being amusing and some simply scurrilous, after the fashion of the time.

Meanwhile, the Piozzis had become tired of travel and wished again to enjoy the luxury of a home. "Prevail on Mr. Piozzi to settle in England," had been Dr. Johnson's parting advice. It was not difficult to do so, and on their return, after a short stay in London, they took up residence in Bath.

Here Madam Piozzi, encouraged by the success of the "Anecdotes," devoted herself to the publication of two volumes of "Letters to and from the late Samuel Johnson." Their preparation for the press was somewhat crude: it consisted largely in making omissions here and there, and substituting asterisks for proper names; but the copyright was sold for five hundred pounds, and the letters showed, if indeed it was necessary to show, how intimate had been the relationship between the Doctor and herself.

As time went on, there awakened in Madam Piozzi a longing for the larger life of Streatham, and her husband, always anxious to accomplish her wishes, decided that she should return to the scene of her former triumphs; but Dr. Johnson, the keystone of her social arch, was gone, and there was no one to take his place. Her husband was a cultured gentleman, but he was not to the English manner born.

The attempt was made, however, and on the seventh anniversary of their wedding day Streatham was thrown open. Seventy people sat down to dinner, the house and grounds were illuminated, and the villagers were made welcome. A thousand people

thronged through the estate. One might have supposed that a young lord had come into his own.

It was a brave effort, but it was soon seen to be unavailing. A man's fame may be like a shuttle-cock,
having constantly to be struck to prevent its falling;
but not a woman's. She had lost caste by her marriage. It was not forgotten that her husband was "a
foreigner," that he had been a "fiddler"; while his
wife had been the object of too much ridicule, the
subject of too many lampoons.

But the lady had resources within herself; she was
an inveterate reader and she had tasted the joys of
authorship. She now published a volume of travels
and busied herself with several other works, the very
names of which are forgotten except by the curious
in such matters.

While she was thus engaged a bitter and scandalous
attack was made upon her by Baretti. Now, Baretti
was a liar, and in proof of her good sense and for-
giving disposition, I offer in evidence the entry that
she made in her journal when she heard of his death.
"Baretti is dead. Poor Baretti! . . . he died as he
lived, less like a Christian than a philosopher, leaving no debts (but those of gratitude) undischarged
and expressing neither regret for the past nor fear for
the future. . . . A wit rather than a scholar, strong
in his prejudices, haughty in spirit, cruel in anger.
He is dead! So is my enmity."

On another occasion she contrived to quiet a hostile
critic who had ridiculed her in verse; much damage

may be done by a couplet, as she well knew, and the lines, —

> See Thrale's grey widow with a satchel roam
> And bring in pomp laborious nothings home, —

were not nice, however true they might be. Madam Piozzi determined to take him in hand. She contrived at the house of a friend to get herself placed opposite to him at a supper-table, and after observing his perplexity with amusement for a time, she raised her wine-glass to him and proposed the toast, "Good fellowship for the future." The critic was glad to avail himself of the dainty means of escape from an awkward situation.

However, it was evident that life at Streatham could not be continued on the old scale. Funds were not as plentiful as in the days of the great brewmaster; so after a few years, when her husband suggested their retiring to her native Wales, she was glad to fall in with the idea. A charming site was selected, and a villa built in the Italian style after her husband's design. It was called "Brynbella," meaning beautiful brow; half Welsh and half Italian, like its owners. I fancy their lives were happier here than they had been elsewhere, for they built upon their own foundation. Piozzi had his piano and his violin, and the lady busied herself with her books; while the monotony of existence was pleasantly broken by occasional visits to Bath, where they had many friends.

And during these years, letters and notes, comment and criticism, dropped from her pen like leaves from a tree in autumn. She lived over again in memory her life in London, reading industriously, and busy in the pleasant and largely profitless way which tends to make days pass into months and months into years and leave no trace of their passing. She must always have had a pen in her hand: it goes without saying that she had kept a diary; in those days everyone did, and most had less than she to record. It was Dr. Johnson who suggested that she get a little book and write in it all the anecdotes she might hear, observations she might make, or verse that might otherwise be lost. These instructions were followed literally, but no little book sufficed. She filled many large quarto volumes, six of which, entitled "Thraliana," passed through the London auction rooms in 1908, bringing £2050. One volume, which perhaps does not belong to the series, but which in every way accords with Dr. Johnson's suggestion, formed part of the late A. M. Broadley's collection until, at his death, it passed with several other items, into that of the writer.

Mr. Broadley took an ardent interest in everything that related to Mrs. Thrale, and published, a few years ago, her "Journal of the Welsh Tour," undertaken in the summer of 1774. Dr. Johnson also kept a diary on this journey, but his is bald and fragmentary, while that of the lady is an intimate and consecutive narrative. The original manuscript volume, in its original dark, limp leather binding is before me.

so much as the thoughts of going to Town thus to settle for the Winter before I have had any Enjoyment of Streatham at all & so all my hopes of Pleasure blow away. I thought to have lived at Streatham in Quiet & comfort have kissed my Children & cuffed them by turns, & had a Place for them always to play in; & here I must be shut up in that odious Dungeon, where nobody will come near me, the Children are to be sick for want of Air, & I am never to see a face but Mr. Johnson's — Oh what a Life that is? and how truly do I abhor it!

at Noon however I saw my Girls, & thought Susan vastly improved. at Evening I saw my Boys & liked them very well too, How much is there always to thank God for! but Dare not enjoy poor Streatham lest I should be forced to quit it.

FACSIMILE, MUCH REDUCED IN SIZE, OF THE LAST PAGE OF MRS. THRALE'S "JOURNAL OF A TOUR IN WALES," UNDERTAKEN IN THE COMPANY OF DR. JOHNSON IN THE SUMMER OF 1774

It comprises ninety-seven pages in Mrs. Thrale's beautiful hand, beginning, "On Tuesday, 5th July, 1774, I began my journey through Wales. We set out from Streatham in our coach and four post horses, accompanied by Dr. Johnson and our eldest daughter. Baretti went with us as far as London, where we left him and hiring fresh horses they carried us to the Mitre at Barnet"; and so on throughout the whole tour, until she made this, her final entry: —

September 30th. When I rose Mr. Thrale informed me that the Parliament was suddenly dissolved and that all the world was bustle; that we were to go to Southwark, not to Streatham, and canvass away. I heard the first part of this report with pleasure, the latter with pain; nothing but a real misfortune could, I think, affect me so much as the thoughts of going to Town thus to settle for the Winter before I have had any enjoyment of Streatham at all; and so all my hopes of pleasure blow away. I thought to have lived in Streatham in quiet and comfort, have kissed my children and cuffed them by turns, and had a place always for them to play in; and here I must be shut up in that odious dungeon, where nobody will come near me, the children are to be sick for want of air, and I am never to see a face but Mr. Johnson's. Oh, what a life that is! and how truly do I abhor it! At noon however I saw my Girls and thought Susan vastly improved. At evening I saw my Boys and liked them very well too. How much is there always to thank God for! But I dare not enjoy poor Streatham lest I should be forced to quit it.

I value this little volume highly, as who, interested in the lady, would not? It is an unaffected record of a journey, of interesting people who met interesting people wherever they went, and its publication by Broadley was a pious act. But that the Broadley volume, published a few years ago, gets its chief value from the sympathetic introduction by Thomas Seccombe, must, I think, be admitted.

It is no longer the fashion to "blush as well as weep for Mrs. Thrale." This silly phrase is Macaulay's. Rather, as Sir Walter Raleigh remarked to me in going over some of her papers in my library, "What a dear, delightful person she was! I have always wanted to meet her." In the future, what may be written of Mrs. Thrale will be written in better taste. At this time of day why should she be attacked because she married a man who did not speak English as his mother tongue, and who was a musician rather than a brewer? One may be an enthusiastic admirer of Dr. Johnson — I confess I am — and yet keep a warm place in one's heart for the kindly and charming little woman. Admit that she was not the scholar she thought she was, that she was "inaccurate in narration": what matters it? She was a woman of character, too. She was not overpowered by Dr. Johnson, as was Fanny Burney, to such a degree that at last she came to write like him, only more so. Mrs. Thrale by her own crisp, vigorous English, influenced the Doctor finally to write as he talked, naturally, without that undue elaboration which was characteristic of his earlier style.

If Johnson mellowed under the benign influence of the lady, she was the gainer in knowledge, especially in such knowledge as comes from books. It was Mrs. Thrale rather than her husband who formed the Streatham library. Her taste was robust, she baulked at no foreign language, but set about to study it. I have never seen a book from her library — and I have seen many — which was not filled with notes written in her clear and beautiful hand. These volumes, like the books which Lamb lent Coleridge, and which he returned with annotations tripling their value, are occasionally offered for sale in those old book-shops where our resolutions not to be tempted are writ in so much water; or they turn up at auction sales and astonish the uninitiated by the prices they bring.

Several of these volumes are in the collection of the writer: her Dictionary, the gift of Dr. Johnson, for instance, and a "Life of Psalmanazar," another gift from the same source; but the book which, above all others, every Johnsonian would wish to own is the property of Miss Amy Lowell of Boston, a poet of rare distinction, a critic, and America's most distinguished woman collector. Who does not envy her the possession of the first edition of Boswell's "Life of Johnson," filled with the marginalia of the one person in the world whose knowledge of the old man rivaled that of the great biographer himself? And to hear Miss Lowell quote these notes in a manner suggestive of the charm of Madam Piozzi herself, is a delight never to be forgotten.

About the time of the Piozzis' removal to Wales,

MISS AMY LOWELL, OF BOSTON, POET, CRITIC, AND AMERICA'S MOST
DISTINGUISHED WOMAN COLLECTOR

they decided to adopt a nephew, the son of Piozzi's brother, who had met with financial reverses in Italy. The boy had been christened John Salusbury in honor of Mrs. Piozzi, and she became greatly attached to the lad and decided to leave him her entire fortune. He was brought up as an English boy, and his education was a matter which gave her serious concern.

Meanwhile, the years that had touched the lady so lightly had left their impress upon her husband, who does not seem to have been strong. He was a great sufferer from gout, and finally died, and was buried in the parish church of Tremeirchion, which years before he had caused to be repaired, and had built there a burial vault in which his remains were placed. They had lived in perfect harmony for twenty-five years, thus effectually overturning the prophecies of their friends. She continued to reside at Brynbella until the marriage of her adopted son, when she generously gave him the estate and removed to Bath, that lovely little city where so many celebrities have gone to pass the closing years of eventful lives.

As a "Bath cat" she continued her interest in men, women, and books until the end. Having outlived all her old friends, she proceeded to make new; and when nearly eighty astonished everyone by showing great partiality for a young and handsome actor, — and, if reports be true, a very bad actor, — named Conway. There was much smoke and doubtless some fire in the affair: letters purporting to be hers to him were published after her death. They may not be genuine, and if they are they show simply, as Leslie Stephen says, that at a very advanced age she became silly.

On her eightieth birthday she gave a ball to six or seven hundred people in the Assembly Rooms at Bath, and led the dancing herself with her adopted son (who by this time was Sir John Salusbury Piozzi), very much to her satisfaction.

A year later she met with an accident, from the effects of which she died. She was buried in Tremeirchion Church beside her husband. A few years ago, on the two hundredth anniversary of the birth of Johnson, a memorial tablet was erected in the quaint old church, reading, —

Near this place are interred the remains of
HESTER LYNCH PIOZZI
Dr. Johnson's Mrs. Thrale
Born 1741, died 1821

Mrs. Piozzi's life is her most enduring work. Trifles were her serious business, and she was never idle. Always a great letter-writer, she set in motion a correspondence which would have taxed the capacity of a secretary with a typewriter. To the last she was a great reader, and observing a remark in Boswell on the irksomeness of books to people of advanced age, she wrote on the margin, "Not to me, at eighty." Her wonderful memory remained unimpaired until

the last. She knew English literature well. She spoke
French and Italian fluently. Latin she transcribed
with ease and grace; of Greek she had a smattering,
and she is said to have had a working knowledge of
Hebrew; but I suspect that her Hebrew would have
set a scholar's hair on end. With all these accom-
plishments, she was not a pedant, or, properly speaking, a Blue-Stocking, or if she was, it was of a very
light shade of blue. She told a capital story, omitted
everything irrelevant and came to the point at once;
in brief, she was a man's woman.

And to end the argument where it began, — for
arguments always end where they begin, — I came
across a remark the other day which sums up my
contention. It was to the effect that, in whatever
company Mrs. Piozzi found herself, others found her
the most charming person in the room.

VIII

A RIDICULOUS PHILOSOPHER

I AM not sure that I know what philosophy is; a philosopher is one who practices it, and we have it on high authority that "there was never yet philosopher that could endure the toothache patiently."

There is an old man in Wilkie Collins's novel, "The Moonstone," the best novel of its kind in the language, who, when in doubt, reads "Robinson Crusoe." In like manner I, when in doubt, turn to Boswell's "Life of Johnson," and there I read that the fine, crusty old doctor was hailed in the Strand one day by a man who half a century before had been at Pembroke College with him. It is not surprising that Johnson did not at first remember his former friend, and he was none too well pleased to be reminded that they were both "old men now." "We are, sir," said Dr. Johnson, "but do not let us discourage one another"; and they began to talk over old times and compare notes as to where they stood in the world.

Edwards, his friend, had practiced law and had made money, but had spent or given away much of it. "I shall not die rich," said he. "But, sir," said Johnson, "it is better to live rich than to die rich." And now comes Edwards's immortal remark, "You are a philosopher, Dr. Johnson. I have tried, too, in my

William Godwin

THE RIDICULOUS PHILOSOPHER

From a drawing by Maclise

time to be a philosopher; but, I don't know how, cheerfulness was always breaking in."

With the word "cheerfulness," Edwards had demolished the scheme of life of most of our professed philosophers, who have no place in their systems for the attribute that goes furthest toward making life worth while to the average man.

Cheerfulness is a much rarer quality than is generally supposed, especially among the rich. It was not common even before we learned that, in spite of Browning, though God may be in his heaven, nevertheless, all is wrong with the world.

If "most men lead lives of quiet desperation," as Thoreau says they do, it is, I suspect, because they will not allow cheerfulness to break in upon them when it will. A good disposition is worth a fortune. Give cheerfulness a chance and let the professed philosopher go hang.

But it is high time for me to turn my attention, and yours, if I may, to the particular philosopher through whom I wish to stick my pen, and whom, thus impaled, I wish to present for your edification — say, rather, amusement. His name was William Godwin; he was the husband of Mary Wollstonecraft and the father-in-law of Shelley.

Godwin was born in Cambridgeshire in 1756, and came of preaching stock. It is related that, when only a lad, he used to steal away, not to go in swimming or to rob an orchard, but to a meeting-house to preach; this at the age of ten. The boy was father to

the man: to the end of his life he never did anything
else. He first preached orthodoxy, later heterodoxy,
but he was always a preacher. I do not like the tribe.
I am using the word as indicating one who elects to
teach by word rather than by example.

When a boy he had an attack of smallpox. Religious scruples prevented him from submitting to vac-
cination, for he said he had no wish to run counter to
the will of God. In this frame of mind he did not long
remain. He seems to have been a hard student —
what we would call a grind. He read enormously, and
by twenty he considered that he was fully equipped
for his life's work. He was as ready to preach as an
Irishman is to fight, for the love of it; but he was
quarrelsome as well as pious, and, falling out with his
congregation, he dropped the title of Reverend and
betook himself to literature and London.

At this time the French Revolution was raging, and
the mental churning which it occasioned had its effect
upon sounder minds than his. Godwin soon became
intimate with Tom Paine and others of like opinions.
Wherever political heresy and schism was talked, there
Godwin was to be found. He stood for everything
which was "advanced" in thought and conduct; he
joined the school which was to write God with a small
g. All the radical visionaries in London were attracted
to him, and he to them. He thought and dreamed and
talked, and finally grew to feel the need of a larger
audience. The result was "An Enquiry Concerning
Political Justice," a book which created a tremendous

sensation in its day. It seemed the one thing needed to bring political dissent and dissatisfaction to a head.

Much was wrong at the time, much is still wrong, and doubtless reformers of Godwin's type do a certain amount of good. They call attention to abuses, and eventually the world sets about to remedy them. A "movement" is in the air; it centres in some man who voices and directs it. For the moment the man and the movement seem to be one. Ultimately the movement becomes diffused, its character changes; frequently the man originally identified with it is forgotten — so it was with Godwin.

"Political Justice" was published in 1793. In it Godwin fell foul of everything. He assailed all forms of government. The common idea that blood is thicker than water, is wrong: all men are brothers; one should do for a stranger as for a brother. The distribution of property is absurd. A man's needs are to be taken as the standard of what he should receive. He that needs most is to be given most — by whom, Godwin did not say.

Marriage is a law and the worst of all laws: it is an affair of property, and like property must be abolished. The intercourse of the sexes is to be like any other species of friendship. If two men happen to feel a preference for the same woman, let them both enjoy her conversation and be wise enough to consider sexual intercourse "a very trivial object indeed."

I have a copy of "Political Justice," before me, with Tom Paine's signature on the title-page. What a whirlwind all this once created, especially with the young! Its author became one of the most-talked-of men of his time, and Godwin's estimate of himself could not have been higher than that his disciples set upon him. Compared with him, "Paine was nowhere and Burke a flashy sophist." He gloried in the reputation his book gave him, and he profited by it to the extent of a thousand pounds; to him it was a fortune.

Pitt, who was then Prime Minister, when his attention was called to the book, wisely remarked, "It is not worth while to prosecute the author of a three-guinea book, because at such a price very little harm can be done to those who have not three shillings to spare."

The following year Godwin published his one other book that has escaped the rubbish heap of time — "The Adventures of Caleb Williams," a novel. It is the best of what might be called "The Nightmare Series," which would begin with "The Castle of Otranto," include his own daughter's "Frankenstein," and end, for the moment, with Bram Stoker's "Dracula." "Caleb Williams" has genuine merit; that it is horrible and unnatural may be at once admitted, but there is a vitality about it which holds your interest to the last; unrelieved by any flash of sentiment or humor, it is still as entirely readable as it was once immensely popular. Colman, the younger, dramatized it under the name of "The Iron Chest," and several generations of playgoers have shuddered at the character of Falkland, the murderer, who, and not Caleb Williams, is the chief character. His other novels are soup made out of the same stock, as a *chef* would say, with a dash of the supernatural added.

Godwin had now written all that he was ever to write on which the dust of years has not settled, to be disturbed only by some curious student of a forgotten literature; yet he supposed that he was writing for posterity!

Meanwhile he, who had been living with his head in the clouds, became aware of the existence of "females." It was an important, if belated, discovery. He was always an inveterate letter-writer, and his curious letters to a number of women have been preserved. He seems to have had more than a passing fancy for Amelia Alderson, afterward Mrs. Opie, the wife of the artist. He was intimate with Mrs. Robinson, the "Perdita" of the period, in which part she attracted the attention of the Prince of Wales. Mrs. Inchbald and Mrs. Reveley were also friends, with whom he had frequent misunderstandings. His views on the subject of marriage being well known, perhaps these ladies, merely to test the philosopher, sought to overcome his objection to "that worst of institutions." If so, their efforts were unsuccessful.

Godwin, however, seems to have exerted a peculiar fascination over the fair sex, and he finally met one with whom, as he says, "friendship melted into love." Godwin, saying he would ne'er consent, consented. Mary Wollstonecraft, the author of the "Rights of Woman," now calling herself Mrs. Imlay, triumphed.

Her period of romance, followed fast by tragedy, was for a brief time renewed with Godwin. She had had one experience, the result of which was a fatherless infant daughter, Fanny; and some time after she took up with Godwin, she urged upon him the desirability of "marriage lines."

Godwin demurred for a time; but when Mary confided to him that she was about to become a mother, a private wedding in St. Pancras Church took place. Separate residence was attempted, in order to conform to Godwin's theory that too close familiarity might result in mutual weariness; but Godwin was not destined to become bored by his wife. She had intelligence and beauty; indeed, it seems likely that he loved her as devotedly as it was possible for one of his frog-like nature to do. Shortly after the marriage a daughter was born, and christened Mary; and a few days later the remains of Mary Wollstonecraft Godwin were interred in the old graveyard of St. Pancras, close by the church which she had recently left as a bride.

No sketch of Godwin's life would be complete without the well-known story of the expiring wife's exclamation: "I am in heaven"; to which Godwin replied, "No, my dear, you only mean that your physical sensations are somewhat easier."

Thus, by that "divinity that shapes our ends rough," Godwin, who did not approve of marriage and who had no place in his philosophy for the domestic virtues, became within a few months a husband, a widower, a stepfather, and a father. Probably no man was less well equipped than he for his immediate responsibilities. He had been living in one house and his wife in another, to save his face, as it were, and also to avoid interruptions; but this scheme of life was no longer possible. A household must be established; some sort of a family nurse became an immediate necessity. One was secured, who tried to marry Godwin out of hand. To escape her attentions he fled to Bath.

But his objections to marriage as an institution were waning, and when he met Harriet Lee, the daughter of an actor, and herself a writer of some small distinction, they were laid aside altogether. His courtship of Miss Lee took the form of interminable letters. He writes her: "It is not what you are but what you might be that charms me"; and he chides her for not being prepared faithfully to discharge the duties of a wife and mother. Few women have been in this humor won; Miss Lee was not among them.

Godwin finally returned to London. He was now a man approaching middle age, cold, methodical, dogmatic, and quick to take offense. He began to live on borrowed money. The story of his life at this time is largely a story of his squabbles. A more industrious man at picking a quarrel one must go far to find; and that the record might remain, he wrote letters — not short, angry letters, but long, serious, disputatious epistles, such as no one likes to receive, and which seem to demand and usually get an immediate answer.

Ritson writes him: "I wish you would make it convenient to return to me the thirty pounds I loaned you. My circumstances are by no means what they were at the time I advanced it, nor did I, in fact, imagine you would have retained it so long." And again: "Though you have not the ability to repay the money I loaned you, you might have integrity enough to return the books you borrowed. I do not wish to bring against you a railing accusation, but am compelled, nevertheless, to feel that you have not acted the part of an honest man."

Godwin seems to have known his weakness, for he writes of himself: "I am feeble of tact and liable to the grossest mistakes respecting theory, taste, and character." And again: "No domestic connection is fit for me but that of a person who should habitually study my gratification and happiness." This sounds ominous from one who was constantly looking for a "female companion"; and it was to prove so.

It is with a feeling of relief that we turn, for a moment, from the sordid life of Godwin the philosopher to Godwin the dramatist. He was sadly in need of funds, and, following the usual custom of an author in distress, had written a tragedy, for which Charles Lamb had provided the epilogue.

John Philip Kemble, seduced by Godwin's flattery and insistence, had finally been prevailed upon to put it on the stage. Kemble had made up his mind that all the good tragedies that could be written had been written, and had not his objections been overruled, the tragedy, "Antonio," would never have been produced, and one of Lamb's most delightful essays, in consequence, never written.

With the usual preliminaries, and after much correspondence and discussion, the night of the play came. It was produced at the Theatre Royal, Drury Lane — what a ring it has! Lamb was there in a box next to the author, who was cheerful and confident.

It is a pity to mutilate Lamb's account of it, but it is too long to quote except in fragments.

The first act swept by solemn and silent . . . applause would have been impertinent, the interest would warm in the next act. . . . The second act rose a little in interest, the audience became complacently attentive. . . . The third act brought the scene which was to warm the piece progressively to the final flaming forth of the catastrophe, but the interest stood stone still. . . .

It was Christmas time and the atmosphere furnished some pretext for asthmatic affections. Some one began to cough, his neighbors sympathized with him, till it became an epidemic; but when from being artificial in the pit the cough got naturalized on the stage, and Antonio himself seemed more intent upon relieving his own lungs than the distress of the author, then Godwin "first knew fear," and intimated that, had he been aware that Mr. Kemble labored under a cold, the performance might possibly have been postponed.

In vain did the plot thicken. The procession of verbiage stalked on, the audience paid no attention whatever to it, the actors became smaller and smaller, the stage receded, the audience was going to sleep, when suddenly Antonio whips out a dagger and stabs his sister to the

NEVER PERFORMED.

Theatre Royal, Drury Lane,

This present SATURDAY, December 13th, 1800,

Their Majesties Servants will act a New Tragedy called

ANTONIO:

by Godwin   OR, *Damned with Universal Consent*

THE SOLDIER'S RETURN.

The Characters by

Mr. WROUGHTON,

Mr. BARRYMORE,

Mr. KEMBLE,

Mr. C. KEMBLE,

Mr. POWELL,

Mr. HOLLAND.

Mr. MADDOCKS,   Mr. FISHER,

Mr. EVANS,   Mr. WEBB,

Mrs. SIDDONS.

The Prologue to be Spoken by Mr. C. KEMBLE,

And the Epilogue by Miss HEARD.

After the Tragedy will be acted a Farce called

The VIRGIN UNMASK'D.

Goodwill, Mr. PACKER,

Blister, Mr. SUETT,

Couper, Mr. BANNISTER, Jun.

Quaver, Mr. DIGNUM,

Thomas, Mr. FISHER,

Miss Lucy by the YOUNG LADY

who performed the Part of Miss Hoyden in the Trip to Scarborough,

(Being her Second Appearance on this Stage.)

The Doors to be opened at a Quarter past FIVE, and to begin at a Quarter past SIX.

Places for the Boxes to be taken of Mr. FOSBROOK, at the Box-Office, in Little Russell-Street.
Boxes 6s. Second Price 3s.   Pit 3s. 6. Second Price 2s.   Gallery 2s. Second Price 1s.
Upper Gallery 1s. Second Price 6d.   NO MONEY TO BE RETURNED.

Printed by C. Lowndes, next the Stage-Door.   *Vivant Rex & Regina.*

The Tragedy of PIZARRO continues to be received with unabating applause, and
will be acted, for the 8th time this Season, on Monday next.
The NEW PANTOMIME
Will be produced on Monday, the 22nd. Instant.

CHARLES LAMB'S PLAY-BILL OF "ANTONIO," BY GODWIN. "DAMNED WITH
UNIVERSAL CONSENT"

heart. The effect was as if a murder had been committed
in cold blood, with the audience betrayed into being ac-
complices. The whole house rose in clamorous indigna-
tion — they would have torn the unfortunate author to
pieces if they could have got him.

The play was hopelessly and forever damned, and
the epilogue went down in the crash.

Over my writing-table hangs a dark oak frame
containing a souvenir of this performance — the
programme which Charles Lamb used on this fateful
evening. It is badly crumpled, crumpled no doubt by
Elia in his agony. No reference is made to the play
being by Godwin except a note in Charles Lamb's
handwriting which reads, "By Godwin," with the sig-
nificant words, "Damned with universal consent."

Godwin bore his defeat with philosophic calm. He
appealed to friends for financial assistance and to
posterity for applause. But it was really a serious
matter. He was on the verge of ruin, and now did
what many another man has done when financial
difficulties crowded thick and fast — he married
again.

A certain Mrs. Clairmont fell in love with Godwin even before she had spoken to him. She was a
fat, unattractive widow, and apparently did all the
courting. She took lodgings close by Godwin's, and
introduced herself — "Is it possible that I behold the
immortal Godwin?"

This is flattery fed with a knife. When a widow
makes up her mind to marry, one of two things must

be done, and quickly — her victim must run or submit. Godwin was unable to run and a marriage was the result. Like his first wedding, it was for a time kept a profound secret.

An idea of Godwin and his wife at this period is to be had from Lamb's letters. He refers constantly to Godwin as the Professor, and to his wife as the Professor's Rib, who, he says, "has turned out to be a damned disagreeable woman, so much so as to drive Godwin's old cronies" — among whom was Lamb — "from his house."

It was a difficult household. Mrs. Godwin had two children by her first husband: a daughter whose right name was Mary Jane, but who called herself Claire — she lived to become the mistress of Lord Byron and the mother of his daughter Allegra; also a son, who was raised a pet and grew up to be a nuisance. Godwin's immediate contribution to the establishment was the illegitimate daughter of his first wife, who claimed Imlay for her father, and his own daughter Mary, whose mother had died in giving her birth. In due course there was born another son, christened William, after his father.

Something had to be done, and promptly. Godwin began a book on Chaucer, of whose life we know almost as little as of Shakespeare's. In dealing with Chaucer, Godwin introduced a method which subsequent writers have followed. Actual material being scanty, they fill out the picture by supposing what he might have done and seen and thought.

Godwin filled two volumes quarto with musings about the fourteenth century, and called it a "Life of Chaucer."

Mrs. Godwin — who was a "managing woman" — had more confidence in trade than in literature. She opened a bookshop in Hanway Street under the name of Thomas Hodgkins, the manager; subsequently in Skinner Street, under her own name, M. J. Godwin. From this shop there issued children's books, the prettiest and wisest, for "a penny plain and tuppence colored," and more. "The Children's Book-Seller," as he called himself, was presently successful, and parents presented his little volumes to their children, with no suspicion that the lessons of piety and goodness which charmed away selfishness were published, revised, and sometimes written by a philosopher whom they would scarcely venture to name. It was Godwin who suggested to Charles Lamb and his sister that the "Tales from Shakespeare" be written. Godwin's own contributions were produced under the name of Baldwin.

Lamb writes: "Hazlitt has written some things and a grammar for Godwin, but the gray mare is the better horse. I do not allude to Mrs. Godwin, but to the word grammar, which comes near gray mare, if you observe." It would certainly surprise Godwin could he know that, while his own "works" are forgotten, some of the little publications issued by the "Juvenile Library," 41 Skinner Street, Snow Hill, are worth their weight in gold.

The years passed on. Godwin lived more or less in constant terror of his wife, of whom Lamb writes: "Mrs. Godwin grows every day in disfavor with God and man. I will be buried with this inscription over me: 'Here lies Charles Lamb, the woman-hater, I mean that hated one woman. For the rest, God bless 'em, and when He makes any more, make 'em prettier.'"

As he grew older Godwin moderated his views of men somewhat, so that "he ceased to be disrespectful to any one but his Maker"; and he once so far forgot himself as to say "God bless you" to a friend, but quickly added, "to use a vulgar expression." He remained, however, always prepared to sacrifice a friend for a principle. He seemed to feel that truth had taken up its abode in him, and that any question which he had submitted to the final judgment of his own breast had been passed upon finally and forever.

This search for truth has a great fascination for a certain type of mind. It does not appear dangerous: all one has to do is thrust one's feet in slippers and muse; but it has probably caused as much misery as the search for the pole. The pole has now been discovered and can be dismissed, but the search for truth continues. It will always continue, for the reason that its location is always changing. Every generation looks for it in a new place.

One night Lamb, dropping in on Godwin, found him discussing with Coleridge his favorite problem, "Man as he is and man as he ought to be." The

March 10, 1818—

Dear Madam

You perhaps recollect an unfortunate female infant, of which I was the father; that you took into your house, & were kind enough to protect for a week, a very few days after its birth. That child proposes to herself the pleasure of putting these lines into your hands. She is married to the eldest son of Sir Timothy Shelley Baronet, & is travelling with her family.

I think I need not request you to receive her with favour & kindness. It has been very often a subject of deep regret to me, that I have never heard of you, except accidentally, since you left England. I trust to have the pleasure of some more direct information, by means of the interview I contemplate between you & my daughter.

Believe me, Dear Madam,
with the sincerest regard yours
W Godwin

LETTER FROM WILLIAM GODWIN

I bought this letter one hundred years to a day after it had been written, for a sum which would have amazed its writer, and temporarily, at least, have relieved him of his financial difficulties.

discussion seemed interminable. "Hot water and its better adjuncts" had been entirely overlooked. Finally Lamb stammered out, "Give me man as he ought *not* to be, and something to drink." It must have been on one of these evenings that Godwin remarked that he wondered why more people did not write like Shakespeare; to which Lamb replied that he could — if he had the mind to.

The older generation was passing away. Long before he died Godwin was referred to as though he were a forgotten classic; but there was to be a revival of interest in him, due entirely to the poet Shelley. The mere mention of Shelley's name produced an explosion. He had been expelled from Oxford for atheism. Reading revolutionary books, as well as writing them, he had come across "Political Justice" and was anxious to meet the author.

He sought him out, eventually made the acquaintance of his daughter Mary, by this time a beautiful and interesting girl of seventeen years, and in due course eloped with her, deserting his wife Harriet. Where was Godwin's philosophy now? we may well ask. At no time in his long life was Godwin so ridiculous as in his relations with Shelley.

In their flight, Shelley and Mary had taken with them Mrs. Godwin's daughter Claire. The mother made after the runaways post-haste and overtook them in Calais, her arrival creating consternation in the camp of the fugitives; but they all declined to return. In such scorn was Shelley generally held, that the rumor that he had bought both Godwin's daughter and his step-daughter for a sum in hand created no amazement, the pity rather than the possibility of it being most discussed.

Financial affairs, too, in Skinner Street were going badly. From the record of notes given and protested at maturity, one might have supposed that Godwin was in active business in a time of panic.

"Don't ask me whether I won't take none or whether I will, but leave the bottle on the chimley-piece and let me put my lips to it when I am so dispoged." Such was the immortal Mrs. Gamp's attitude toward gin. Godwin's last manner in money matters was much the same: money he would take from any one and in any way when he must, but, like Mrs. Gamp, he was "dispoged" to take it indirectly.

Indignant with Shelley, whose views on marriage were largely of his teaching, Godwin refused to hold any communication with him except such as would advance his (Godwin's) fortunes at Shelley's expense. Their transactions were to be of a strictly business character (business with Shelley!). We find Godwin writing him and returning a check for a thousand pounds because it was drawn to his order. How sure he must have been of it! "I return your cheque because no consideration can induce me to utter a cheque drawn by you and containing my name. To what purpose make a disclosure of this kind to your banker? I hope you will send a duplicate of it by the post which will reach me on Saturday morning.

You may make it payable to Joseph Hume or James Martin or any other name in the whole directory." And then Godwin would forge the name of "Joseph Hume or James Martin or any other name in the whole directory," and guarantee the signature by his own indorsement, and the business transaction would be complete. Pretty high finance this, for a philosopher!

Not until after the death of Harriet, when Shelley's connection with Mary was promptly legalized, would Godwin consent to receive them. He then expressed his great satisfaction, and wrote to his brother in the country that his daughter had married the eldest son of a wealthy baronet.

If this world affords true happiness, it is to be found in a home where love and confidence increase with years, where the necessities of life come without severe strain, where luxuries enter only after their cost has been carefully considered. We are told that wealth is a test of character — few of us have to submit to it. Poverty is the more usual test. It is difficult to be very poor and maintain one's self-respect. Godwin found it impossible.

He, whose chief wish it had been to avoid domestic entanglements and who wanted his gratification and happiness studied habitually, was living in a storm-centre of poverty, misery, and tragedy. Claire was known to have had a baby by Lord Byron, who had deserted her; Harriet Shelley had drowned herself in the Serpentine; Fanny Godwin, his step-daughter,

took poison at Bristol. The philosopher, almost overcome, sought to conceal his troubles with a lie. To
one of his correspondents he refers to Fanny's having been attacked in Wales with an inflammatory
fever "which carried her off."

Meanwhile, the sufferings of others he bore with
splendid fortitude. In a very brief letter to Mary
Shelley, answering hers in which she told him of
the death of her child, he said, "You should recollect
that it is only persons of a very ordinary sort and
of a pusillanimous disposition that sink long under a
calamity of this nature." But he covered folio sheets
in his complainings to her, counting on her sensitive
heart and Shelley's good-nature for sympathy and
relief.

With the death of Shelley, Godwin's affairs became desperate. Taking advantage of some defect in
the title of the owner of the property which he had
leased, he declined for some time to pay any rent,
meanwhile carrying on a costly and vexatious lawsuit. Curiously enough, in the end, justice triumphed.
Godwin was obliged to pay two years' arrears of rent
and the costs of litigation. Of course, he looked upon
this as an extreme hardship, as another indication
of the iniquity of the law. But he was now an old
man; very little happiness had broken in upon him,
and his friends took pity on him. Godwin was most
ingenious in stimulating them to efforts on his behalf. A subscription was started under his direction.
He probably felt that he knew best how to vary his

appeals and make them effective. So much craft one
would not have suspected in the old beggar.

One thing he always was — industrious. He finished a wretched novel and at once began a "History
of the Commonwealth." He finished "The Lives
of the Necromancers," and promptly began a novel;
but with all his writings he has not left one single
phrase with which his name can be associated, or a
single thought worth thinking.

It is almost superfluous to say that he had no sense
of humor. With his head in the clouds and his feet
in his slippers, he mused along.

Hazlitt tells a capital story of him. Godwin was
writing a "Life of Chatham," and applied to his acquaintances to furnish him with anecdotes. Among
others, a Mr. Fawcett told him of a striking passage
in a speech by Lord Chatham on General Warrants,
at the delivery of which he (Mr. Fawcett) had been
present. "Every man's house has been called his
castle. And why is it called his castle? Is it because
it is defended by a wall, because it is surrounded with
a moat? No, it may be nothing more than a straw-
built shed. It may be open to all the elements; the
wind may enter it, the rain may enter — but the king
cannot enter."

Fawcett thought that the point was clear enough;
but when he came to read the printed volume, he
found it thus: "Every man's house is his castle. And
why is it called so? Is it because it is defended by a
wall, because it is surrounded with a moat? No, it

may be nothing more than a straw-built shed. It may be exposed to all the elements; the rain may enter into it, all the winds of heaven may whistle around it, but the king cannot," — and so forth.

Things were going from bad to worse. Most of his friends were dead or estranged from him. He had made a sad mess of his life and he was very old. Finally, an appeal on his behalf was made to the government, the government against which he had written and talked so much. It took pity on him. Lord Grey conferred on him the post of Yeoman Usher of the Exchequer, whatever that may be, with a residence in New Palace Yard. The office was a sinecure, "the duties performed by menials." For this exquisite phrase I am indebted to his biographer, C. Kegan Paul. It seems to suggest that a "menial" is one who does his duty. Almost immediately, however, a reformed Parliament abolished the office, and Godwin seemed again in danger; but men of all creeds were now disposed to look kindly on the old man. He was assured of his position for life, and writing to the last, in 1836 he died, at the age of eighty, and was buried by the side of Mary Wollstonecraft in St. Pancras Churchyard.

If there is to be profit as well as pleasure in the study of biography, what lesson can be learned from such a life?

Many years before he died Godwin had written a little essay on "Sepulchres." It was a proposal for erecting some memorial to the dead on the spot where their remains were interred. Were one asked to suggest a suitable inscription for Godwin's tomb it might be

HOW NOT TO DO IT.

In the ever-delightful "Angler," speaking of the operation of baiting a hook with a live frog, Walton finally completes his general instructions with the specific advice to "use him as though you loved him." In baiting my hook with a dead philosopher I have been unable to accomplish this. I do not love him; few did; he was a cold, hard, self-centred man who did good to none and harm to many. As a husband, father, friend, he was a complete failure. His search for truth was as unavailing as his search for "gratification and happiness." He is all but forgotten. It is his fate to be remembered chiefly as the husband of the first suffragette.

What has become of the

> Wonderful things he was going to do
> All complete in a minute or two?

Where are now his novel philosophies and theories? To ask the question is to answer it.

Constant striving for the unobtainable frequently results in neglect of important matters close at hand — such things as bread and cheese and children are neglected. Some happiness comes from the successful effort to make both ends meet habitually and lap over occasionally. My philosophy of life may be called smug, but it can hardly be called ridiculous.

IX

A GREAT VICTORIAN

FOR a time after the death of any author, the world, if it has greatly admired that author, begins to feel that it has been imposed upon, becomes a little ashamed of its former enthusiasm and ends by neglecting him altogether. This would seem to have been Anthony Trollope's case, to judge from the occasional comment of English critics, who, if they refer to him at all, do so in some such phrase as, "About this time Trollope also enjoyed a popularity which we can no longer understand." From one brief paper purporting to be an estimate of his present status, these nuggets of criticism are extracted: —

Mr. Trollope was not an artist.

Trollope had something of the angry impatience of the middle-class mind with all points of view not his own.

"Tancred" is as far beyond anything that Trollope wrote as "Orley Farm" is superior to a Chancery pleading.

We have only to lay "Alroy" on the same table with "The Prime Minister" to see where Anthony Trollope stands.

It is not likely that Trollope's novels will have any vogue in the immediate future; *every page brings its own flavor of unreality.* [Italics mine.]

And in referring to Plantagenet Palliser, who figures largely in so many of his novels, the author says: —

Some nicknames are engaging; "Planty Pall" is not one of these. The man is really not worth writing about.

"Is He Popenjoy?" is perhaps the most readable of all Mr. Trollope's works. It is shorter than many.

Finally, when it is grudgingly admitted that he did some good work, the answer to the question, "Why is such work neglected?" is, "Because the world in which Trollope lived has passed away." It would seem that absurdity could go no further.

American judgment is in general of a different tenor, although Professor Phelps, of Yale, in his recent volume, "The Advance of the English Novel," dismisses Trollope with a single paragraph, in which is embedded the remark, "No one would dare call Trollope a genius." Short, sharp and decisive work this; but Professor Phelps is clearing the decks for Meredith, to whom he devotes twenty or more pages. I respect the opinion of college professors as much as Charles Lamb respected the equator; nevertheless, I maintain that, if Trollope was not a genius, he was a very great writer; and I am not alone.

Only a few days ago a cultivated man of affairs, referring to an interesting contemporary caricature of Dickens and Thackeray which bore the legend, "Two Great Victorians," remarked, "They were great Victorians, indeed, but I have come to wonder in these later years whether Anthony Trollope will not outlive them both." And while the mere book-collector should be careful how he challenges the opinion of "one who makes his living by reading books and

Anthony Trollope

FROM A PHOTOGRAPH BY MESS^{RS} ELLIOTT & FRY

then writing about them," — the phrase is Professor Phelps's, — nevertheless, when one's opinion is supported, as mine is, by the authority of such a novelist as our own Howells, he may perhaps be forgiven for speaking up.

Mr. Howells not long ago, in a criticism of the novels of Archibald Marshall, refers to him as a "disciple of Anthony Trollope," whom he calls "the greatest of the Victorians." This is high praise — perhaps too high. Criticism is, after all, simply the expression of an opinion; the important question is, whether one has a right to an opinion. It is easy to understand why the author of "Silas Lapham" should accord high place to Trollope.

Trollope can never be popular in the sense that Dickens is popular, nor is it so necessary to have him on the shelves as to have Thackeray; but any one who has not made Trollope's acquaintance has a great treat in store; nor do I know an author who can be read and re-read with greater pleasure. But to fall completely under the lure of his — genius, I was going to say, but I must be careful — he should be read quietly — and thoroughly: that is to say, some thirty or forty volumes out of a possible hundred or more.

It may at once be admitted that there are no magnificent scenes in Trollope as there are in Thackeray; as, for example, where Rawdon Crawley in "Vanity Fair," coming home unexpectedly, finds Becky entertaining the Marquis of Steyne. On the other hand, you will not find in any of his best stories anything so deadly dull as the endless talk about Georgie Osborne, aged variously five, seven, or ten years, in the same volume. How often have I longed to snatch that infant from his nurse and impale him on the railings of St. James's Park!

For the most part, people in Trollope's stories lead lives very like our own, dependent upon how our fortunes may be cast. They have their failures and their successes, and fall in love and fall out again, very much as we do. At last we begin to know their peculiarities better than we know our own, and we think of them, not as characters in a book, but as friends and acquaintances whom we have grown up with. Some we like and some bore us exceedingly — just as in real life. His characters do not lack style, — the Duke of Omnium is a very great person indeed, — but Trollope himself has none. He has little or no brilliancy, and we like him the better for it. The brilliant person may become very fatiguing to live with — after a time.

It is, however, in this country rather than in England that Trollope finds his greatest admirers. To-day the English call him "mid-Victorian." Nothing worse can be said. Even Dickens and Thackeray have to fight against an injunction to this effect, which I cannot believe is to be made permanent. Nothing is more seductive and dangerous than prophecy, but one more forecast will not greatly increase its bulk, and so I venture to say that, Dickens and Thackeray aside, Trollope will outlive all the other novelists of his time.   Dickens has come to stay; Thackeray will join the immortals with two novels under his arm, and perhaps one novel of George Eliot and one by Charles Reade will survive; but Beaconsfield, Bulwer-Lytton, Kingsley, and a host of others once famous, will join the long procession headed for oblivion, led by Ann Radcliffe.

And if it be Trollope's fate to outlast all but the greatest of his contemporaries, it will be due to the simplicity and lack of effort with which he tells his tale.   There is no straining after effect — his characters are real, live men and women, without a trace of caricature or exaggeration. His humor is delicious and his plots sufficient, although he has told us that he never takes any care with them; and aside from his character-drawing, he will be studied for the life-like pictures of the upper- and middle-class English society of his time. Not one only, but all of his novels might be called "The Way We Live Now." Someone has said that he is our greatest realist since Fielding; he has been compared with Jane Austen, lacking her purity of style, but dealing with a much larger world.

"I do not think it probable that my name will remain among those who in the next century will be known as the writers of English prose fiction." So wrote Trollope in the concluding chapter of his autobiography. And he adds: "But if it does, that permanency of success will probably rest on the characters of Plantagenet Palliser, Lady Glencora, and the Reverend Mr. Crawley." Now it is as certain that Trollope is remembered as it is that we are in the next century; but it is not so much for any single character, or group of characters, or, indeed, any single book, that he is remembered, as it is for the qualities I have referred to. We may not love the English people, but we all love England; we love to go there and revel in its past; and the England that Trollope described so accurately is rapidly passing away; it was going perhaps more quickly than the English people themselves knew, even before this war began.

To read Trollope is to take a course in modern English history — social history to be sure, but just as important as political, and much more interesting. He has written a whole series of English political novels, it is true, but their interest is entirely aside from politics. It may be admitted that there are dreary places in Trollope, as there are dreary reaches on the lovely Thames, but they can be skipped, and more rapidly; and, as Dr. Johnson says, "Who but a fool reads a book through?"

The reason so many American girls marry, or at least used to marry, Englishmen, was because they found them different from the men whom they had grown up with; not finer, not as fine, perhaps, but more interesting. It is for some such reason as this that we get more pleasure out of Trollope than we do out of Howells, whose work, in some respects, resembles his. And Trollope, although he frequently stops the progress of his story to tell us what a fine thing an English gentleman is, never hesitated to "Paint the warts," and it is not altogether unpleasant to see the warts — on others.

Trollope takes, or appears to take, no care with his plots. The amazing thing about him is that he sometimes gives his plot away; but this seems to make no difference. In the dead centre of "Can You Forgive Her?" Trollope says that you must forgive her if his book is written aright. Lady Mason, in "Orley Farm," confesses to her ancient lover that she is guilty of a crime; but when she comes to be tried for it, the interest in her trial is intense; so in "Phineas Redux," where Phineas is tried for murder, the reader is assured that he is not guilty and that it will come out all right in the end; but this does not in the least detract from the interest of the story. Compare with this Wilkie Collins's "Moonstone," probably the best plot in English fiction. The moment that you know who stole the diamond and how it was stolen, the interest is at an end.

I have referred to the trial in "Orley Farm." It is, in my judgment, the best trial scene in any novel. I made this statement once to a well-read lawyer, and he was inclined to dispute the point, and of course mentioned "Pickwick." I reminded him that I had said the best, not the best known. Bardell *vs.* Pickwick is funny, inimitably funny, never to be forgotten, but burlesque. The trial in "A Tale of Two Cities" is heroic romance; but the trial in "Orley Farm" is real life. The only trial which can be compared to it is Effie Deans's, which I confess is infinitely more pathetic, too much so to be thoroughly enjoyed.

In "Orley Farm" one can see and hear Mr. Furnival, with his low voice and transfixing eye; one knows that the witness in his hands is as good as done for; and as for Mr. Chaffanbrass, — and did Dickens ever invent a better name? — he knew his work was cut out for him, and he did it with horrible skill. One sees plainly that the witnesses were trying to tell the truth, but that Chaffanbrass, intent on winning his case, would not let them: he was fighting, not for the truth, but for victory. The sideplay is excellent, the suppressed excitement in the court-room, the judge, the lawyers, are all good.

At last Mr. Furnival rises: "Gentlemen of the jury," he said, "I never rose to plead a client's cause with more confidence than I now feel in pleading that of my friend, Lady Mason." And after three hours he closes his great speech with this touching bit: "And now I shall leave my client's case in your hands. As to the verdict which you will give, I have no apprehension. You know as well as I do that she has not been guilty of this terrible crime. That you will so pronounce I do not for a moment doubt. But I do hope that the verdict will be accompanied by some expression on your part which may show to the world at large how great has been the wickedness displayed in the accusation."

And Trollope adds: "And yet as he sat down he

knew that she had been guilty! To his ear her guilt
had never been confessed; but yet he knew that it was
so, and knowing that, he had been able to speak as
though her innocence were a thing of course. That
those witnesses had spoken the truth he also knew,
and yet he had been able to hold them up to the exe-
cration of all around them as though they had committed the worst of crimes from the foulest of mo-
tives! And more than this, stranger than this, worse
than this, — when the legal world knew, — as the
legal world soon did know, — that all this had been
so, the legal world found no fault with Mr. Furnival,
conceiving that he had done his duty by his client in
a manner becoming an English barrister and an English gentleman."

I have frequently heard people say that they would
like to attend a trial. It is not worth while: trials
are either shocking or stupid; the best way to see a
trial is to read "Orley Farm."

Those of us who love Trollope love him for those
very qualities which cause fatigue in others. Our
lives, it may be, are fairly strenuous; it is hardly
necessary for us to have our feelings wrung of an evening. When the day is done and I settle down in my
arm-chair by the crackling wood fire, I am no longer
inclined to problems, real or imaginary. I suppose the
average man does his reading with what comfort he
may after dinner; it is the time for peace — and
Trollope. It may be that the reader falls asleep.
What matter? Better this, I should say, than that he

should be kept awake by the dissection of a human
soul. This vivisection business is too painful. No,
give me those long descriptions of house-parties,
those chapters made up of dinner conversations, of
endless hunting scenes, of editorials from newspapers,
of meetings of the House, of teas on the Terrace, and
above all, give me the clergy — not in real life for a
minute, but in the pages of Trollope.

But nothing happens, you say. I admit that there
is very little blood and no thunder; but not all of us
care for blood and thunder. Trollope interests one in
a gentler way; in fact, you may not know that you
have been interested until you look at your watch and
find it past midnight. And you can step from one
book to another almost without knowing it. The
characters, the situations repeat themselves over and
over again; your interest is not always intense, but it
never entirely flags. You are always saying to yourself, I'll just read one more chapter.

After you have read fifteen or twenty of his novels,
— and you will surely read this number if you read
him at all, — you will find that you are as intimate
with his characters as you are with the members of
your own family, and you will probably understand
them a great deal better. Professor Phelps says that
he is constantly besieged with the question: "Where
can I find a really good story?" I would recommend
that he keep a list of Trollope's best novels at hand.
Surely they are in accord with his own definition of
what a novel should be — a good story well told. I

will make such a list for him if he is in any difficulty about it.

I am told by those who know, that Trollope's sporting scenes are faultless. Never having found a horse with a neck properly adjusted for me to cling to, I have given up riding. Seated in my easy-chair, novel in hand, in imagination I thrust my feet into riding-boots and hear the click of my spurs on the gravel, as I walk to my mount; for some one has "put me up"; forgetful of my increasing girth, I rather fancy myself in my hunting clothes. Astride my borrowed mount, following a pack of hounds, I am off in the direction of Trumpeton Wood.

Fox-hunting, so fatiguing and disappointing in reality, becomes a delight in the pages of Trollope. The fox "breaks" at last, the usual accident happens, someone misjudges a brook or a fence and is thrown. If the accident is serious, they have a big man down from London. I know just who he will be before he arrives; and when the services of a solicitor or man of business are required, he turns out to be an old friend.

Although I have never knowingly killed a grouse or a partridge, being utterly unfamiliar with the use of shooting irons of any kind, Trollope makes me long for the first of August, that I may tell my man to pack my box and take places in the night mail for Scotland.

And then comes the long hoped-for invitation to spend a week end at Matching Priory; or, it may be that the Duke of Omnium's great establishment, Gatherum Castle, is to be open to me. Dukes and duchesses, lords and ladies, M.P.'s, with the latest news from town, of ministries falling and forming — I have been through it all before. I know the company; when a man enters the room, I know in advance just what turn the gossip will take.

But, above all, the clergy! Was there ever a more wonderful gallery of portraits? Balzac, you will say. I don't know — perhaps; but beginning with the delightful old Warden, his rich, pompous, but very human son-in-law, Archdeacon Grantley, Bishop Proudie and his shrewish lady, and that Uriah Heep of clergymen, Mr. Slope — it is a wonderful assemblage of living men and women leading everyday lives without romance, almost without incident.

Trollope was the painter, perhaps I should say the photographer, *par excellence* of his time. He set up his camera and took his pictures from every point of view. Possibly he was not a very great artist, but he was a wonderfully skillful workman. As he says of himself, he was at his writing-table at half-past five in the morning; he required of himself 250 words every quarter of an hour; his motto was *nulla dies sine linea* — no wet towel around his brow. He went "doggedly" at it, as Dr. Johnson says, and wrote an enormous number of books for a total of over seventy thousand pounds. He looked upon the result as comfortable, but not splendid.

"You are defied to find in Trollope a remark or an

action out of keeping with the character concerned. I would give a pound for every such instance found by an objector, if he would give me a penny for every strictly consistent speech or instance I might find in return." I am quoting from a little book of essays by Street; and it seems to me that he has here put his finger upon one of Trollope's most remarkable qualities: his absolute faithfulness. He was a realist, if I understand the word, but he did not care to deal much with the disagreeable or the shocking, as those whom we call realists usually do.

His pictures of the clergy, of whom he says that, when he began to write, he really knew very little, delighted some and offended others. An English critic, Hain Friswell, a supreme prig, says they are a disgrace, almost a libel; but the world knows better. On the whole his clergy are a very human lot, with faults and weaknesses just like our own. To my mind Mrs. Proudie, the bishop's lady, is a character worthy of Dickens at his very best. There is not a trace of caricature or exaggeration about her, and the description of her reception is one of the most amusing chapters ever written. In another vein, and very delicate, is the treatment of Mrs. Proudie's death. The old Bishop feels a certain amount of grief: his mainstay, his life-long partner has been taken from him; but he remembers that life with her was not always easy; one feels that he will be consoled.

Trollope tells an amusing story of Mrs. Proudie. He was writing one day at the Athenæum Club when two clergymen entered the room, each with a novel in his hand. Soon they began to abuse what they were reading, and it turned out that each was reading one of his novels. Said one, "Here is that Archdeacon whom we have had in every novel that he has ever written." "And here," said the other, "is that old Duke whom he talked about till everyone is tired of him. If I could not invent new characters I would not write novels at all." Then one of them fell foul of Mrs. Proudie. It was impossible for them not to be overheard. Trollope got up and, standing between them, acknowledged himself to be the culprit; and as to Mrs. Proudie, said he, "I'll go home and kill her before the week is out."

"The biographical part of literature is what I love most." After his death in 1882, his son published an autobiography which Trollope had written some years before. Swinburne calls it "exquisitely comical and conscientiously coxcombical." Whatever this may mean, it is generally thought to have harmed his reputation somewhat. In it he speaks at length of his novels: tells us how and when and where he wrote them; expressing his opinion as dispassionately as if he were discussing the work of an author he had never seen. Painstaking and conscientious he may have been, but in his autobiography he shows no sign of it — on the contrary, he stresses quantity rather than quality.

For this very reason a set — what the publishers call a "definitive edition" — of Trollope will never

be published. There is no demand for one. Editions
of him in sumptuous binding, gilt-top, with uncut
(and unopened) edges, under glass, will not be found
in the houses of those who select their books at the
same time they make their choice of the equipment
of their billiard-room. The immortality of morocco
Trollope will never have; but on the open shelves of
the man or woman whose leisure hours are spent in
their libraries, who know what is best in English fiction, there will be found invariably six or ten of his
novels in cloth, by this publisher or that, worn and
shapeless from much reading.

There is frequently some discussion as to the se-
quence in which Trollope's books should be read.
Especially is this true of what his American publishers, Dodd, Mead & Co., call the "Barsetshire"
series and the "Parliamentary" series. The novels
forming what they term the "Manor House" series
have no particular connection with each other. They
recommend the following order: —

THE BARSETSHIRE NOVELS

The Warden
Barchester Towers
Dr. Thorne
Framley Parsonage
The Small House at Allington
The Last Chronicle of Barset

THE PARLIAMENTARY NOVELS

The Eustace Diamonds
Can You Forgive Her?

Phineas Finn
Phineas Redux
The Prime Minister
The Duke's Children

THE MANOR-HOUSE NOVELS

Orley Farm
The Vicar of Bullhampton
Is He Popenjoy?
John Caldigate
The Belton Estate

Good stories all of them; and the enthusiastic Trollopian may wish also to read "The Three Clerks," in which Chaffanbrass is introduced for the first time; "The Bertrams," of which Trollope says, "I do not remember ever to have heard even a friend speak well of it"; "Castle Richmond," which is hard going: "Miss MacKenzie," in which there is a description of a dinner-party *à la Russe*, not unworthy of the author of Mrs. Proudie's reception in "Barchester Towers."

The list is by no means complete, but by this time we may have enough and not wish to make Lotta Schmidt's acquaintance, or give a hoot "Why Frau Frohman Raised Her Prices." I once knew but have forgotten.

Personally, Trollope was the typical Englishman: look at his portrait. He was dogmatic, self-assertive, rather irritable and hard to control, as his superiors in the Post-Office, in which he spent the greater part of his life, well knew; not altogether an amiable character, one would say. His education was by no means first-class, and his English is the English we talk rather than the English we write; but he was able to use it in a way sufficient for his purpose.

Listen to the conclusion of his Autobiography: —

It will not, I trust, be supposed by any reader that I have intended in this so-called autobiography to give a record of my inner life. No man ever did so truly — and no man ever will. Rousseau probably attempted it, but who doubts but that Rousseau has confessed in much the thoughts and convictions, rather than the facts, of his life? If the rustle of a woman's petticoat has ever stirred my blood; if a cup of wine has been a joy to me; if I have thought tobacco at midnight in pleasant company to be one of the elements of an earthly paradise; if, now and again, I have somewhat recklessly fluttered a five-pound note over a card-table — of what matter is that to any reader? I have betrayed no woman. Wine has brought me no sorrow. It has been the companionship of smoking that I have loved, rather than the habit. I have never desired to win money, and I have lost none. To enjoy the excitement of pleasure, but to be free from its vices and ill effects — to have the sweet, and leave the bitter untasted — that has been my study. The preachers tell us that this is impossible. It seems to me that hitherto I have succeeded fairly well. I will not say that I have never scorched a finger — but I carry no ugly wounds.

For what remains to me of life I trust for my happiness still chiefly to my work — hoping that when the power of work is over with me, God may be pleased to take me from a world in which, according to my view, there can be no joy; secondly, to the love of those who love me; and then to my books. That I can read and be happy while I am reading, is a great blessing. Could I remember, as some men do, what I read, I should have been able to call myself an educated man.

To trust for happiness chiefly to work and books, — to taste the sweet and leave the bitter untasted, — some may call such a scheme of life commonplace; but the most eventful lives are not the happiest — probably few authors have led happier lives than Anthony Trollope.

One final word I am forced to say. Since this awful war broke out, I read him in a spirit of sadness. The England that he knew and loved and described with such pride is gone forever. It will, to the coming generation, seem almost as remote as the England of Elizabeth. The Church will go, the State will change, and the common people will come into their own. The old order of things among the privileged class, much pay for little work, will be reversed. It will be useless to look for entailed estates and a leisure class — for all that made England a delightful retreat to us. If England is to continue great and powerful, as I earnestly hope and believe she is, England must be a better place for the poor and not so enervating for the rich, or both rich and poor are valiantly fighting her battles in vain.

> For the row that I prize is yonder,
> Away on the unglazed shelves;
> The bulged and the bruised octavos,
> The dear and the dumpy twelves.
>
>   Austin Dobson.

X

TEMPLE BAR THEN AND NOW

THE King of England is not a frequent visitor to the
City of London, meaning by "the City" that square
mile or so of old London whose political destinies
are in the keeping of the Lord Mayor, of which the
Bank of England is almost the exact centre, St. Paul's
the highest ground, and Temple Bar the western
boundary.

It might be said that the King is the only man in
England who has no business in the City. His duties
are in the West End — in Westminster; but to the
City he goes on state occasions; and it so happened
that several years ago I chanced to be in London on
one of them.

I had reached London only the night before, and
I did not know that anything out of the ordinary was
going on, until over my breakfast of bacon and eggs
— and such bacon! — I unfolded my "Times" and
learned that their Majesties were that morning going
in state to St. Paul's Cathedral to give thanks for
their safe return from India. It was not known that
they had been in any great peril in India; but royal
progresses are, I suppose, always attended with a certain amount of danger. At any rate the King and
Queen had reached home safely, and wanted to give

thanks, according to historic precedent, in St. Paul's; and the ceremony was set for that very morning.

Inquiring at the office of my hotel in Pall Mall, I learned that the Royal procession would pass the doors in something over an hour, and that the windows of a certain drawing-room were at my disposal. It would have been more comfortable to view the Royal party from a drawing-room of the Carlton; but what I wanted to see would take place at Temple Bar; so, my breakfast dispatched, I sallied forth to take up my position in the crowded street.

It was in February — a dark, gloomy, typical London morning. The bunting and decorations, everywhere apparent, had suffered sadly from the previous night's rain and were flapping dismally in the cold, raw air; and the streets, though crowded, wore a look of hopeless dejection.

I am never so happy as in London. I know it well, if a man can be said to know London well, and its streets are always interesting to me; but the Strand is not my favorite street. It has changed its character sadly in recent years. The Strand no longer suggests interesting shops and the best theatres, and I grieve to think of the ravages that time and Hall Caine have made in the Lyceum, which was once Irving's, where I saw him so often in his, and my, heyday. However, my way took me to the Strand, and, passing Charing Cross, I quoted to myself Dr. Johnson's famous remark: "Fleet Street has a very animated appearance; but the full tide of human existence is at Charing

TEMPLE BAR AS IT IS TO-DAY

Cross." As I neared the site of Temple Bar, however, I observed that, for this morning, at any rate,
the tide was setting toward the City.

My progress through the crowd was slow, but I
finally reached my objective point, the Griffin, which
marks the spot where for many centuries Temple Bar
stood. Taking up my position just in front of the
rather absurd monument, which forms an "island"
in the middle of the street, I waited patiently for
the simple but historic and picturesque ceremony to
begin.

Before long the city dignitaries began to arrive.
First came the Sheriffs and Aldermen in coaches of
state, wearing their scarlet-and-ermine robes. Finally, a coach appeared, out of the window of which
protruded the end of the great mace, emblem of
City authority; and at last the Lord Mayor himself,
in all his splendor, in a coach so wonderful in its gold
and color that one might have supposed it had been
borrowed from Cinderella for the occasion.

While I was wondering how many times and under
what varying conditions this bit of pageantry had
been enacted on this very spot, a slight wave of cheering down the Strand apprised me of the approach of
the Royal procession. The soldiers who lined both
sides of the street became, at a word of command,
more immovable than ever, standing at "attention,"
if that is the word which turns men into statues. At
the same time a band began the national anthem, and
this seemed the signal for the Mayor and his attend-

ants to leave their coaches and group themselves just east of the monument. A moment later the Royal party, in carriages driven by postilions with outriders, swept by; but the state carriage in which sat the King and Queen was brought to a halt immediately in front of the City party.

The Lord Mayor, carrying his jeweled sword in his hand, bowed low before his sovereign, who remained seated in the open carriage. Words, I presume, were spoken. I saw the Lord Mayor extend his greetings and tender his sword to the King, who, saluting, placed his hand upon its hilt and seemed to congratulate the City upon its being in such safe keeping. The crowd cheered — not very heartily; but history was in the making, and the true Londoner, although he might not like to confess it, still takes a lively interest in these scenes which link him to the past.

While the City officials, their precious sword — it was a gift from Queen Elizabeth — still in their keeping, were returning to their coaches and taking their places, there was a moment's delay, which gave me a good opportunity of observing the King and his consort, who looked very much like the pictures of them we so frequently see in the illustrated papers. The King looked bored, and I could not help noticing that he was not nearly as interested in me as I was in him. I felt a trifle hurt until I remembered that his father, King Edward, had in the same way ignored Mark Twain, that day when the King was leading a procession in Oxford Street, and Mark was on top of an omnibus, dressed to kill in his new top-coat. Evidently kings do not feel bound to recognize men in the street whom they have never seen before.

The Lord Mayor and his suite, having resumed their places, were driven rapidly down Fleet Street toward St. Paul's, the Royal party following them. The whole ceremony at Temple Bar, the shadow of former ceremonies hardly more real, had not occupied much over five minutes. The crowd dispersed, Fleet Street and the Strand immediately resumed their wonted appearance except for the bunting and decorations, and I was left to discuss with myself the question, what does this King business really mean?

Many years ago Andrew Carnegie wrote a book, "Triumphant Democracy," in which, as I vaguely remember, he likened our form of government to a pyramid standing on its base, while a pyramid representing England was standing on its apex. There is no doubt whatever that a pyramid looks more comfortable on its base than on its apex; but let us drop these facile illustrations of strength and weakness and ask ourselves, "In what way are we better off, politically, than the English?"

In theory, the king, from whom no real authority flows, may seem a little bit ridiculous, but in practice how admirably the English have learned to use him! If he is great enough to exert a powerful influence on the nation for good, his position gives him an immense opportunity. How great his power is, we do not know, — it is not written down in books, —

but he has it. If, on the other hand, he has not the full confidence of the people, if they mistrust his judgment, his power is circumscribed: wise men rule and Majesty does as Majesty is told to do.

"We think of our Prime Minister as the wisest man in England for the time being," says Bagehot. The English scheme of government permits, indeed, necessitates, her greatest men entering politics, as we call it. Is it so with us?

Our plan, however excellent it may be in theory, in practice results in our having constantly to submit ourselves — those of us who must be governed — to capital operations at the hands of amateurs who are selected for the job by drawing straws. That we escape with our lives is due rather to our youth and hardy constitution than to the skill of the operators.

To keep the king out of mischief, he may be set the innocuous task of visiting hospitals, opening expositions, or laying corner-stones. Tapping a block of granite with a silver trowel, he declares it to be "well and truly laid," and no exception can be taken to the masterly manner in which the work is done. Occasionally, once a year or so, plain Bill Smith, who has made a fortune in the haberdashery line, say, bends the knee before him and at a tap of a sword across his shoulder arises Sir William Smith. Bill Smith was not selected for this honor by the king himself; certainly not! the king probably never heard of him; but the men who rule the nation, those in authority, for reasons sufficient if not good, selected

Smith for "birthday honors," and he is given a stake in the nation.

And so it goes. The knight may become a baronet, the baronet a baron, the baron a duke — this last not often now, only for very great service rendered the Empire; and with each advance in rank comes increases of responsibility — in theory, at least. Have our political theories worked out so well that we are justified in making fun of theirs as we sometimes do? I think not. After our country has stood as well as England has the shocks which seven or ten centuries may bring it, we may have the right to say, "We order these things better at home."

While musing thus, the Strand and Temple Bar of a century and a half ago rise up before me, and I notice coming along the footway a tall, burly old man, walking with a rolling gait, dressed in a brown coat with metal buttons, knee-breeches, and worsted stockings, with large silver buckles on his clumsy shoes. He seems like a wise old fellow, so I approach him and tell him who I am and of my perplexities.

"What! Sir, an American? They are a race of convicts and ought to be thankful for anything we allow them short of hanging." And then, seeing me somewhat disconcerted, he adds less ferociously: "I would not give half a guinea to live under one form of government rather than another." Saying which, he turns into a court off Fleet Street and is lost to view.

It was only after he had disappeared that I realized that I had been speaking to Dr. Johnson.

Just when the original posts, bars, and chains gave way to a building known as Temple Bar, we have no means of knowing. Honest John Stow, whose effigy in terra cotta still looks down on us from the wall of the Church of St. Andrew Undershaft, published his famous "Survey of [Elizabethan] London" in 1598. In it he makes scant mention of Temple Bar; and this is the more remarkable because he describes so accurately many of the important buildings, and gives the exact location of every court and lane, every pump and well, in the London of his day.

Stow assures his readers that his accuracy cost him many a weary mile's travel and many a hard-earned penny, and his authority has never been disputed. He refers to the place several times, but not to the gate itself. "Why this is, I have not heard, nor can I conjecture," to use a phrase of his; but we know that a building known as Temple Bar must have been standing when the "Survey" appeared; for it is clearly indicated in Aggas's pictorial map of London, published a generation earlier; otherwise we might infer that in Stow's time it was merely what he terms it, a "barre" separating the liberties of London from Westminster — the city from the shire. It is obvious that it gets its name from that large group of buildings known as the Temple, which lies between Fleet Street and the river, long the quarters of the Knights

Templar, and for centuries past the centre of legal learning in England.

Referring to the "new Temple by the Barre," Stow tells us that "over against it in the high streets stand a payre of stockes"; and adds that the whole street "from the Barre to the Savoy was commanded to be paved in the twenty-fourth year of the reign of King Henry the Sixt" (this sturdy lad, it will be remembered, began to "reign" when he was only nine months old), with "tole to be taken towards the charges thereof." This practice of taking "tole" from all non-freemen at Temple Bar continued until after the middle of the nineteenth century, and fine confusion it must have caused. The charge of two pence each time a cart passed the City boundary finally aroused such an outcry against the "City turnpike" that it was done away with. Whoever received this revenue must have heartily bewailed the passing of the good old days; for a few years before the custom was abandoned, the toll collected amounted to over seven thousand pounds per annum.

The first reference which seems to suggest a building dates back to the time when "Sweet Anne Bullen" passed from the Tower to her coronation at Westminster, at which time the Fleet Street conduit poured forth red wine, and the city waits — or minstrels — "made music like a heavenly noyse." We know, too, that it was "a rude building," and that it was subsequently replaced by a substantial timber structure of classic appearance, with a pitched roof, spanning the street and gabled at each end. Old prints show us that it was composed of three arches — a large central arch for vehicular traffic, with smaller

OLD TEMPLE BAR
Demolished in 1666

arches, one on each side, over the footway. All of the arches were provided with heavy oaken doors, studded with iron, which could be closed at night, or when unruly mobs, tempted to riot, threatened — and frequently carried out their threat — to disturb the peace of the city.

The City proper terminated at Lud Gate, about halfway up Ludgate Hill; but the jurisdiction of the City extended to Temple Bar, and those residing between the two gates were said to be within the liberties of the City and enjoyed its rights and privileges, among them that of passing through Temple Bar without paying toll. Although Lud Gate was the most important gate of the old city, originally forming a part of the old London wall, from time immemorial Temple Bar has been the great historic entrance to the City. At Temple Bar it was usual, upon an accession to the throne, the proclamation of a peace, or the overthrow of an enemy, for a state entry to be made into the City. The sovereign, attended by his trumpeters, would proceed to the closed gate and demand entrance. From the City side would come the inquiry, "Who comes here?" and the herald having made reply, the Royal party would be admitted and conducted to the lord mayor.

With the roll of years this custom became slightly modified. When Queen Elizabeth visited St. Paul's to return thanks for the defeat of the Spanish Armada, we read that, upon the herald and trumpeters having announced her arrival at the Gate, the Lord Mayor advanced and surrendered the city sword to the Queen, who, after returning it to him, proceeded to St. Paul's. On this occasion — as on all previous occasions — the sovereign was on horseback, Queen

Elizabeth having declined to ride, as had been suggested, in a vehicle drawn by horses, on the ground that it was new-fangled and effeminate. For James I, for Charles I and Cromwell and Charles II, similar ceremonies were enacted, the coronation of Charles II being really magnificent and testifying to the joy of England in again having a king.

Queen Anne enters the City in a coach drawn by eight horses, "none with her but the Duchess of Marlborough, in a very plain garment, the Queen full of jewels," to give thanks for the victories of the duke abroad; and so the stately historic procession winds through the centuries, always pausing at Temple Bar, right down to our own time.

But to return to the actual "fabrick," as Dr. Johnson would have called it. We learn that, soon after the accession of Charles II, old Temple Bar was marked for destruction. It was of wood, and, although "newly paynted and hanged" for state occasions, it was felt that something more worthy of the great city, to which it gave entrance, should be erected. Inigo Jones was consulted and drew plans for a new gate, his idea being the erection of a really triumphant arch; but, as he died soon after, his plan was abandoned. Other architects with other plans came forward. At length the King became interested in the project and promised money toward its accomplishment; but Charles II was an easy promiser, and as the money he promised belonged to someone else, nothing came of it. While the project was being thus discussed, the plague broke out, followed by the fire which destroyed so much of old London, and public attention was so earnestly directed to the rebuilding of London itself that the gate, for a time, was forgotten.

Temple Bar had escaped the flames, but the rebuilding of London occasioned by the fire gave Christopher Wren his great opportunity. A new St. Paul's with its "mighty mothering dome," a lasting monument to his genius, was erected, and churches innumerable, the towers and spires of which still point the way to heaven — instructions which, we may suspect, are neglected when we see how deserted they are; but they serve, at least, to add charm and interest to a ramble through the City.

Great confusion resulted from the fire, but London was quick to see that order must be restored, and it is much to be regretted that Wren's scheme for replanning the entire burned district was not carried out. Fleet Street was less than twenty-four feet wide at Temple Bar — not from curb to curb, for there was none, but from house to house. This was the time to rebuild London; although something was done, much was neglected, and Wren was finally commissioned to build a new gate of almost the exact dimensions of the old one.

The work was begun in 1670 and progressed slowly, for it was not finished until two years later. What a fine interruption to traffic its rebuilding must have occasioned! Constructed entirely of Portland stone, the same material as St. Paul's, it consisted, like the old one, of three arches — a large flattened centre

TEMPLE BAR IN DR. JOHNSON'S TIME

arch, with small semicircular arches on either side. Above the centre arch was a large window, which gave light and air to a spacious chamber within; while on either side of the window were niches, in which were placed statues of King James and his Queen, Anne

of Denmark, on the City side and of Charles I and
Charles II on the Westminster side.

The curious may wish to know that the mason was
Joshua Marshall, whose father had been master-
mason to Charles I; that the sculptor of the statues
was John Bushnell, who died insane; and that the
cost of the whole, including the statues at four hundred and eighty pounds, was but thirteen hundred
and ninety-seven pounds, ten shillings.

The fog and soot and smoke of London soon give
the newest building an appearance of age, and mercifully bring it into harmony with its surroundings.
Almost before the new gate was completed, it had
that appearance; and before it had a chance to grow
really old, there arose a demand for its removal altogether. Petitions praying for its destruction were cir-
culated and signed. Verse, if not poetry, urging its
retention was written and printed.

If that Gate is pulled down, 'twixt the Court and the City,
You'll blend in one mass, prudent, worthless and witty.
If you league cit and lordling, as brother and brother,
You'll break order's chain and they'll war with each other.
Like the Great Wall of China, it keeps out the Tartars
From making irruptions, where industry barters,
Like Samson's Wild Foxes, they'll fire your houses,
And madden your spinsters, and cousin your spouses.
They'll destroy in one sweep, both the Mart and the Forum,
Which your fathers held dear, and their fathers before 'em.

But, attacked by strong city men and defended
only by sentiment, Temple Bar still continued to
impede traffic and shut out light and air, while the

generations who fought for its removal passed to their rest. It became the subject of jokes and conundrums. Why is Temple Bar like a lady's veil? it was asked; the answer being that both must be raised (razed) for busses. The distinction between a buss and a kiss, suggested by Herrick, of whom the eighteenth-century City man never heard, would have been lost; but we know that —

> Kissing and bussing differ both in this,
> We buss our wantons and our wives we kiss.

No account of Temple Bar would be complete without reference to the iron spikes above the centre of the pediment, on which were placed occasionally the heads of persons executed for high treason. This ghastly custom continued down to the middle of the eighteenth century, and gave rise to many stories, most of them legendary, but which go to prove, were proof necessary, that squeamishness was not a common fault in the days of the Georges.

To refer, however briefly, to the taverns which clustered east and west of Temple Bar and to the authors who frequented them, would be to stop the progress of this paper — and begin another. Dr. Johnson only voiced public opinion when he said that a tavern chair is a throne of human felicity. For more than three centuries within the shadow of Temple Bar there was an uninterrupted flow of wine and wit and wisdom, with, doubtless, some wickedness. From Ben Jonson, whose favorite resort was The Devil, adjoining the Bar on the south side, down to Tennyson, who frequented The Cock, on the north, came the same cry, for good talk and good wine.

> O plump head-waiter at the Cock,
> To which I most resort,
> How goes the time? 'Tis five o'clock —
> Go fetch a pint of port.

This does not sound like the author of "Locksley Hall," but it is; and while within the taverns, "the chief glory of England, its authors," were writing and talking themselves into immortality, just outside there ebbed and flowed beneath the arches of Temple Bar, east in the morning and west at night, the human stream which is one of the wonders of the world.

On Thursday evening last, some gentlemen, who supped and spent some agreeable hours at The Devil Tavern near Temple Barr, upon calling for the bill of expenses had the following given them by the landlord, viz.:

	£	s.	d
For geese, the finest ever seen By Duke or Duchess, King or Queen,	o.	6.	6.
For nice green peas, as plump and pretty, Better ne'er ate in London City,	o.	3.	9.
For charming gravy, made to please, With butter, bread & Cheshire cheese,	o.	3.	o.
For honest porter, brown and stout, That cheers the heart, & cures the gout,	o.	1.	5.
For unadulterated wine; Genuine! Noble! Pure! Divine!	o.	6.	o.
For my Nan's punch (and Nan knows how To make good punch, you'll all allow)	o.	7.	o.
For juniper, most clear and fine, That looks and almost tastes, like wine,	o.	1.	4.
For choice tobacco, undefiled Harmless and pleasant, soft and mild	o.	o.	2.
	£1.	9.	2.

CLIPPING FROM A NEWSPAPER PUBLISHED IN 1767

Meanwhile the importance of Temple Bar as a city gate was lessening; "a weak spot in our defenses," a wit calls it, and points out that the enemy can dash around it through the barber's shop, one door of which opens into the City, and the other into the "suburbs"; but down to the last it continued to play a part in City functions. In 1851 it is lit with twenty thousand lamps as the Queen goes to a state ball in Guildhall. A few months later, it is draped in black as the remains of the Iron Duke pause for a moment under its arches, on the way to their final resting-place in St. Paul's Cathedral. In a few years we see it draped with the colors of England and Prussia, when the Princess Royal, as the bride of Frederick William, gets her "Farewell" and "God bless you" from the City, on her departure for Berlin. Five years pass and the young Prince of Wales and his beautiful bride, Alexandra, are received with wild applause by the mob as their carriage halts at Temple Bar; and once again when, in February, 1872, Queen Victoria, the Prince and Princess of Wales, and their Court go to St. Paul's to return thanks for the Prince's happy recovery from a dangerous illness.

With this event the history of Temple Bar in its old location practically ceases. It continued a few years longer a "bone in the throat of Fleet Street"; but at last its condition became positively dangerous, its gates were removed because of their weight, and its arches propped up with timbers. Finally, in 1877, its removal was decided upon, by the Corporation of London, and Temple Bar, from time immemorial one of London's most notable landmarks, disappears and the Griffin on an "island" rises in its stead.

"The ancient site of Temple Bar has been disfigured by Boehm with statues of the Queen and the Prince of Wales so stupidly modeled that they look like statues out of Noah's Ark. It is bad enough that we should have German princes foisted upon us, but German statues are worse."

In this manner George Moore refers to the Memorial commonly called the Griffin, which, shortly after the destruction of the old gate, was erected on the exact spot where Temple Bar formerly stood.

It is not a handsome object; indeed, barring the Albert Memorial, it may be said to represent Victorian taste at its worst. It is a high, rectangular pedestal, running lengthwise with the street, placed on a small island which serves as a refuge for pedestrians crossing the busy thoroughfare. On either side are niches in which are placed the lifesize marble figures described by Moore. But this is not all: there are bronze tablets let into the masonry, showing in *basso-rilievo* incidents in the history of old Temple Bar, with portraits, medallions, and other things. This base pedestal, if so it may be called, is surmounted by a smaller pedestal on which is placed a heraldic dragon or griffin, — a large monster in bronze, — which is supposed to guard the gold of the City.

We do not look for beauty in Fleet Street, and we know that only in the Victorian sense is this monument a work of art; but it has the same interest for us as a picture by Frith — it is a human document. Memories of the past more real than the actual present crowd upon us, and we turn under an archway into the Temple Gardens, glad to forget the artistic sins of Boehm and his compeers.

Ask the average Londoner what has become of old Temple Bar, and he will look at you in blank amazement, and then, with an effort of memory, say, "They've put it up somewhere in the north." And so it is.

On its removal the stones were carefully numbered, with a view to reërection, and there was some discussion as to where the old gate should be located. It is agreed now that it should have been placed in the Temple Gardens; but for almost ten years the stones, about one thousand in number, were stored on a piece of waste ground in the Farrington Road. Finally, they were purchased by Sir Henry Meux, the rich brewer, whose brewery, if out of sight, still indicates its presence by the strong odor of malt, at the corner of Oxford Street and Tottenham Court Road. Sir Henry Meux was the owner of a magnificent country seat, Theobald's Park, near Waltham Cross, about twelve miles north of London; and he determined to make Temple Bar the principal entrance gate to this historic estate.

So to Theobald's Park, anciently Tibbals, I bent my steps one morning. Being in a reminiscent mood, I had intended to follow in the footsteps of Izaak Walton, from the site of his shop in Fleet Street just east of Temple Bar, and having, in the words of the gentle angler, "stretched my legs up Tottenham Hill," to take the high road into Hertfordshire; but the English spring having opened with more than its customary severity, I decided to go by rail. It was raining gently but firmly when my train reached its destination, Waltham Cross, and I was deprived of the pleasure I had promised myself of reaching Temple Bar on foot. An antique fly, drawn by a superannuated horse, was secured at the railway station, and after a short drive I was set down before old Temple Bar, the gates of which were closed as securely against me as ever they had been closed against an unruly mob in its old location.

Driving along a flat and monotonous country road, one comes on the old gate almost suddenly, and experiences a feeling, not of disappointment but of surprise. The gate does not span the road, but is set back a little in a hedge on one side of it, and seems large for its setting. One is prepared for a dark, grimy portal, whereas the soot and smoke of London have been erased from it, and, instead, one sees an antique, creamy-white structure tinted and toned with the green of the great trees which overhang it.

Prowling about in the drenching rain, I looked in vain for some sign of life. I shouted to King James, who looked down on me from his niche; and receiving no reply, addressed his consort, inquiring how I was to secure admittance.

A porter's lodge on one side, almost hidden in the trees, supplied an answer to my question, and on my giving a lusty pull at the bell, the door was opened and a slatternly woman appeared and inquired my business. "To look over Temple Bar," I replied. "Hutterly himpossible," she said; and I saw at once that tact and a coin were required. I used both. "Go up the drive to the great 'ouse and hask for the clerk [pronounced clark] of the works, Mr. 'Arrison; 'e may let ye hover."

I did as I was told and had little difficulty with Mr. Harrison. The house itself was undergoing extensive repairs and alterations. It has recently passed, under the will of Lady Meux, to its present owner, together with a fortune of five hundred thousand pounds in money.

Many years ago Henry Meux married the beautiful and charming Valerie Langton, an actress, — a Gaiety girl, in fact, — but they had had no children, and when he died in 1900, the title became extinct. Thereafter Lady Meux, enormously wealthy, without relatives, led a retired life, chiefly interested in breeding horses. A chance courtesy paid her by the wife of Sir Hedworth Lambton, who had recently married, together with the fact that he had established a reputation for ability and courage, decided her in her thought to make him her heir.

Sir Hedworth, a younger son of the second Earl of Durham, had early adopted the sea as his profession. He had distinguished himself in the bombardment of Alexandria, and had done something wonderful at Ladysmith. He was a hero, no longer a young man, without means — who better fitted to succeed to her wealth and name? In 1911 Lady Meux died, and this lovely country seat, originally a hunting-lodge of King James, subsequently the favorite residence of Charles I, and with a long list of royal or noble owners, became the property of the gallant sailor. All that he had to do was to forget that the name of Meux suggested a brewery and exchange his own for it, and the great property was his. It reads like a chapter out of a romance. Thus it was that the house was being thoroughly overhauled for its new owner at the time of my visit.

But I am wandering from Temple Bar. Armed with a letter from Mr. Harrison, I returned to the gate. First, I ascertained that the span of the centre arch, the arch through which for two centuries the traffic of London had passed, was but twenty-one feet "in the clear," as an architect would say; next, that the span of the small arches on either side was only four feet six inches. No wonder that there was always congestion at Temple Bar.

I was anxious also to see the room above, the room in which formerly Messrs. Child, when it had adjoined their banking-house, had stored their old ledgers and cash-books. Keys were sought and found, and I was admitted. The room was bare except for a large table in the centre, on which were quill pens and an inkstand in which the ink had dried up years before. One other thing there was, a visitor's book, which, like a new diary, had been started off bravely years before, but in which no signature had recently been written. I glanced over it and noticed a few well-known names — English names, not American, such as one usually finds, for I was off the beaten track of the tourist. The roof was leaking here and there, and little pools of water were forming on the floor. It was as cold as a tomb. I wished that a tavern, the Cock, the Devil, or any other, had been just outside, as in the old days when Temple Bar stood in Fleet Street.

The slatternly woman clanked her keys; she too was cold. I had seen all there was to see. The beauty of Temple Bar is in its exterior, and, most of all, in its wealth of literary and historic associations. I could muse elsewhere with less danger of pneumonia, so I said farewell to the kings in their niches, who in this suburban retreat seemed like monarchs retired from business, and returned to my cab.

The driver was asleep in the rain. I think the horse was, too. I roused the man and he roused the beast, and we drove almost rapidly back to the station; no, not to the station, but to a public house close by it, where hot water and accompaniments were to be had.

"When is the next train up to London?" I asked an old man at the station.

"In ten minutes, but you 'll find it powerful slow."

I was not deceived; it took me over an hour to reach London.

As if to enable me to bring this story to a fitting close, I read in the papers only a few days ago: "Vice-

Admiral Sir John Jellicoe was to-day promoted to the rank of Admiral, and Sir Hedworth Meux, who until now has been commander-in-chief at Portsmouth, was appointed Admiral of the Home Fleet." [1]

Good luck be with him! Accepting the burdens which properly go with rank and wealth, he is at this moment cruising somewhere in the cold North Sea, in command of perhaps the greatest fleet ever assembled. Upon the owner of Temple Bar, at this moment, devolves the duty of keeping watch and ward over England.

[1] This was written in April, 1915. Sir Hedworth Meux is not now in active service.

XI

A MACARONI PARSON

IT will hardly be questioned that the influence of the priesthood is waning. Why this is so, it is not within the province of a mere book-collector to discuss; but the fact will, I think, be admitted. In the past, however, every country and almost every generation has produced a type of priest which seems to have been the special product of its time. The soothsayer of old Rome, concealed, perhaps, in a hollow wall, whispered his warning through the marble lips of a conveniently placed statue, in return for a suitable present indirectly offered; while to-day Billy Sunday, leaping and yelling like an Apache Indian, shrieks his admonitions at us, and takes up a collection in a clothes-basket. It is all very sad and, as Oscar Wilde would have said, very tedious.

Priests, prophets, parsons, or preachers! They are all human, like the rest of us. Too many of them are merely insurance agents soliciting us to take out policies of insurance against fire everlasting, for a fee commensurate, not with the risk, but with our means. It is a well-established trade, in which the representatives of the old-line companies, who have had the cream of the business, look with disapproval upon new methods, as well they may, their own having

worked so well for centuries. The premiums collected
have been enormous, and no evidence has ever been
produced that the insurer took any risk whatever.

And the profession has been, not only immensely
lucrative, but highly honorable. In times past priests
have ranked with kings: sometimes wearing robes of
silk studded with jewels; on fortune's cap the top-
most button, exhibit Wolsey; sometimes appearing
in sackcloth relieved by ashes; every man in his
humor. But it is not my purpose to inveigh against
any creed or sect; only I confess my bewilderment at
the range of human interest in questions of doctrine,
while simple Christianity stands neglected.

The subject of this paper, however, is not creeds
in general or in particular, but an eighteenth-century
clergyman of the Church of England. It will not, I
think, be doubted by those who have given the subject any attention that religious affairs in England
in the eighteenth century were at a very low ebb indeed. Carlyle, as was his habit, called that century
some hard names; but some of us are glad occasionally
to steal away from our cares and forget our present
"efficiency" in that century of leisure. Perhaps not
for always, but certainly for a time, it is a relief to

> . . . live in that past Georgian day
> When men were less inclined to say
> That "Time is Gold," and overlay
> With toil, their pleasure.

And to quote Austin Dobson again, with a slight
variation: —

Seventeen hundred and twenty-nine: —
That is the date of this tale of mine.

First great George was buried and gone;
George the Second was plodding on.

Whitefield preached to the colliers grim;
Bishops in lawn sleeves preached at him;

Walpole talked of "a man and his price";
Nobody's virtue was over-nice: —

certainly not that of the clergyman of whom I am
about to speak.

And now, without further delay, I introduce William Dodd. Doctor Dodd, he came to be called; subsequently, the "unfortunate Doctor Dodd," which he certainly considered himself to be, and with good reason, as he was finally hanged.

William Dodd was born in Lincolnshire, in 1729, and was himself the son of a clergyman. He early became a good student, and entering Clare Hall, Cambridge, at sixteen, attracted some attention by his close application to his studies. But books alone did not occupy his time: he attained some reputation as a dancer and was noted for being very fond of dress. He must have had real ability, however, for he was graduated with honors, and his name appears on the list of wranglers. Immediately after receiving his Arts degree, he set out to make a career for himself in London.

Young Dodd was quick and industrious: he had good manners and address, made friends quickly, and was possessed of what, in those days, was called "a lively imagination," which seems to have meant a fondness for dissipation; with friends to help him, he soon knew his way about the metropolis. Its many pitfalls he discovered by falling into them, and the pitfalls for a gay young blade in London in the middle of the eighteenth century were many and sundry.

But whatever his other failings, of idleness Dodd could not be accused. He did not forget that he had come to London to make a career for himself. He had already published verse; he now began a comedy, and the death of the Prince of Wales afforded him a subject for an elegy. From this time on he was prepared to write an ode or an elegy at the drop of a hat. The question, should he become author or minister, perplexed him for some time. For success in either direction perseverance and a patron were necessary. Perseverance he had, but a patron was lacking.

While pondering these matters, Dodd seemed to have nipped his career in the bud by a most improvident marriage. His wife was a Mary Perkins, which means little to us. She may have been a servant, but more likely she was the discarded mistress of a nobleman who was anxious to see her provided with a husband. In any event, she was a handsome woman, and his marriage was not his greatest misfortune.

Shortly after the wedding, we hear of them living in a small establishment in Wardour Street, not then, as now, given over to second-hand furniture shops, but rather a good quarter frequented by literary men and artists. Who supplied the money for this venture we do not know; it was probably borrowed from some-one, and we may suspect that Dodd already was headed the wrong way — or that, at least, his father thought so ; for we hear of his coming to London to persuade his son to give up his life there and return to Cambridge to continue his studies.

Shortly after this time he published two small vol-umes of quotations which he called "Beauties of Shakespeare." He was the first to make the discovery that a book of quotations "digested under proper heads" would have a ready sale. Shakespeare in the dead centre of the eighteenth century was not the colossal figure that he is seen to be as we celebrate the tercentenary of his death. I suspect that my friend Felix Schelling, the great Elizabethan scholar, feels that anyone who would make a book of quota-tions from Shakespeare deserves Dodd's end, namely, hanging; indeed, I have heard him suggest as much; but we cannot all be Schellings. The book was well received and has been reprinted right down to our own time. In the introduction he refers to his at-tempt to present a collection of the finest passages of the poet, "who was ever," he says, "of all modern authors, my first and greatest favorite"; adding that "it would have been no hard task to have multiplied notes and parallel passages from Greek, Latin and English writers, and thus to have made no small dis-play of what is commonly called learning"; but that he had no desire to perplex the reader. There is much good sense in the introduction, which we must also think of as coming from a young man little more than a year out of college.

As it was his first, so he thought it would be his last, serious venture into literature, for in his preface he says: "Better and more important things henceforth demand my attention, and I here, with no small pleasure, take leave of Shakespeare and the critics: as this work was begun and finish'd before I enter'd upon the sacred function in which I am now happily employ'd."

Dodd had already been ordained deacon and settled down as a curate in West Ham in Essex, where he did not spare himself in the dull round of parochial drudgery. So passed two years which, looking back on them from within the portals of Newgate Prison, he declared to have been the happiest of his life. But he soon tired of the country, his yearning for city life was not to be resisted, and securing a lectureship at St. Olave's, Hart Street, he returned to London and relapsed into literature.

A loose novel, "The Sisters," is credited to him. Whether he wrote it or not is a question, but he may well have done so, for some of its pages seem to have inspired his sermons. Under cover of being a warning to the youth of both sexes, he deals with London life in a manner which would have put the author of "Peregrine Pickle" to shame; but as nobody's virtue was over-nice, nobody seemed to think it particularly strange that a clergyman should have written such a book. In many respects he reminds us of his more gifted rival, Laurence Sterne.

Dodd's great chance came in 1758, when a certain Mr. Hingley and some of his friends got together three thousand pounds and established an asylum for Magdalens, presumably penitent. The scheme was got under way after the usual difficulties; and as, in the City, the best way to arouse public interest is by a dinner, so in the West End a sermon may be made to serve the same purpose. Sterne had talked a hundred and sixty pounds out of the pockets of his hearers for the recently established Foundling Hospital; Dodd, when selected to preach the inaugural sermon at Magdalen House, got ten times as much. Who had the greater talent? Dodd was content that the question should be put. The charity became immensely popular. "Her Majesty" subscribed three hundred pounds, and the cream of England's nobility, feeling a personal interest in such an institution, and perhaps a personal responsibility for the urgent need of it, made large contributions. The success of the venture was assured.

Dodd was made Chaplain. At first this was an honorary position, but subsequently a small stipend was attached to it. The post was much to his liking, and it became as fashionable to go to hear Dodd and see the penitent magdalens on Sunday, as to go to Ranelagh and Vauxhall with, and to see, impenitent magdalens during the week. Services at Magdalen House were always crowded: royalty attended; everybody went.

Sensational and melodramatic, Dodd drew vivid
pictures of the life from which the women and young
girls had been rescued: the penitents on exhibition
and the impenitents in the congregation, alike, were
moved to tears. Frequently a woman swooned, as
was the fashion in those days, and her stays had to be
cut; or someone went into hysterics and had to be
carried screaming from the room. Dodd must have
felt that he had made no mistake in his calling.
Horace Walpole says that he preached very eloquently
in the French style; but it can hardly have been in the
style of Bossuet, I should say. The general wanton-
ness of his subject he covered by a veneer of decency;
but we can guess what his sermons were like, without
reading them, from our knowledge of the man and the
texts he chose. "These things I command you, that
ye love one another," packed the house; but his
greatest effort was inspired by the text, "Whosoever
looketh on a woman." It does not require much imagination to see what he would make out of that!

But for all his immense popularity Dodd was getting very little money. His small living in the country and his hundred guineas or so from the Magdalen
did not suffice for his needs. He ran into debt, but he
had confidence in himself and his ambition was
boundless; he even thought of a bishopric. Why not?
It was no new way to pay old debts. Influence in high
places was his; but first he must secure a doctor's degree. This was not difficult. Cambridge, if not exactly proud of him, could not deny him, and Dodd got

his degree. The King was appealed to, and he was appointed a Royal Chaplain. It was a stepping-stone to something better, and Dodd, always industrious, now worked harder than ever. He wrote and published incessantly: translations, sermons, addresses, poems, odes, and elegies on anybody and everything: more than fifty titles are credited to him in the British Museum catalogue.

And above all things, Dodd was in demand at a "city dinner." His blessings — he was always called upon to say grace — were carefully regulated according to the scale of the function. A brief "Bless, O Lord, we pray thee" sufficed for a simple dinner; but when the table was weighted down, as it usually was, with solid silver, and the glasses suggested the variety and number of wines which were to follow one another in orderly procession until most of the company got drunk and were carried home and put to bed, then Dodd rose to the occasion, and addressed a sonorous appeal which began, "Bountiful Jehovah, who has caused to groan this table with the abundant evidences of thy goodness."

The old-line clergy looked askance at all these doings. Bishops, secure in their enjoyment of princely incomes, and priests of lesser degree with incomes scarcely less princely, regarded Dodd with suspicion. Why did he not get a good living somewhere, from someone; hire a poor wretch to mumble a few prayers to half-empty benches on a Sunday while he collected the tithes? Why this zeal? When a substantial

banker hears of an upstart guaranteeing ten per cent
interest, he awaits the inevitable crash, certain that,
the longer it is postponed, the greater the crash will
be. In the same light the well-beneficed clergyman
regarded Dodd.

Dodd himself longed for tithes; but as they were
delayed in coming, he, in the meantime, decided to
turn his reputation for scholarship to account, and
accordingly let it be known that he would board and
suitably instruct a limited number of young men; in
other words, he fell back upon the time-honored custom of taking pupils. He secured a country house at
Ealing and soon had among his charges one Philip
Stanhope, a lad of eleven years, heir of the great Earl
of Chesterfield, who was so interested in the worldly
success of his illegitimate son, to whom his famous
letters were addressed, that he apparently gave himself little concern as to the character of instruction
that his lawful son received.

Dodd's pupils must have brought a substantial increase of his small income, which was also suddenly
augmented in another way. About the time he began
to take pupils, a lady to whom his wife had been a
sort of companion died and left her, quite unexpectedly, fifteen hundred pounds. Nor did her good
fortune end there. As she was attending an auction
one day, a cabinet was put up for sale, and Mrs. Dodd
bid upon it, until, observing a lady who seemed anxious to obtain it, she stopped bidding, and it became
the property of the lady, who in return gave her a lot-

tery ticket, which drew a prize of a thousand pounds for Mrs. Dodd.

With these windfalls at his disposal, Dodd embarked upon a speculation quite in keeping with his tastes and abilities. He secured a plot of ground not far from the royal palace, and built upon it a chapel of ease which he called Charlotte Chapel, in honor of the Queen. Four pews were set aside for the royal household, and he soon had a large and fashionable congregation. His sermons were in the same florid vein which had brought him popularity, and from this venture he was soon in receipt of at least six hundred pounds a year. With his increased income his style of living became riotous. He dined at expensive taverns, set up a coach, and kept a mistress, and even tried to force himself into the great literary club which numbered among its members some of the most distinguished men of the day; but this was not permitted.

For years Dodd led, not a double, but a triple life. He went through the motions of teaching his pupils. He preached, in his own chapels and elsewhere, sermons on popular subjects, and at the same time managed to live the life of a fashionable man about town. No one respected him, but he had a large following and he contrived every day to get deeper into debt.

It is a constant source of bewilderment to those of us who are obliged to pay our bills with decent regularity, how, in England, it seems to have been so easy to live on year after year, paying apparently nothing to anyone, and resenting the appearance of a bill-collector as an impertinence. When Goldsmith died, he owed a sum which caused Dr. Johnson to exclaim, "Was ever poet so trusted before?" and Goldsmith's debts were trifling in comparison with Dodd's. But, at the moment when matters were becoming really serious, a fashionable living — St. George's — fell vacant, and Dodd felt that if he could but secure it his troubles would be over.

The parish church of St. George's, Hanover Square, was one of the best known in London. It was in the centre of fashion, and then, as now, enjoyed almost a monopoly of smart weddings. Its rector had just been made a bishop. Dodd looked upon it with longing eyes. What a plum! It seemed beyond his reach, but nothing venture, nothing have. On investigation Dodd discovered that the living was worth fifteen hundred pounds a year and that it was in the gift of the Lord Chancellor. The old adage, "Give thy present to the clerk, not to the judge," must have come into his mind; for, not long after, the wife of the Chancellor received an anonymous letter offering three thousand pounds down and an annuity of five hundred a year if she would successfully use her influence with her husband to secure the living for a clergyman of distinction who should be named later. The lady very properly handed the letter to her husband, who at once set inquiries on foot. The matter was soon traced to Dodd, who promptly put the blame on his wife, saying that he had not been aware of the officious zeal of his consort.

The scandal became public, and Dodd thought it best to go abroad. His name was removed from the list of the King's chaplains. No care was taken to disguise references to him in the public prints. Libel laws in England seem to have been circumvented by the use of asterisks for letters: thus, Laurence Sterne would be referred to as "the Rev. L. S*****," coupled with some damaging statement; but in Dodd's case precaution of this sort was thought unnecessary. He was bitterly attacked and mercilessly ridiculed. Even Goldsmith takes a fling at him in "Retaliation," which appeared about this time. It remained, however, for Foote, the comedian, to hold him up to public scorn in one of his Haymarket farces, in which the parson and his wife were introduced as Dr. and Mrs. Simony. The satire was very coarse; but stomachs were strong in those good old days, and the whole town roared at the humor of the thing, which was admitted to be a great success.

On Dodd's return to London his fortunes were at a very low ebb indeed. A contemporary account says that, although almost overwhelmed with debt, his extravagance continued undiminished until, at last, "he descended so low as to become the editor of a newspaper." My editorial friends will note well the depth of his infamy.

After a time the scandal blew over, as scandal will when the public appetite has been appeased, and Dodd began to preach again: a sensational preacher will always have followers. Someone presented him to a small living in Buckinghamshire, from which he had a small addition to his income; but otherwise he was almost neglected.

At last he was obliged to sell his interest in his chapel venture, which he "unloaded," as we should say to-day, on a fellow divine by misstating its value as a going concern, so that the purchaser was ruined by his bargain. But he continued to preach with great pathos and effect, when suddenly the announcement was made that the great preacher, Dr. Dodd, the Macaroni Parson, had been arrested on a charge of forgery; that he was already in the Compter; that he had admitted his guilt, and that he would doubtless be hanged.

The details of the affair were soon public property. It appears that, at last overwhelmed with debt, Dodd had forged the name of his former pupil, now the Earl of Chesterfield, to a bond for forty-two hundred pounds. The bond had been negotiated and the money paid when the fraud was discovered. A warrant for his arrest was at once made out, and Dodd was taken before Justice Hawkins (Johnson's first biographer), who sat as a committing magistrate, and held him for formal trial at the Old Bailey. Meanwhile all but four hundred pounds of the money had been returned; for a time it seemed as if this small sum could be raised and the affair dropped. This certainly was Dodd's hope; but the law had been set in motion, and justice, rather than mercy, was allowed to take its course. The crime had been committed early in February. At the trial a few weeks later, the Earl of Chesterfield, disregarding Dodd's plea, appeared against him, and he was sentenced to death; but some legal point had been raised in his favor, and it was several months before the question was finally decided adversely to him.

Dodd was now in Newgate Prison. There he was indulged in every way, according to the good old custom of the time. He was plentifully supplied with money, and could secure whatever money would buy. Friends were admitted to see him at all hours, and he occupied what leisure he had with correspondence, and wrote a long poem, "Thoughts in Prison," in five parts. He also projected a play and several other literary ventures.

Meanwhile a mighty effort was set on foot to secure a pardon. Dr. Johnson was appealed to, and while he entertained no doubts as to the wisdom of capital punishment for fraud, forgery, or theft, the thought of a minister of the Church of England being publicly haled through the streets of London to Tyburn and being there hanged seemed horrible to him, and he promised to do his best. He was as good as his word. With his ready pen he wrote a number of letters and petitions which were conveyed to Dodd, and which, subsequently copied by him, were presented to the King, the Lord Chancellor, to any one, in fact, who might have influence and be ready to use it. He even went so far as to write a letter which, when transcribed by Mrs. Dodd, was presented to the Queen. One

4

To the King's &c

It is most humbly represented to your Majesty by William Dodd, the unhappy Convict now lying under Sentence of death.

That William Dodd acknowledging the justice of the Sentence denounced against him, has no hope or refuge but in your Majesty's clemency:

That, though to recollect or mention the usefulness of his former life, or the efficacy of his ministry, must overwhelm him in his present condition with shame and sorrow, he yet humbly hopes that his past labours will not wholly be forgotten, and that the zeal with which he has exhorted others to a good life, though it does not extenuate his crime, may mitigate his punishment.

That debased as he is by ignominy, and distressed as he is by poverty, scorned by the world and detested by himself, deprived of all external comforts, and afflicted by the consciousness of guilt, he can derive no hope from earthly life, but that of

FACSIMILE OF THE FIRST PAGE OF DR. JOHNSON'S PETITION TO THE KING
ON BEHALF OF DR. DODD

petition, drawn by Johnson, was signed by twenty-three thousand people; but the King — under the influence of Lord Mansfield, it is said — declined to interest himself.

And this brings me to a point where I must explain my peculiar interest in this thoroughgoing scoundrel. I happen to own a volume of manuscript letters written by Dodd, from Newgate Prison, to a man named Edmund Allen; and as not every reader of Boswell can be expected to remember who Edmund Allen was, I may say that he was Dr. Johnson's neighbor and landlord in Bolt Court, a printer by trade and an intimate friend of the Doctor. It was Allen who gave the dinner to Johnson and Boswell which caused the old man to remark, "Sir, we could not have had a better dinner had there been a Synod of Cooks." The Dodd letters to Allen, however, are only a part of the contents of the volume. It contains also a great number of Johnson's letters to Dodd, and the original drafts of the petitions which he drew up in his efforts to secure mitigation of Dodd's punishment. The whole collection came into my possession many years ago, and has afforded me a subject of investigation on many a winter's evening when I might otherwise have occupied myself with solitaire, did I happen to know one card from another.

Allen appears to have been an acquaintance of Dodd's, and, I judge from the letters before me, called on Johnson with a letter from a certain Lady Harrington, who for some reason which does not appear, was greatly interested in Dodd's fate. Boswell records that Johnson was much agitated at the interview, walking up and down his chamber saying, "I will do what I can." Dodd was personally unknown to Johnson and had only once been in his presence; and while an elaborate correspondence was being carried on between them, Johnson declined to go to see the prisoner, and for some reason wished that his name should not be drawn into the affair; but he did not relax his efforts. Allen was the go-between in all that passed between the two men. In the volume before me, in all of Dodd's letters to Allen, Johnson's name has been carefully blotted out, and Johnson's letters intended for Dodd are not addressed to him, but bear the inscription, "This may be communicated to Dr. Dodd." Dodd's letters to Johnson were delivered to him by Allen and were probably destroyed, Allen having first made the copies which are now in my possession. Most of Dodd's letters to Allen appear to have been preserved, and Johnson's letters to Dodd, together with the drafts of his petitions, were carefully preserved by Allen, Dodd being supplied with unsigned copies. Allen in this way carried out Johnson's instructions to "tell nobody."

Dodd's letters seem for the most part to have been written at night. The correspondence began early in May, and his last letter was dated June 26, a few hours before he died. None of Dodd's letters seem to have been published, and Johnson's, although of supreme interest, do not appear to have been known

in their entirety either to Hawkins, Boswell, or Boswell's greatest editor, Birkbeck Hill. The petitions, so far as they have been published, seem to have been printed from imperfect copies of the original drafts. Boswell relates that Johnson had told him he had written a petition from the City of London, but they *mended* it. In the original draft there are a few *repairs*, but they are in Dr. Johnson's own hand. The petition to the King evidently did not require mending, as the published copies are almost identical with the original.

In the petition which he wrote for Mrs. Dodd to copy and present to the Queen, Johnson, not knowing all the facts, left blank spaces in the original draft for Mrs. Dodd to fill when making her copy; thus the original draft reads: —

To the Queen's Most Excellent Majesty

MADAM: —

It is most humbly represented by —— Dodd, the Wife of Dr. William Dodd, now lying in prison under Sentence of death.

That she has been the Wife of this unhappy Man for more than — years, and has lived with him in the greatest happiness of conjugal union, and the highest state of conjugal confidence.

That she has been therefore for — years a constant Witness of his unwearied endeavors for publick good and his laborious attendance on charitable institutions. Many are the Families whom his care has relieved from want; many are the hearts which he has freed from pain, and the Faces which he has cleared from sorrow.

That therefore she most humbly throws herself at the feet of the Queen, earnestly entreating that the petition of a distressed Wife asking mercy for a husband may be considered as naturally exciting the compassion of her Majesty, and that when her Wisdom has compared the offender's good actions with his crime, she will be graciously pleased to represent his case in such terms to our most gracious Sovereign, as may dispose him to mitigate the rigours of the law.

The case of the unfortunate Dr. Dodd was by now the talk of the town. If agitation and discussion and letters and positions could have saved him, saved he would have been, for all London was in an uproar, and efforts of every kind on his behalf were set in motion. He can hardly have been blamed for feeling sure that they would never hang him. Johnson was not so certain, and warned him against over-confidence.

Rather curiously, merchants, "city people," who, one might suppose, would be inclined to regard the crime of forgery with severity, were disposed to think that Dodd's sufferings in Newgate were sufficient punishment for any crime he had committed. After all, it was said, the money, most of it, had been returned; so they signed a monster petition; twenty-three thousand names were secured without difficulty. But the West End was rather indifferent, and Dr. Johnson finally came to the conclusion that, while no effort should be relaxed (in a letter to Mr. Allen he says, "Nothing can do harm, let everything be tried"), it was time for Dodd to prepare himself for his fate. He thereupon wrote the following letter, which we may suppose Allen either transcribed or read to the unfortunate prisoner: —

SIR: —

You know that my attention to Dr. Dodd has incited me to enquire what is the real purpose of Government; the dreadful answer I have put into your hands.

Nothing now remains but that he whose profession it has been to teach others to dye, learn how to dye himself.

It will be wise to deny admission from this time to all who do not come to assist his preparation, to addict himself wholly to prayer and meditation, and consider himself as no longer connected with the world. He has now nothing to do for the short time that remains, but to reconcile himself to God. To this end it will be proper to abstain totally from all strong liquors, and from all other sensual indulgences, that his thoughts may be as clear and calm as his condition can allow.

If his Remissions of anguish, and intervals of Devotion leave him any time, he may perhaps spend it profitably in writing the history of his own depravation, and marking the gradual declination from innocence and quiet to that state in which the law has found him. Of his advice to the Clergy, or admonitions to Fathers of families, there is no need; he will leave behind him those who can write them. But the history of his own mind, if not written by himself, cannot be written, and the instruction that might be derived from it must be lost. This therefore he must leave if he leaves anything; but whether he can find leisure, or obtain tranquillity sufficient for this, I cannot judge. Let him however shut his doors against all hope, all trifles and all sensuality. Let him endeavor to calm his thoughts by abstinence, and look out for a proper director in his penitence, and May God, who would that all men shall be saved, help him with his Holy Spirit, and have mercy on him for Jesus Christ's Sake.

I am, Sir,

Your most humble Servant,

SAM JOHNSON.

June 17, 1777.

Then, in response to a piteous appeal, Johnson wrote a brief letter for Dodd to send to the King, begging him at least to save him from the horror and ignominy of a public execution; and this was accompanied by a brief note.

SIR: —

I most seriously enjoin you not to let it be at all known that I have written this letter, and to return the copy to Mr. Allen in a cover to me. I hope I need not tell you that I wish it success, but I do not indulge hope.

SAM JOHNSON.

As the time for Dodd's execution drew near, he wrote a final letter to Johnson, which, on its delivery, must have moved the old man to tears. It was written at midnight on the 25th of June, 1777.

Accept, thou great and good heart, my earnest and fervent thanks and prayers for all thy benevolent and kind efforts in my behalf. Oh! Dr. Johnson! as I sought your knowledge at an early hour in life, would to heaven I had cultivated the love and acquaintance of so excellent a man! I pray God most sincerely to bless you with the highest transports — the infelt satisfaction of humane and benevolent exertions! And admitted, as I trust I shall be, to the realms of bliss before you, I shall hail your arrival there with transports, and rejoice to acknowledge that you were my Comforter, my Advocate and my Friend! God be ever with you!

June 25, Midnight.

Accept, thou great and good Heart, my earnest and fervent Thanks and Prayers for all thy benevolent and kind Efforts on my Behalf. — Oh! Dr Johnson, as I sought your Knowledge at an early Hour in Life, would to Heaven I had cultivated the Love and Acquaintance of so excellent a Man! — I pray, God most sincerely to bless You with the highest Transports, — the infelt Satisfaction of humane and benevolent Exertions! — and admitted, as I trust I shall be, to the Realms of Bliss before You, I shall hail your Arrival there with Transport and rejoyce to acknowledge that You was my Comforter, my Advocate, and my Friend.

God be ever with You!

For Dr Johnson.

To Mr Allen.

Add, Dear Sir, to the many other Favours conferred on Your unfortunate Friend, that of delivering my dying Thanks to the worthiest of Men.

W. D.

12 o'Clock, Wednesday Night

MR. ALLEN'S COPY OF THE LAST LETTER DR. DODD SENT DR. JOHNSON. DODD WAS HANGED ON JUNE 27, 1777

The original letter in Dodd's handwriting was kept by Johnson, who subsequently showed it to Boswell, together with a copy of his reply which Boswell calls "solemn and soothing," giving it at length in the "Life." My copy is in Allen's hand, but there is a note to Allen in Dodd's hand which accompanied the original, reading: "Add, dear sir, to the many other favors conferred on your unfortunate friend that of delivering my dying thanks to the worthiest of men. W. D."

Two other things Johnson did: he wrote a sermon, which Dodd delivered with telling effect to his fellow convicts, and he prepared with scrupulous care what has been called Dr. Dodd's last solemn declaration. It was without doubt intended to be read by Dodd at the place of execution, but unforeseen circumstances prevented. Various versions have been printed in part. The original in Johnson's hand is before me and reads: —

To the words of dying Men regard has always been paid. I am brought hither to suffer death for an act of Fraud of which I confess myself guilty, with shame such as my former state of life naturally produces; and I hope with such sorrow as The Eternal Son, he to whom the Heart is known, will not disregard. I repent that I have violated the laws by which peace and confidence are established among men; I repent that I have attempted to injure my fellow creatures, and I repent that I have brought disgrace upon my order, and discredit upon Religion. For this the law has sentenced me to die. But my offences against God are without name or number, and can admit only of general confession and general repentance. Grant,

Almighty God, for the Sake of Jesus Christ, that my repentance however late, however imperfect, may not be in vain.

The little good that now remains in my power, is to warn others against those temptations by which I have been seduced. I have always sinned against conviction; my principles have never been shaken; I have always considered the Christian religion, as a revelation from God, and its Divine Author, as the Saviour of the world; but the law of God, though never disowned by me, has often been forgotten. I was led astray from religious strictness by the Vanity of Show and the delight of voluptuousness. Vanity and pleasure required expense disproportionate to my income. Expense brought distress upon me, and distress impelled me to fraud.

For this fraud, I am to die; and I die declaring that however I have offended in practice, deviated from my own precepts, I have taught others to the best of my knowledge the true way to eternal happiness. My life has been hypocritical, but my ministry has been sincere. I always believed and I now leave the world declaring my conviction. that there is no other name under heaven by which we can be saved, but only the name of the Lord Jesus, and I entreat all that are here, to join with me, in my last petition that for the Sake of Christ Jesus my sins may be forgiven.

Anything more gruesome and demoralizing than an eighteenth-century hanging it would be impossible to imagine. We know from contemporary accounts of Dodd's execution that it differed only in detail from other hangings, which were at the time a common occurrence. His last night on earth was made hideous by the ringing of bells. Under the window of his cell a small bell was rung at frequent intervals by the watch, and he was reminded that he was soon to die, and that the time for repentance was short. At daybreak the great bell of St. Sepulchre's Church just over the way began to toll, as was customary whenever prisoners in Newgate were being rounded up for execution.

"Hanging Days" were usually holidays. Crowds collected in the streets, and as the day wore on, they became mobs of drunken men, infuriated or delighted at the proceedings, according to their interest in the prisoners. At nine o'clock the Felon's Gate was swung open and the prisoners were brought out. On this occasion, there were only two; frequently there were more — once indeed as many as fifteen persons were hanged on the same day. This was counted a great event.

Dodd was spared the ignominy of the open cart in which the ordinary criminal was taken to the gallows, and a mourning coach drawn by four horses was provided for him by some of his friends. This was followed by a hearse with an open coffin. The streets were thronged. After the usual delays the procession started, but stopped again at St. Sepulchre's, that he might receive a nosegay which was presented him, someone having bequeathed a fund to the church so that this melancholy custom could be carried out. Farther on, at Holborn Bar, it was usual for the cortège to stop, that the condemned man might be regaled with a mug of ale.

Ordinarily the route from Newgate to Tyburn was

very direct, through and along the Tyburn Road, now Oxford Street; but on this occasion it had been announced that the procession would follow a roundabout course through Pall Mall. Thus the pressure of the crowd would be lessened and everyone would have an opportunity of catching a glimpse of the unfortunate man; and everyone did. The streets were thronged, stands were erected and places sold, windows along the line of march were let at fabulous prices. In Hyde Park soldiers — two thousand of them — were under arms to prevent a rescue. The authorities were somewhat alarmed at the interest shown, and it was thought best to be on the safe side; the law was not to be denied.

Owing to the crowds, the confusion, and the out-of-the-way course selected, it was almost noon when the procession reached Tyburn. We do not often think, as we whirl in our taxis along Oxford Street in the vicinity of Marble Arch, that this present centre of wealth and fashion was once Tyburn. There is nothing now to suggest that it was, a century or two ago, an unlovely and little-frequented outskirt of the great city, given over to "gallows parties."

At Tyburn the crowd was very dense and impatient: it had been waiting for hours and rain had been falling intermittently. As the coach came in sight, the crowd pressed nearer; Dodd could be seen through the window. The poor man was trying to pray. More dead than alive, he was led to the cart, on which he was to stand while a rope was placed about his neck. There was a heavy downpour of rain, so there was no time for the farewell address which Dr. Johnson had so carefully prepared. A sudden gust of wind blew off the poor man's hat, taking his wig with it: it was retrieved, and someone clapped it on his head backwards. The crowd was delighted; this was a hanging worth waiting for. Another moment, and Dr. Dodd was swung into eternity.

Let it be said that there were some who had their doubts as to the wisdom of such exhibitions. Might not such frequent and public executions have a bad effect upon public taste and morals? "Why no, sir," said Dr. Johnson; "executions are intended to draw spectators. If they do not draw spectators they do not answer their purpose. The old method is satisfactory to all parties. The public is gratified by a procession, the criminal is supported by it." And his biographer, Hawkins, remarks complacently: "We live in an age in which humanity is the fashion."

"And so they have hanged Dodd for forgery, have they?" casually remarked the Bishop of Bristol, from the depths of his easy-chair. "I'm sorry to hear it."

"How so, my Lord?"

"Because they have hanged him for the least of his crimes."

XII

OSCAR WILDE

MY interest in Oscar Wilde is a very old story: I went to hear him lecture when I was a boy, and, boy-like, I wrote and asked him for his autograph, which he sent me and which I still have.

It seems strange that I can look back through thirty years to his visit to Philadelphia, and in imagination see him on the platform of old Horticultural Hall. I remember, too, the discussion which his visit occasioned, preceded as it was by the publication in Boston of his volume of poems, the English edition having been received with greater cordiality than usually marks a young poet's first production — for such it practically was.

At the time of his appearance on the lecture platform he was a large, well-built, distinguished-looking man, about twenty-six years old, with rather long hair, generally wearing knee-breeches and silk stockings. Any impressions which I may have received of this lecture are now very vague. I remember that he used the word "renaissance" a good deal, and that at the time it was a new word to me; and it has always since been a word which has rattled round in my head very much as the blessed word "Mesopotamia" did in the mind of the old lady, who

CARICATURE OF OSCAR WILDE

From an original drawing by Aubrey Beardsley

remarked that no one should deprive her of the hope of eternal punishment.

Now, it would be well at the outset, in discussing Oscar Wilde, to abandon immediately all hope of eternal punishment — for others. My subject is a somewhat difficult one, and it is not easy to speak of Wilde without overturning some of the more or less fixed traditions we have grown up with. We all have a lot of axioms in our systems, even if we are discreet enough to keep them from our tongues; and to do Wilde justice, it is necessary for us to free ourselves of some of these. To make my meaning clear, take the accepted one that genius is simply the capacity for hard work. This is all very well at the top of a copy-book, or to repeat to your son when you are didactically inclined; but for the purposes of this discussion, this and others like it should be abandoned. Having cleared our minds of cant, we might also frankly admit that a romantic or sinful life is, generally speaking, more interesting than a good one.

Few men in English literature have lived a nobler, purer life than Robert Southey, and yet his very name sets us a-yawning, and if he lives at all it is solely due to his little pot-boiler, become a classic, the "Life of Nelson." The two great events in Nelson's life were his meeting with Lady Emma Hamilton and his meeting with the French. Now, disguise it as we may, it still remains true that, in thinking of Nelson, we think as much of Lady Emma as we do of Trafalgar. Of course, in saying this I realize that I am not an Englishman making a public address on the anniversary of the great battle.

Southey's life gives the lie to that solemn remark about genius being simply a capacity for hard work: if it were so, he would have ranked high; he worked incessantly, produced his to-day neglected poems, supported his family and contributed toward the support of the families of his friends. He was a good man, and worked himself to death; but he was not a genius.

On the other hand, Wilde was; but his life was not good, it was not pure; he did injury to his friends; and to his wife and children, the greatest wrong a man could do them, so that she died of a broken heart, and his sons live under an assumed name; yet, notwithstanding all this, perhaps to some extent by reason of it, he is a most interesting personality, and no doubt his future place in literature will be to some extent influenced by the fate which struck him down just at the moment of his greatest success.

Remembering Dr. Johnson's remark that in lapidary work a man is not upon oath, it has always seemed to me that something like the epitaph he wrote for Goldsmith's monument in Westminster Abbey might with equal justice have been carved upon Wilde's obscure tombstone in a neglected corner of Bagneux Cemetery in Paris. The inscription I refer to translates: "He left scarcely any style of writing untouched and touched nothing that he did not adorn."

I am too good a Goldsmithian to compare Goldsmith, with all his faults and follies, to Wilde, with his faults and follies, and vices superadded; but Wilde wrote "Dorian Gray," a novel original and powerful in conception, as powerful as "Dr. Jekyll and Mr. Hyde"; and remembering that Wilde was also an essayist, a poet, and a dramatist, I think we may fairly say that he too touched nothing that he did not adorn.

But, to begin at the beginning. Wilde was not especially fortunate in his parents. His father was a surgeon-oculist of Dublin, and was knighted by the Lord Lieutenant of Ireland — just why, does not appear, nor is it important; his son always seemed a little ashamed of the incident. His mother was the daughter of a clergyman of the Church of England. She was "advanced" for her time, wrote prose and verse, under the *nom de plume* of "Speranza," which were published frequently in a magazine, which was finally suppressed for sedition. If Lady Wilde was emancipated in thought, of her lord it may be said that he put no restraint whatever upon his acts. They were a brilliant, but what we would call to-day a Bohemian, couple. I have formed an impression that the father, in spite of certain weaknesses of character, was a man of solid attainments, while of the mother someone has said that she reminded him of a tragedy queen at a suburban theatre. This is awful.

Oscar Wilde was a second son, born in Dublin, on the 16th of October, 1854. He went to a school at

Enniskillen, afterwards to Trinity College, Dublin, and finally to Magdalen College, Oxford. He had already begun to make a name for himself at Trinity, where he won a gold medal for an essay on the Greek comic poets; but when, in June, 1878, he received the Newdigate Prize for English verse for a poem, "Ravenna," which was recited at the Sheldonian Theatre at Oxford, it can fairly be said that he had achieved distinction.

While at Magdalen, Wilde is said to have fallen under the influence of Ruskin, and spent some time in breaking stones on the highways, upon which operation Ruskin was experimenting. It may be admitted that the work for its own sake never attracted Wilde: it was the reward which followed — breakfast-parties, with informal and unlimited talk, in Ruskin's rooms.

One does not have to read much of Wilde to discover that he had as great an aversion to games, which kept him in the open, as to physical labor. Bernard Shaw, that other Irish enigma, who in many ways of thought and speech resembles Wilde, when asked what his recreations were, replied, "Anything except sport." Wilde said that he would not play cricket because of the indecent postures it demanded; fox-hunting — his phrase will be remembered — was "the unspeakable after the uneatable." But he was the leader, if not the founder, of the æsthetic cult, the symbols of which were peacock-feathers, sunflowers, lilies, and blue china. His rooms, perhaps the most talked about in Oxford, were beautifully paneled in oak, decorated with porcelain supposed to be very valuable, and hung with old engravings. From the windows there was a lovely view of the River Cherwell and the beautiful grounds of Magdalen College.

He soon made himself the most talked-of person in the place: abusing his foes, who feared his tongue. His friends, as he later said of someone, did not care for him very much — no one cares to furnish material for incessant persiflage.

When he left Oxford Oscar Wilde was already a well-known figure: his sayings were passed from mouth to mouth, and he was a favorite subject for caricature in the pages of "Punch." Finally, he became known to all the world as Bunthorne in Gilbert and Sullivan's opera, "Patience." From being the most talked-of man in Oxford, he became the most talked-of man in London — a very different thing: many a reputation has been lost on the road between Oxford and London. His reputation, stimulated by long hair and velveteen knee-breeches, gave Whistler a chance to say, "Our Oscar is knee plush ultra." People compared him with Disraeli. When he first became the talk of the town, great things were expected of him; just what, no one presumed to say. To keep in the going while the going was good, Wilde published his volume of Poems (1881); it followed that everyone wanted to know what this singular young man had to say for himself, and paid half a

"OUR OSCAR" AS HE WAS WHEN
WE LOANED HIM TO AMERICA

From a contemporary English caricature

guinea to find out. The volume immediately went through several editions, and, as I have mentioned, was reprinted in this country.

Of these poems the "Saturday Review" said, — and I thank the "Saturday Review" for teaching me these words, for I think they fitly describe nine tenths of all the poetry that gets itself published, — "Mr. Wilde's verses belong to a class which is the special terror of the reviewers, the poetry which is neither good nor bad, which calls for neither praise nor blame, and in which one searches in vain for any personal touch of thought or music."

It was at this point in his career that Wilde determined to show himself to us: he came to America to lecture; was, of course, interviewed on his arrival in New York, and spoke with the utmost disrespect of the Atlantic.

Considering how little ballast Wilde carried, his lectures here were a great success: "Nothing succeeds like excess." He spoke publicly over two hundred times, and made what was, for him, a lot of money. Looking back, it seems a daring thing to do; but Wilde was always doing daring things. To lecture in New York, Philadelphia, and Boston was all very well; but it would seem to have required courage for Wilde, fresh from Oxford, his reputation based on impudence, long hair, knee-breeches, a volume of poems, and some pronounced opinions on art, to take himself, seriously, west to Omaha and Denver, and north as far as Halifax. However, he went and returned alive, with at least one story which will never die. It was Wilde who said that he had seen in a dance-hall in a mining-camp the sign, "Don't shoot the pianist; he is doing his best." The success of this story was instant, and probably prompted him to invent the other one, that he had heard of a man in Denver who, turning his back to examine some lithographs, had been shot through the head, which gave Wilde the chance of observing how dangerous it is to interest one's self in bad art. He remarked also that Niagara Falls would have been more wonderful if the water had run the other way.

On his return to England he at once engaged attention by his remark, "There is nothing new in America — except the language." Of him, it was observed that Delmonico had spoiled his figure. From London he went almost immediately to Paris, where he found sufficient reasons for cutting his hair and abandoning his pronounced habiliments. Thus he arrived, as he said of himself, at the end of his second period.

Wilde spoke French fluently and took steps to make himself at home in Paris; with what success, is not entirely clear. He made the acquaintance of distinguished people, wrote verses, and devoted a good deal of time to writing a play for Mary Anderson, "The Duchess of Padua," which was declined by her and was subsequently produced in this country by Lawrence Barrett and Mimma Gale. In spite of their efforts, it lived for but a few nights.

Meanwhile it cost money to live in Paris, especially to dine at fashionable cafés, and Wilde decided to return to London; but making ends meet is no easier there than elsewhere. He wrote a little, lectured when he could, and having spent the small inheritance he had received from his father, it seemed that "Exit Oscar" might fairly be written against him.

But to the gratification of some, and the surprise of all, just about this time came the announcement of his marriage to a beautiful and charming lady of some fortune, Constance Lloyd, the daughter of a deceased barrister. Whistler sent a characteristic wire to the church: "May not be able to reach you in time for ceremony; don't wait." Indeed, it may here be admitted that in an encounter between these wits it was Jimmie Whistler who usually scored.

Of Whistler as an artist I know nothing. My friends the Pennells, at the close of their excellent biography, say, "His name and fame will live forever." This is a large order, but of Whistler, with his rapier-like wit, it behooved all to beware. In a weak moment Wilde once voiced his appreciation of a good thing of Whistler's with, "I wish I had said that." Quick as a flash, Jimmie's sword was through him, and forever: "Never mind, Oscar, you will." It may be that the Pennells are right.

But to return. With Mrs. Wilde's funds, her husband's taste, and Whistler's suggestions, a house was furnished and decorated in Tite Street, Chelsea, and for a time all went well. But it soon became evident that some fixed income, certain, however small, was essential; fugitive verse and unsigned articles in magazines afford small resource for an increasing family. Two sons were born, and, driven by the spur of necessity, Wilde became the Editor of "The Woman's World," and for a time worked as faithfully and diligently as his temperament permitted; but it was the old story of Pegasus harnessed to the plough.

Except for editorial work, the next few years were unproductive. "Dorian Gray," Wilde's one novel, appeared in the summer of 1890. It is exceedingly difficult to place: his claim that it was the work of a few days, written to demonstrate to some friends his ability to write a novel, may be dismissed as untrue — there is internal evidence to the contrary. It was probably written slowly, as most of his work was. In its first form it appeared in "Lippincott's Magazine" for July, 1890; but it was subjected to careful revision for publication in book form. Wilde always claimed that he had no desire to be a popular novelist — "It is far too easy," he said.

"Dorian Gray" is an interesting and powerful, but artificial, production, leaving a bitter taste, as of aloes in the mouth: one feels as if one had been handling a poison. The law compels certain care in the use of explosives, and poisons, it is agreed, are best kept in packages of definite shape and color, that they may by their external appearance challenge the attention of the thoughtless. Only Roosevelt can tell without looking what book should and what should not bear the governmental stamp, "Guaranteed to be pure and wholesome under the food and drugs act." Few, I think, would put this label on "Dorian Gray." Wilde's own criticism was that the book was inartistic because it has a moral. It has, but it is likely to be overlooked in its general nastiness. In "Dorian Gray" he betrays for the first and perhaps the only time the decadence which was subsequently to be the cause of his undoing.

I have great admiration for what is called, and frequently ridiculed as, the artistic temperament, but I am a believer also in the sanity of true genius, especially when it is united, as it was in the case of Charles Lamb, with a fine, manly, honest bearing toward the world and the things in it; but alone it may lead us to yearn with Wilde

> To drift with every passion till my soul
> Is a stringed lute on which all winds can play.

It has been suggested on good authority that it is very unpleasant to wear one's heart upon one's sleeve. To expose one's soul to the elements, however interesting in theory, must be very painful in practice: Wilde was destined to find it so.

Why the story escaped success at the hands of the adapter for the stage, I never could understand. The clever talk of the characters in the novel should be much more acceptable in the quick give-and-take of a society play than it is in a narrative of several hundred pages; moreover, it abounds in situations which are intensely dramatic, leading up to an overwhelming climax; probably it was badly done.

It is with a feeling of relief that one turns from "Dorian Gray" — which, let us agree, is a book which a young girl would hesitate to put in the hands of her mother — to Wilde's other prose work, so different in character. Of his shorter stories, his fairy tales and the rest, it would be a delight to speak: many of them are exquisite, and all as pure and delicate as a flower, with as sweet a perfume. They do not know Oscar Wilde who have not read "The Young King and the Star Child," and the "Happy Prince." That they are the work of the same brain that produced "Dorian Gray" is almost beyond belief.

What a baffling personality was Wilde's! Here is a man who has really done more than William Morris to make our homes artistic, and who is at one with Ruskin in his effort that our lives should be beautiful; he had a message to deliver, yet, by reason of his flippancy and his love of paradox, he is not yet rated at his real worth. It is difficult for one who is first of all a wit to make a serious impression on his listeners. I think it is Gilbert who says, "Let a professed wit say, 'pass the mustard,' and the table roars."

Wilde was a careful and painstaking workman, serious as an artist, whatever he may have been as a man; and in the end he became a great master of English prose, working in words as an artist does in color, trying first one and then another until he had secured the desired effect, the effect of silk which

Seccombe speaks of. But he affected idleness. A story is told of his spending a week-end at a country house. Pleading the necessity of working while the humor was on, he begged to be excused from joining the other guests. In the evening at dinner his hostess asked him what he had accomplished, and his reply is famous. "This morning," he said, "I put a comma in one of my poems." Surprised and amused, the lady inquired whether the afternoon's work had been equally exhausting. "Yes," said Wilde, passing his hand wearily over his brow, "this afternoon I took it out again."

Just about the time that London had made up its mind that Wilde was nothing but a clever man about town, welcome as a guest because of the amusement he afforded, "The Soul of Man Under Socialism" appeared in the "Fortnightly Magazine" for February, 1891. London was at once challenged and amazed. This essay opens with a characteristic statement, one of those peculiarly inverted paradoxes for which Wilde was shortly to become famous. "Socialism," he says, "would relieve us from the sordid necessity of living for others"; and what follows is Wilde at his very best.

What is it all about? I am not sure that I know: it seems to be a plea for the individual, perhaps it is a defense of the poor; it is said to have been translated into the languages of the downtrodden, the Jew, the Pole, the Russian, and to be a comfort to them; I hope it is. Do such outpourings do any good, do they change conditions, is the millennium brought nearer thereby? I hope so. But if it is comforting for the downtrodden, whose wants are ill supplied, it is a sheer delight for the downtreader who, free from anxiety, sits in his easy-chair and enjoys its technical excellence.

I know nothing like it: it is as fresh as paint, and like fresh paint it sticks to one; in its brilliant, serious, and unexpected array of fancies and theories, in truths inverted and distorted, in witticisms which are in turn tender and hard as flint, one is delighted and bewildered. Wilde has only himself to blame if this, a serious and beautiful essay, was not taken seriously. "The Soul of Man Under Socialism" is the work of a consummate artist who, taking his ideas, disguises and distorts them, polishing them the while until they shine like jewels in a rare and unusual setting. Naturally, almost every other line in such a work is quotable: it seems to be a mass of quotations which one is surprised not to have heard before.

Interesting as Wilde's other essays are, I will not speak of them; with the exception of "Pen, Pencil and Poison," a study of Thomas Griffiths Wainewright, the poisoner, they will inevitably be forgotten.

Of Wilde's poems I am not competent to speak: they are full of Arcady and Eros; nor am I of those who believe that "every poet is the spokesman of God." A book-agent once called on Abraham Lincoln and sought to sell him a book for which the President had no use. Failing, he asked Lincoln if he would not

write an indorsement of the work which would enable
him to sell it to others. Whereupon the President,
always anxious to oblige, with a humor entirely his
own, wrote, "Any one who likes this kind of book will
find it just the kind of book they like." So it is with
Wilde's poetry: by many it is highly esteemed, but
I am inclined to regard it as a part of his "literary
wild oats."

After several attempts in the field of serious
drama, in which he was unsuccessful, by a fortunate
chance he turned his attention to the lighter forms of
comedy, in which he was destined to count only the
greatest as his rivals. Pater says these comedies have
been unexcelled since Sheridan; this is high praise,
though not too high; but it is rather to contrast than
to compare such a grand old comedy as the "School
for Scandal" with, say, "The Importance of Being
Earnest." They are both brilliant, both artificial;
they both reflect in some manner the life and the atmosphere of their time; but the mirror which Sheridan holds up to nature is of steel and the picture is
hard and cold; Wilde, on the other hand, uses an ex-
aggerating glass, which seems specially designed to
reflect warmth and fluffiness.

Wilde was the first to produce a play which depends almost entirely for its success on brilliant talk.
In this field Shaw is now conspicuous: he can grow
the flower now because he has the seed. It was Wilde
who taught him how, Wilde who, in four light comedies, gave the English stage something it had been

without for a century. His comedies are irresistibly clever, sparkle with wit, with a flippant and insolent levity, and withal have a theatrical dexterity which Shaw's are almost entirely without. While greatly inferior in construction to Pinero's, they are as brilliantly written; the plots amount to almost nothing: talk, not the play, is the thing; and but for their author's eclipse they would be as constantly on the boards to-day in this country and in England as they are at present on the Continent.

The first comedy, "Lady Windermere's Fan," was produced at the St. James's, February 22, 1892. Its success, despite the critics, was instant: full of saucy repartee, overwrought with epigrams of the peculiar kind conspicuous in the "Soul of Man," it delighted the audience. "Punch" made a feeble pun about Wilde's play being tame, forgetting the famous dictum that the great end of a comedy is to make the audience merry; and this end Wilde had attained, and he kept his audiences in the same humor for several years — until the end. Of his plays this is, perhaps, the best known in this country. It was successfully given in New York, Philadelphia, and elsewhere, only a year or two ago. It might, I think, be called his "pleasant play": for a time it looks as if a pure wife were going astray, but the audience is not kept long in suspense: the plot can be neglected and the lines enjoyed, with the satisfactory feeling that it will all come out right in the end.

"A Woman of No Importance" is in my judgment

the least excellent of his four comedies; it might be
called his "unpleasant" play: it is two acts of sheer
talk, in Wilde's usual vein, and two acts of acting.
The plot is, as usual, insignificant. A certain lazy
villain in high official position meets a young fellow
and offers him a post as his secretary. The boy, much
pleased, introduces his mother, and the villain dis-
covers that the boy is his own son. The son insists
that the father should marry his mother, but she
declines. The father offers to make what amends he
can, loses his temper, and refers to the lady as a
woman of no importance; for which he gets his face
well smacked. The son marries a rich American Puri-
tan. This enables Wilde to be very witty at the expense of American fathers, mothers, and daughters.
Tree played the villain very well, it is said.

Never having seen Wilde's next play acted, I once
innocently framed this statement for the domestic
circle: "I have never seen 'An Ideal Husband'"; and
when my wife sententiously replied that she had never
seen one either, I became careful to be more explicit
in future statements. No less clever than the others,
it has plot and action, and is interesting to the end.
Of all his plays it is the most dramatic. On its
first production it was provided with a splendid cast,
including Lewis Waller, Charles Hawtrey, Julia
Neilson, Maude Millett, and Fanny Brough. In the
earlier plays all the characters talked Oscar Wilde; in
this Wilde took the trouble, for it must have been to
him a trouble, to conceal himself and let his people

speak for themselves: they stay in their own characters in what they do as well as in what they say. "An Ideal Husband" was produced at the Haymarket early in 1895, and a few weeks later, at the St. James's, "The Importance of Being Earnest."

Wilde called this a trivial comedy for serious people. It is clever beyond criticism; but, as one critic says, one might as well sit down and gravely discuss the true inwardness of a soufflé. In it Wilde fairly lets himself loose; such talk there never was before; it fairly bristles with epigram; the plot is a farce; it is a mental and verbal extravaganza. Wilde was at his best, scintillating as he had never done before, and doing it for the last time. He is reported to have said that the first act is ingenious, the second beautiful, and the third abominably clever. Ingenious it is, but its beauty and cleverness are beyond praise. To have seen the lovely Miss Millard as Cecily, the country girl, to have heard her tell Gwendolen, the London society queen (Irene Vanbrugh), that "flowers are as common in the country as people are in London," is a delight never to be forgotten.

Wilde was now at the height of his fame. That the licenser of the stage had forbidden the performance of "Salome" was a disappointment; but Sarah Bernhardt had promised to produce it in Paris, and, not thinking that when his troubles came upon him she would break her word, he was able to overcome his chagrin.

Only a year or two before, he had been in need, if

not in abject poverty. He was now in receipt of large royalties. No form of literary effort makes money faster than a successful play. Wilde had two, running at the best theatres. His name was on every lip in London; even the cabbies knew him by sight; he had arrived at last, but his stay was only for a moment. Against the advice and wishes of his friends, with "fatal insolence," he adopted a course which, had he been capable of thought, he must have seen would inevitably lead to his destruction.

To those mental scavengers, the psychologists, I leave the determination of the exact nature of the disease which was the cause of Wilde's downfall: it is enough for me to know that whom the gods would destroy they first make mad.

The next two years Wilde spent in solitary and degrading seclusion; his sufferings, mental and physical, can be imagined. Many have fallen from heights greater than his, but none to depths more humiliating. Many noble men and dainty women have been subjected to greater indignities than he, but they have been supported by their belief in the justice or honor of the cause for which they suffered.

Wilde was not, however, sustained by the consciousness of innocence, nor was he so mentally dwarfed as to be unable to realize the awfulness of his fate. The literary result was "De Profundis." Written while in prison, in the form of a letter to his friend Robert Ross, it was not published until five years after his death: indeed, only about one third of the whole has as yet appeared in English.

"De Profundis" may be in parts offensive, but as a specimen of English prose it is magnificent; it is by way of becoming a classic: no student of literature can neglect this cry of a soul lost to this world, intent upon proving — I know not what — that art is greater than life, perhaps. Much has been written in regard to it: by some it is said to show that even at the time of his deepest degradation he did not appreciate how low he had fallen; that to the last he was only a *poseur* — a phrase-maker; that, genuine as his sorrow was, he nevertheless was playing with it, and was simply indulging himself in rhetoric when he said, "I, once a lord of language, have no words in which to express my anguish and my shame."

One would say that it was not the sort of book which would become popular; nevertheless, more than twenty editions have been published in English, and it has been translated into French, German, Italian, and Russian.

It was inevitable that "De Profundis" should become the subject of controversy: Oscar Wilde's sincerity has always been challenged; he was called affected. His answer to this charge is complete and conclusive: "The value of an idea has nothing whatever to do with the sincerity of the man who expresses it."

For many years, indeed until quite recently, his name cast a blight over all his work. This was inevitable, but it was inevitable also that the work of such a genius should sooner or later be recognized.

Only a few years ago I heard a cultured lady say, "I never expected to hear his name mentioned in polite society again." But the time is rapidly approaching when Oscar Wilde will come into his own, when he will be recognized as one of the greatest and most original writers of his time. When shall we English-speaking people learn that a man's work is one thing and his life another?

It is much to be regretted that Wilde's life did not end with "De Profundis"; but his misfortunes were to continue. After his release from prison he went to France, where he lived under the name of Sebastian Melmoth: but as Sherard, his biographer, says, "He hankered after respectability." It was no longer the social distinction which the unthinking crave when they have all else: this great writer, he who had been for a brief moment the idol of cultured London, sought mere respectability, and sought it in vain.

Only when he was neglected and despised, miserable and broken in spirit, sincere feeling at last overcame the affectation which was his real nature and he wrote his one great poem, "The Ballad of Reading Gaol." No longer could the "Saturday Review" "search in vain for the personal touch of thought and music": the thought is there, very simple and direct and personal without a doubt: the music is no longer the modulated noise of his youth. The Ballad is an almost faultless work of art. What could be

more impressive than the description of daybreak
in prison: —

> At last I saw the shadowed bars,
> Like a lattice wrought in lead,
> Move right across the whitewashed wall
> That faced my three-plank bed,
> And I knew that somewhere in the world
> God's dreadful dawn was red.

The life begun with such promise drew to a close:
an outcast, deserted by his friends, the few who
remained true to him he insulted and abused. He
became dissipated, wandered from France to Italy
and back again. In mercy it were well to draw the
curtain. The end came in Paris with the close of
the century he had done so much to adorn. He died
on November 30, 1900, and was buried, by his faithful friend, Robert Ross, in a grave which was leased
for a few years in Bagneux Cemetery.

The kindness of Robert Ross to Oscar Wilde is
one of the most touching things in literary history.
The time has not yet come to speak of it at length,
but the facts are known and will not always be with-
held. Owing largely to his efforts, a permanent resting-place was secured a few years ago in the most
famous cemetery in France, the Père Lachaise.
There, in an immense sarcophagus of granite, curiously carved, were placed the remains of him who
wrote: —

"Society, as we have constituted it, will have no
place for me, has none to offer; but Nature, whose
sweet rains fall on unjust and just alike, will have

clefts in the rock where I may hide, and sweet valleys in whose silence I may weep undisturbed. She will hang the night with stars so that I may walk abroad in the darkness without stumbling, and send the wind over my footprints so that none may track me to my hurt; she will cleanse me in great waters and with bitter herbs make me whole."

It is too early to judge Wilde's work entirely apart from his life: to do so will always be difficult: we could do so the sooner if we had a Dr. Johnson among us to speak with authority and say, "Let not his misfortunes be remembered, he was a very great man."

John Ehret.

Dickinson

from his

friend

Oscar Wilde

XIII

A WORD IN MEMORY

To have been born and lived all his life in Philadelphia, yet to be best known in London and New York; to have been the eldest son of a rich man and the eldest grandson of one of the richest men in America, yet of so quiet and retiring a disposition as to excite remark; to have been but a few years out of college, yet to have achieved distinction in a field which is commonly supposed to be the browsing-place of age; to have been relatively unknown in his life and to be immortal in his death — such are the brief outlines of the career of Harry Elkins Widener.

It is a curious commentary upon human nature that the death of one person well known to us affects us more than the deaths of hundreds or thousands not known to us at all. It is for this reason, perhaps, at a time when the papers bring us daily their record of human suffering and misery from the war in Europe, that I can forget the news of yesterday and live over again the anxious hours which followed the brief announcement that the Titanic, on her maiden voyage, the largest, finest, and fastest ship afloat, had struck an iceberg in mid-ocean, and that there were grave fears for the safety of her passengers and crew. There the first news ceased.

The accident had occurred at midnight; the sea was perfectly calm, the stars shone clearly; it was bitter cold. The ship was going at full speed. A slight jar was felt, but the extent of the injury was not realized and few passengers were alarmed. When the order to lower the boats was given there was little confusion. The order went round, "Women and children first." Harry and his father were lost, his mother and her maid were rescued.

In all that subsequently appeared in the press, — and for days the appalling disaster was the one subject of discussion, — the name of Harry Elkins Widener appeared simply as the eldest son of George D. Widener. Few knew that, quite aside from the financial prominence of his father and the social distinction and charm of his mother, Harry had a reputation which was entirely of his own making. He was a born student of bibliography. Books were at once his work, his recreation, and his passion. To them he devoted all his time; but outside the circle of his intimate friends few understood the unique and lovable personality of the man to whom death came so suddenly on April 15, 1912, shortly after he had completed his twenty-seventh year.

His knowledge of books was truly remarkable. In the study of rare books, as in the study of an exact science, authority usually comes only with years. With Harry Widener it was different. He had been collecting only since he left college, but his intense enthusiasm, his painstaking care, his devo-

HARRY ELKINS WIDENER

tion to a single object, his wonderful memory, and, as he gracefully says in the introduction to the catalogue of some of the more important books in his library, "The interest and kindness of my grandfather and my parents," had enabled him in a few years to secure a number of treasures of which any collector might be proud.

Harry Elkins Widener was born in Philadelphia on January 3, 1885. He received his early education at the Hill School, from which he was graduated in 1903. He then entered Harvard University, where he remained four years, receiving his bachelor's degree in 1907. It was while a student at Harvard that he first began to show an interest in book-collecting; but it was not until his college days were over that, as the son of a rich man, he found, as many another man has done, that the way to be happy is to have an occupation.

He lived with his parents and his grandfather in their palatial residence, Lynnewood Hall, just outside Philadelphia. He was proud of the distinction of his relatives, and used to say, "We are a family of collectors. My grandfather collects paintings, my mother collects silver and porcelains, Uncle Joe collects everything," — which indeed he does, — "and I, books."

Book-collecting soon became with him a very serious matter, a matter to which everything else was subordinated. He began, as all collectors do, with unimportant things at first; but how rapidly his taste developed may be seen from glancing over the pages of the catalogue of his library, which, strictly speaking, is not a library at all — he would have been the last to call it so. It is but a collection of perhaps three thousand volumes; but they were selected by a man of almost unlimited means, with rare judgment and an instinct for discovering the best. Money alone will not make a bibliophile, although, I confess, it develops one.

His first folio of Shakespeare was the Van Antwerp copy, formerly Locker Lampson's, one of the finest copies known; and he rejoiced in a copy of "Poems Written by Wil. Shakespeare, Gent," 1640, in the original sheepskin binding. His "Pickwick," if possibly inferior in interest to the Harry B. Smith copy, is nevertheless superb: indeed he had two, one "in parts as published, with all the points," another a presentation copy to Dickens's friend, William Harrison Ainsworth. In addition he had several original drawings by Seymour, including the one in which the shad-bellied Mr. Pickwick, having with some difficulty mounted a chair, proceeds to address the Club. The discovery and acquisition of this drawing, perhaps the most famous illustration ever made for a book, is indicative of Harry's taste as a collector.

One of his favorite books was the Countess of Pembroke's own copy of Sir Philip Sidney's "Arcadia," and it is indeed a noble volume; but Harry's love for his mother, I think, invariably led him, when he was showing his treasures, to point out a sentence written in his copy of Cowper's "Task." The book had once been Thackeray's, and the great novelist had written on the frontispiece, "A great point in a great man, a great love for his mother. A very fine and true portrait. Could artist possibly choose a better position than the above? W. M. Thackeray." "Is n't that a lovely sentiment?" Harry would say; "and yet they say Thackeray was a cynic and a snob." His "Esmond" was presented by Thackeray to Charlotte Brontë. His copy of the "Ingoldsby Legends" was unique. In the first edition, by some curious oversight on the part of the printer, page 236 had been left blank, and the error was not discovered until a few sheets had been printed. In a presentation copy to his friend, E. R. Moran, on this blank page, Barham had written: —

> By a blunder for which I have only myself to thank,
> Here's a page has been somehow left blank.
> Aha! my friend Moran, I have you. You'll look
> In vain for a fault in one page of my book!

signing the verse with his *nom de plume*, Thomas Ingoldsby.

Indeed, in all his books, the utmost care was taken to secure the copy which would have the greatest human interest: an ordinary presentation copy of the first issue of the first edition would serve his purpose only if he were sure that the dedication copy was unobtainable. His Boswell's "Life of Johnson" was the dedication copy to Sir Joshua Reynolds, with an inscription in the author's hand.

He was always on the lookout for rarities, and Dr.
Rosenbach, in the brief memoir which serves as an
introduction to the Catalogue of his Stevenson collection, says of him: —

"I remember once seeing him on his hands and
knees under a table in a bookstore. On the floor was
a huge pile of books that had not been disturbed for
years. He had just pulled out of the débris a first
edition of Swinburne, a presentation copy, and it was
good to behold the light in his face as he exclaimed,
'This is better than working in a gold mine.' To
him it was one."

His collection of Stevenson is a monument to his
industry and patience, and is probably the finest collection in existence of that much-esteemed author.
He possessed holograph copies of the Vailima Letters
and many other priceless treasures, and he secured the
manuscript of, and published privately for Stevenson
lovers, in an edition of forty-five copies, an autobiography written by Stevenson in California in the
early eighties. This item, under the title of "Memoirs
of Himself," has an inscription, "Given to Isobel
Stewart Strong . . . for future use, when the under-
writer is dead. With love, Robert Louis Stevenson."
The catalogue of his Stevenson collection alone, the
painstaking work of his friend and mentor, Dr. Rosenbach, makes an imposing volume and is an invaluable
work of reference for Stevenson collectors.

Harry once told me that he never traveled without
a copy of "Treasure Island," and knew it practically

by heart. I, myself, am not averse to a good book as a traveling companion; but in my judgment, for constant reading, year in and year out, it should be a book which sets you thinking, rather than a narrative like "Treasure Island," but — *chacun à son goût.*

But it were tedious to enumerate his treasures, nor is it necessary. They will ever remain, a monument to his taste and skill as a collector, in the keeping of Harvard University — his

MEMOIRS OF HIMSELF

BY

ROBERT LOUIS STEVENSON

PRINTED FROM THE ORIGINAL MANUSCRIPT
IN THE POSSESSION OF

HARRY ELKINS WIDENER

PHILADELPHIA
FOR PRIVATE DISTRIBUTION ONLY
1912

Alma Mater. It is, however, worth while to attempt to fix in some measure the individuality, the rare personality of the man. I cannot be mistaken in thinking that many, looking at the wonderful library erected in Cambridge by his mother in his memory, may wish to know something of the man himself.

There is in truth not much to tell. A few dates have already been given, and when to these is added the statement that he was of retiring and studious disposition, considerate and courteous, little more remains to be said. He lived with and for his books, and was never so happy as when he was saying, "Now if you will put aside that cigar for a moment, I will show you something. Cigar ashes are not good for first editions"; and a moment later some precious volume would be on your knees. What collector does not enjoy showing his treasures to others as appreciative as himself? Many delightful hours his intimates have passed in his library, which was also his bedroom, — for he wanted his books about him, where he could play with them at night and where his eye might rest on them the first thing in the morning, — but this was a privilege extended only to true booklovers. To others he was unapproachable and almost shy. Of unfailing courtesy and an amiable and loving disposition, his friends were very dear to him. "Bill," or someone else, "is the salt of the earth," you would frequently hear him say.

"Are you a book-collector, too?" his grandfather once asked me across the dinner-table.

Laughingly I said, "I thought I was, but I am not in Harry's class."

To which the old gentleman replied, — and his eye beamed with pride the while, — "I am afraid that Harry will impoverish the entire family."

I answered that I should be sorry to hear that, and suggested that he and I, if we put our fortunes together, might prevent this calamity.

His memory was most retentive. Once let him get a fact or a date imbedded in his mind and it was there

BEVERLY CHEW, OF NEW YORK, WHO COMBINES A PROFOUND LOVE
OF ENGLISH LITERATURE WITH AN INEXHAUSTIBLE KNOWLEDGE
OF FIRST EDITIONS

forever. He knew the name of every actor he had ever seen, and the part he had taken in the play last year and the year before. He knew the name of every baseball player and had his batting and running average. When it came to the chief interest of his life, his thirst for knowledge was insatiable. I remember one evening when we were in New York together, in Beverly Chew's library, Harry asked Mr. Chew some question about the eccentricities of the title-pages of the first edition of Milton's "Paradise Lost." Mr. Chew began rolling off the bibliographical data, like the ripe scholar that he is, when I suggested to Harry that he had better make a note of what Mr. Chew was saying. He replied, "I should only lose the paper; while if I get it in my head I will put it where it can't be lost; that is," he added, "as long as I keep my head."

And his memory extended to other collections than his own. For him to see a book once was for him to remember it always. If I told him I had bought such and such a book, he would know from whom I bought it and all about it, and would ask me if I had noticed some especial point, which, in all probability, had escaped me.

He was a member of several clubs, including the Grolier Club, the most important club of its kind in the world. The late J. P. Morgan had sent word to the chairman of the membership committee that he would like Harry made a member. The question of his seconder was waived: it was understood that Mr.

Morgan's endorsement of his protégé's qualifications was sufficient.

It was one night, when we were in New York together during the first Hoe sale, that I had a conversation with Harry, to which, in the light of subsequent events, I have often recurred. We had dined together at my club and had gone to the sale; but there was nothing of special interest coming up, and after a half hour or so, he suggested that we go to the theatre. I reminded him that it was quite late, and that at such an hour a music-hall would be best. He agreed, and in a few moments we were witnessing a very different performance from the one we had left in the Anderson auction rooms; but the performance was a poor one. Harry was restless and finally suggested that we take a walk out Fifth Avenue. During this walk he confessed to me his longing to be identified and remembered in connection with some great library. He expanded this idea at length. He said: "I do not wish to be remembered merely as a collector of a few books, however fine they may be. I want to be remembered in connection with a great library, and I do not see how it is going to be brought about. Mr. Huntington and Mr. Morgan are buying up all the books, and Mr. Bixby is getting the manuscripts. When my time comes, if it ever does, there will be nothing left for me — everything will be gone!"

We spent the night together, and after I had gone to bed he came to my room again, and calling me by a nick-name, said, "I have got to do something in

MR. HUNTINGTON AMONG HIS BOOKS

connection with books to make myself remembered. What shall it be?"

I laughingly suggested that he write one, but he said it was no jesting matter. Then it came out that he thought he would establish a chair at Harvard for the study of bibliography in all its branches. He was much disturbed by the lack of interest which great scholars frequently evince toward his favorite subject.

With this he returned to his own room, and I went to sleep; but I have often thought of this conversation since I, with the rest of the world, learned that his mother was prepared, in his memory, to erect the great building at Harvard which is his monument. His ambition has been achieved. Associated with books, his name will ever be. The great library at Harvard is his memorial. In its *sanctum sanctorum* his collection will find a fitting place.

We lunched together the day before he sailed for Europe, and I happened to remark at parting, "This time next week you will be in London, probably, lunching at the Ritz."

"Yes," he said, "very likely with Quaritch."

While in London Harry spent most of his time with that great bookseller, the second to bear the name of Quaritch, who knew all the great book-collectors the world over, and who once told me that he knew no man of his years who had the knowledge and taste of Harry Widener. "So many of your great American collectors refer to books in terms of steel rails; with Harry it is a genuine and all-absorbing passion, and he is so entirely devoid of side and affectation." In this he but echoed what a friend once said to me at Lynnewood Hall, where we were spending the day: "The marvel is that Harry is so entirely unspoiled by his fortune."

Harry was a constant attendant at the auction rooms at Sotheby's in London, at Anderson's in New York, or wherever else good books were going. He chanced to be in London when the first part of the Huth library was being disposed of, and he was anxious to get back to New York in time to attend the final Hoe sale, where he hoped to secure some books, and bring to the many friends he would find there the latest gossip of the London auction rooms.

Alas! Harry had bought his last book. It was an excessively rare copy of Bacon's "Essaies," the edition of 1598. Quaritch had secured it for him at the Huth sale, and as he dropped in to say good-bye and give his final instructions for the disposition of his purchases, he said: "I think I'll take that little Bacon with me in my pocket, and if I am shipwrecked it will go with me." And I know that it was so. In all the history of book-collecting this is the most touching story.

The death of Milton's friend, Edward King, by drowning, inspired the poet to write the immortal elegy, "Lycidas."

Who would not sing for Lycidas? —
He must not float upon his watery bier
Unwept.

When Shelley's body was cast up by the waves on the shore near Via Reggio, he had a volume of Keats's poems in his pocket, doubled back at "The Eve of St. Agnes." And in poor Harry Widener's pocket there was a Bacon, and in this Bacon we might have read, "The same man that was envied while he lived shall be loved when he is gone."

INDEX

INDEX

A'BECKET, GILBERT, *Comic History of Rome*, 78; *Comic History of England*, 78.

ADAM, ROBERT B., 184 *n.*

ADAMS, JOHN, 58.

ADVERTISEMENTS, importance of, in verifying first editions of certain books, 79.

AINSWORTH, W. H., 346.

ALBERT, PRINCE CONSORT. *See* MARTIN, SIR THEODORE.

ALBERT MEMORIAL, 285.

ALDERSON, AMELIA (Mrs. Opie), 232.

ALDINES, 5, 88.

ALEXANDRA, PRINCESS OF WALES, 284.

ALKEN, HENRY, *Analysis of the Hunting Field*, and *Life of John Mytton*, illustrated by, 77.

ALLAN, JOHN, 83, 84, 85.

ALLEN, EDMUND, 21, 307 *ff.*

ALLEN, JOHN, *Memorial* of, 57.

ALLIS, WILLIAM E., 115, 116.

American Book Prices Current, 103.

ANDERSON, MARY, 327.

ANDERSON'S AUCTION ROOMS, 103, 354.

ANDREWS, WILLIAM LORING, *Gossip about Book-collecting*, 51.

ANNE, QUEEN, 278.

ANNE OF DENMARK, Queen of James I, 280.

ARBLAY, MADAME D'. *See* Burney, Fanny.

ARGYLE, ARCHIBALD CAMPBELL, Duke of, 150.

ARNOLD, WILLIAM HARRIS, *Record of Books and Letters*, 18, 103–106; *First Report of a Book-collector*, 101, 102.

ASSOCIATION BOOKS 1, 107 *ff.*

Athenæum, The, 106 *n.*

AUCHINLECK, ALEXANDER BOSWELL,

LORD, his death, 173; mentioned, 150, 165, 166, 172.

AUCHINLECK, Boswell's birthplace, the author's visit to, 181–184.

AUCTION CATALOGUES, 30.

AUCTION SALES, 59, 60.

AUDUBON, JOHN J., *Birds of North America*, 5.

AULUS GELLIUS, *Noctes Atticæ*, 90.

AUSTEN, JANE, 186, 187, 253.

BACON, FRANCIS, LORD, quoted, 7; and Shakespeare, 92; *Essaies* (1598), Widener's last purchase, 354, 355.

BAGEHOT, WALTER, 272.

BANGS & Co., 104.

Bank of North America, History of the, 57, 58.

BARCLAY, ALEXANDER, 91.

BARCLAY and PERKINS'S, 195.

BARETTI, GIUSEPPE M. A., attacks Mrs. Piozzi, 216; mentioned, 194, 198.

BARHAM, THOMAS, *Ingoldsby Legends*, unique presentation copy of first edition, 347.

BARRETT, LAWRENCE, 327.

BARRIE, SIR JAMES M., *What Every Woman Knows*, 196.

BARTLETT, HENRIETTA, 72.

BARTON, BERNARD, 135.

BEACONSFIELD, BENJAMIN DISRAELI, Earl of. *See* Disraeli.

BEARD, TOM, presentation copy of *A Christmas Carol* to, 116.

BEARDSLEY, AUBREY, caricature of O. Wilde, 114, 319.

BEAUCLERK, LADY DIANA, 179.

BECKFORD, WILLIAM, presentation copy of Disraeli's *Henrietta Temple* to, 29.

BOWDEN, A. J., 75.
BRADFORD CLUB, 57.
BRANDT, SEBASTIAN, *The Ship of Fools*, 91, 92.
BRISTOL, BISHOP OF, 317.
BRITISH MUSEUM, 43, 101, 111.
BROADLEY, A. M., published Mrs. Thrale's *Journal of a Tour in Wales*, 218, 221.
BRONTÉ, CHARLOTTE, presentation copy of *Henry Esmond* to, 347; mentioned, 83.
BRONTÉ, EMILY, 187.
BRONTÉ MUSEUM, 83.
BRONTÉ SISTERS, 186, 187. *See* Bell, Currer, etc.
BROOKS, EDMUND D., bookseller, 53, 54, 83.
BROUGH, FANNY, 336.
BROWNING, ARABEL, 26.
BROWNING, ELIZABETH BARRETT, letter of, 26, 27; mentioned, 186, 187.
BROWNING, ROBERT, *Pauline*, 103; mentioned, 26, 27, 91, 228.
BULWER-LYTTON, SIR EDWARD, 253.
BUNBURY, HENRY W., 32.
BURKE, EDMUND, inscription to, from Boswell, 185; mentioned, 151, 181, 187, 188, 194, 221.
BURNEY, DR. CHARLES, 194, 208.
BURNEY, FANNY (Madame d'Arblay), *Evelina*, 46, 127, 199, 200; her *Diary*, quoted, on life at Streatham Park, 199 *ff.*; mentioned, 186, 187, 204, 209, 221.
BURNS, ROBERT, *Poems*, first Edinburgh edition, 83, 84; Kilmarnock edition, 83–86, 103.
BURNS MUSEUM, 86.
BUSHNELL, JOHN, 281.
BUTLER, SAMUEL, *The Way of all Flesh*, 124.
BYRON, ALLEGRA, 238, 244.
BYRON, GEORGE GORDON, LORD, copy of Thomson's *Seasons* presented by, to Frances W. Webster, 29; mentioned, 238.

CAINE, HALL, 268.
CARLTON HOTEL, London, 268.
CARLYLE, THOMAS, presentation copy of Dickens's *American Notes* to, 115; on Boswell, 154; mentioned, 185, 293.
CARNEGIE, ANDREW, *Triumphant Democracy*, quoted, 271.
CASSATT, A. J., 54.
CATALOGUES of second-hand books, 30 *ff.*, 65 *ff.*; amusing blunders in, 62, 113.
CAXTON, WILLIAM, his books in general, 8, 72; his edition of *Tully, his Treatises on Old Age and Friendship*, 22; mentioned, 91.
CAXTON HEAD, Sign of the, 30.
CHAFFANBRASS, MR., 256, 264.
CHAPMAN, GEORGE, translation of Homer, 102.
CHARING CROSS, 268.
CHARING CROSS ROAD, the book-lover's happy hunting-ground, 15, 16.
CHARLES I, 278, 281.
CHARLES II, 278, 282.
CHARLOTTE, Queen of George III, Dodd's letter to, 309; mentioned, 21, 306.
CHATHAM, WILLIAM PITT, Earl of, 246.
CHAUCER, GEOFFREY, *Works*, 102.
CHESTERFIELD, PHILIP DORMER STANHOPE, fourth Earl of, 21, 301.
CHESTERFIELD, PHILIP STANHOPE, fifth Earl of, 305, 306.
CHEW, BEVERLY, 7, 75, 87, 102, 103, 351.
Christ Church, History of, 58.
CHRIST'S HOSPITAL, 53.
CICERO, *Cato Major*, Franklin's edition of, 9; *Treatises of Old Age and Friendship* (Caxton), 22.
"CITY" OF LONDON, royal visit to, 266 *ff.*; physical boundaries and jurisdiction of, 277.
CLAIRMONT, MRS. M. J., Godwin's second wife, 237. *See* Godwin, Mrs. M. J.
CLAIRMONT, MARY JANE (Claire), Lord Byron's mistress, 238, 242, 243, 244.